I'LL POINT
TO *Heaven*
We Will be Together Again

BY RHETT WINTCH

ACKNOWLEDGMENTS

*N*ow that my novel is complete, I would feel remiss if I didn't mention all those who helped me along the way. First and foremost is God, our Eternal Father, who inspired me that night after my mother's funeral, to lay the foundation of I'll Point to Heaven. He continued guiding and comforting me even through my battles with cancer and rheumatoid arthritis to bring this work to completion.

My angel wife, Lisa, who gave up years of dates and together time, and to add to her bigheartedness, she proofread and edited the manuscript four times. When I fell ill, she loved and cared for me, and nursed me back to good health. Her care was exceptional—she's a registered nurse. I'll love and adore her forever.

I'm grateful for my sisters Char and Pam for always encouraging and reassuring me. They have taken over mothering me since the passing of my mother. Even at the age of fifty-six, I'm fine with that.

I'd also like to thank my daughters Cherie and Nicole, and my daughter-in-law, Brittany. Each of them helped me with scene selection and plot design. I dedicated a chapter to each of them. Furthermore, my friends and work associates provided unwavering backing and praise.

Thanks to Amy Wadsworth and Heidi Brockbank (at Angela Eschler Editing), who helped me lay the foundation of I'll Point to Heaven, and my friend and long-time editor, Fred Roth, who taught me volumes.

And a huge thank-you to my publisher, Xulon Press.

TABLE OF CONTENTS

Table of Contents

CHAPTER 1
THE BOOK

$\mathcal{I}$ gripped the steering wheel a little tighter, and looked at my dad, who was sitting in the passenger seat. For three months now, every other week, I'd made the four-hour trip from my home in Las Vegas to visit him.

He'd insisted that he spend the remainder of his days in the Panguitch Care Center in southern Utah. It was the closest care center to the land he loved with all his heart—a rural untamed country with three small towns: Tropic, Cannonville, and Henrieville, all connected with a winding two-lane road, and nestled under the majestic orange spires of Bryce Canyon National Park. In these towns he'd received an education, learned the true meaning of work, and courted the love of his life. And from the bits and pieces I'd heard, their courtship was one for the ages. I'd pick him up, he'd pick a location, and we would drive. He would bask in the memories of a distant life that once resonated young love, vibrancy, and zeal; and I would spend the hours and minutes pondering whether Dad could soothe my aching heart.

Six months ago, my husband Richard had passed away suddenly from a massive stroke. How could someone be laughing with you one minute, and gone the next? Richard had been the anchor in my life. Without him, I found I was adrift in a sea of emptiness and mounting questions. Was this the end? Till death do us part? All that love and commitment—gone?

Hopelessness was beginning to suffocate me. My prayers were becoming desperate, and if Heavenly Father was sending me answers, I certainly wasn't hearing them. Unless . . .

Ask your father.

When it came, it wasn't a voice, exactly, or even a thought, but more a feeling. And suddenly, I found myself pouring out all my grief and sorrow to my ninety-two-year-old father, as if we'd taken a trip back in time, and I was still a little girl and he was in his early prime, and not a frail senior who lived more in his memories than in the present.

And yet, there was a quiet reverence about him. He wore his years with dignity. He sat with his hands folded on his lap, his silvery white hair glistening in the morning sun, and his thick glasses giving him a look of wisdom.

We drove in silence. There was something different about this drive. Again I glanced at him. He seemed shaken. Why, I wondered? He knows the pleadings of my heart. More than anyone in this world he could answer my questions. He lost his precious wife five years ago. They had a romance so intimate and tender, that they could hardly talk of it. Surely he felt that sixty-nine years of loyalty, commitment, passion, and devotion didn't suddenly halt with her passing. They lost my little brother when Sammy was just two. No doubt Dad pondered if Sammy would be part of the family again, or if they could raise him in the life hereafter.

"Char, my girl." Dad's voice shook me from my train of thought, "The tunnels are coming up. Whose turn is it?"

The tunnels in the middle of Red Canyon were a landmark, a precursor to the real bravura of Bryce Canyon, which was about ten miles further. "It's your turn, Dad." I rolled the windows down a couple inches.

Hoooonk, hoooonk. Dad pressed on the horn, and the sound echoed off the red rock tunnel walls.

"We'll never get tired of that, Dad. Looks like you've instilled a tradition in all of your children."

"I'm glad. It's as thrilling to me now as it was a hundred years ago."

"Oh, Dad, you're not that old."

"Well, it seems like it."

"Dad, there's something . . . special about today. Do you feel it?"

"Every day with you is special, my dear."

"Oh, Dad, you're a big tease."

I took in a deep breath, tears near the surface. Dad was going to skirt my questions again. I looked away. I'd never feel that peace and contentment. For some reason, God wasn't going to answer my questions—at least not through Dad. We drove in silence.

After a few moments, I looked back to find Dad looking intently at me. His countenance was soft, his eyes loving, but he had focus.

"I'm so sorry, my dear—so sorry. I can see how much this pains you. Your mom, the night before she died, asked me to share our story with you. I've been wanting to. With all my heart I've wanted to."

"But something holds me back. I can't figure it. I do have the answers you seek. I've known them since even before your mother passed. But I've felt constrained. I know deep in my heart that I can answer your questions with sound witness from my life. You, and anyone else with similar questions, will have sure understanding that God is our Father, and that the family is central to his plan of happiness. The very reason He sent us to earth is so we may learn to be good husbands and fathers, wives and mothers—family people. His first commandment to Adam and Eve was to multiply and replenish the earth. Why else would He prefer always to be referred to as . . . our Father?"

Dad's words lit a flame of hope in my heart. It was as if I was hearing something I'd always known. I'd read the Bible many times, and I felt the answers were there, if only I understood it better. But why had Dad felt restrained from helping me?

Dad continued. "I've felt for some time that the right time to share it would come. I believed that sharing your mom's and my courtship and our life would set every anxiety of your heart to rest, and bathe your soul with light and truth. I guess . . . I guess I just miss my book."

Now I was really puzzled. What book?

"Do you know what it's like to work for years and accomplish a masterpiece, and then in one moment have it rooted out of your life forever?"

11

Yes, I thought. My marriage with Richard—years of hard work and sacrifice and letting life grind away our rough edges until we felt more like one person in two bodies.

"I'm not really sure," I said.

"Ah, that's fine my dear. But it happened to me."

I wasn't quite sure where this was leading, but I gently encouraged him. "Is that why you haven't shared your story with us children?"

"I suppose it has something to do with it. Let's continue to Tropic, and I'll figure out how to begin."

"Okay." A million questions sprang to mind, but I held my peace. Dad was never one to be rushed. He became pensive and remained quiet. After some time, he looked over at me. "Do you remember the terrible fight your mom and I had after Sammy died? You would have been six."

"You and Mom never fought—not once."

"Do you remember when Sammy died?"

"A little."

"Well, no matter. You see, I wrote a book while I was overseas during World War II. It was a dismal time. With death and despair all around me, it was easy to become depressed and disheartened. But the book! Each time I penned the romance and excitement of my courtship with your mother, I was enveloped in a world of bliss and peace. And to top it off, I felt that God wanted me to write it. The words and feelings flowed as if I was divinely inspired."

I stayed silent, hanging on every precious word of the story I had yearned so long to hear.

"Your mom and I loved that book. It was a sacred reminder to us of the great gift of our love, and the vows we had taken. We read it over and over. Then came that terrible day that your little brother was sick again. I gave permission for the doctor to remove his tonsils. Your mom was against it from the start, but I persisted. Sammy died after the surgery. It was the only black moment in our marriage. She was furious with me. She took the book and threw it in the garbage just as the garbage truck was coming down the road. My book was gone forever."

A cloud immediately cast itself over me. Or was it a dark memory? I did remember this fight. It was as if Sammy's death was a whirlwind, tearing our family apart. My mild, sweet mother, who never raised her voice to anyone, was screaming at Dad. I hid behind the rocker chair. Dad went into the bedroom crying, and Mom came out with something tucked in her arms, covered with a pillow case, and marched out to the trash can. Mom came back in crying and went to a back bedroom. I retrieved the pillowcase just before the garbage truck arrived. I had no idea what it was, but I remembered feeling absolutely certain that it was important and I must keep it safe. And the safest place I knew was under my mattress.

Frantically I searched for a turnout. I skidded to a stop at the side of the road and began sobbing. "Dad, your book! It's not lost."

"What? How on earth can that be?"

I fought to regain my composure. Dad's heart would soar if I could just get the words out. Still breathing heavily, I leaned my head on the steering wheel and whispered, "Oh, Dad, the book is not lost. I got it out of the garbage can."

"You what?" Dad was breathing heavily. "You did?" Color flooded his face, and his eyes filled with tears. "I knew it couldn't be lost forever. Char, my sweet girl—where is it?"

I hesitated, my mind whirling in every direction. "Dad . . . I, I'm not sure. I don't remember anything past the mattress."

"Keep thinking, my girl."

I did so, but it was no use. I looked over at Dad—his eyes pleading. I had to look away. I felt sick at heart. It seemed like Dad was granted his life's true dream, only to have it dashed to bits seconds later.

At last I had to admit defeat. "I'm sorry, Dad. I just can't remember." Once more, I wondered what the point of everything was. Why did life taunt us with hope, with answers that never came? What good did saving the book do, if I couldn't give it to the person it meant so much to? I pulled back onto the highway. "So we're going to your old home in Tropic?"

"I suppose." Dad sounded despondent. "But, I think I'd rather go on to Cannonville and Heaven's Rock."

"Heaven's Rock, that's the big rocky ledge up above Cannonville, isn't it?"

"Yes."

I drove on, memories flirting around me like falling feathers in the wind. Coming then going, appearing then disappearing. Suddenly my mind was filled with detailed images. A rock, a slit in the rock—up above Cannonville. That's where I hid it! "Dad, I know where I put it," I gasped, pulling off the road again. "I put it in the slit of a rock above Cannonville!"

I looked at Dad. His head was bent over, his lips moving slightly. He was thanking his Father in Heaven that his book was not lost. His shoulders shook with silent sobs.

I gently rubbed his back.

After a good while he looked up, his eyes full of longing and hope.

"Yes, yes, that's where I put it. I went to visit Aunt Pam in Cannonville, and I sneaked up there and hid it."

"Let's go get my book!"

I began to worry. It had been nearly sixty-six years. "Dad, I shouldn't mention this, but . . ."

"I know, I know, my dear. There's a chance that it's gone. Well, there's a chance that it's still there too." He looked down at his feet; his countenance becoming concerned. "You know I can't make it up there. Will you go for me?"

"Of course, but I don't remember the way."

"Well, then I'll tell you. You enter the crevice and walk on the sand until it turns to rock. Gradually ascend until you top out. Turn due east until you are looking out over Cannonville, then turn north. Walk sixty steps to the place where the rock juts about eight feet higher. Down below that is a sandy area, from there look at the rock wall and at your eye level you'll notice a slit in the rock. I once showed it to you after the war. That must be how you knew about it."

"I guess so," I said. "I don't remember any of that. But you sure remember the place well."

"That I do, my girl." He remained quiet for several moments. We still had a few miles to go.

"Can you imagine that I was once young and strong, and full of vigor?"

"Dad, I feel your young spirit all over this country."

"That's sweet, my girl. You're truly right. And there's the spirit of a boy and girl falling into never-ending love. A love that would stand any test—any obstacle or roadblock." He chuckled. "But now comes the kicker. There were two girls I loved, and there were two of us boys that loved them. We all knew of Heaven's Rock and the secret hiding place. We knew this whole area from Panguitch to the Paria. Which girl do you think ended up being my . . . forever sweetheart?"

This was news to me. Now there was another young lady in the picture, as well as another young man. Who were they?

We entered the little town of Cannonville. The air was brisk, and no one was out playing or walking. The trees were sprouting new green buds but hadn't filled in to proclaim their beauty. A road swung under the cliff.

"Park over there," Dad said.

I grabbed a pair of gloves and made my way toward the rocks. I looked back at Dad before I entered the crevice. He was watching me intently.

I walked along the sandy bottom, then began ascending the gradual slope, and soon topped out. It was hard. I had to stop to catch my breath. Seventy-two was no spring chicken.

I made my way to the cliff, and sure enough, found that I needed to go north fifty yards or so. Arriving at the little sandy patch, I looked around. I could see the slit in the rock wall. I was scared. I had built Dad's hopes up so much! If it wasn't there . . .

Donning my gloves, I waved my hand back and forth over the opening. I was plenty scared of spiders and snakes. Drawing in a deep breath, I cautiously stuck my hand in, and . . . felt nothing. *Please*, I prayed. I was about to withdraw my hand when, from somewhere deep down I felt prompted to try one more time. I felt the rock to the sides—no further crevices, I inched my way back. Nearly at the end of my reach, my fingers brushed against something other than rock. The book! I pulled it out, still wrapped in the pillow case—now stained and tattered. Gently uncovering it, I peered at the pages, yellowed with age and written with Dad's own stylish handwriting. I dropped to my knees in the sand, and looked heavenward. "Thank you, God! Thank you!" I felt something immediately—a warmth, a realization. This sandy patch of ground was a sacred place.

I stood up, placed Dad's book under my arm, and started back to the crevice. My feet hardly seemed to touch the rock. I was somewhere far away, high up in the puffy clouds. I now knew, the deepest yearnings of my heart would be answered. My life would never be the same.

CHAPTER 2
DAD'S PLAN

$\mathcal{U}$pon descending to the sandy floor and rounding the bottom of the cliff, I could see Dad standing at the side of my SUV—his hand eagerly clutching the door handle.

I held it high and waved it for him to see. When I got to him, tears were streaming down his face. He grabbed it and held it close, and then he pulled me close. I could hear him trying to enunciate words, but they were just garbled cries. A lifetime of hope and dream answered, and it was my answer as well.

I helped him back in, then hurried around and settled into my seat. Dad gently and lovingly opened the thick black cover. It was a large book about an inch thick of lined paper resembling a journal. It had no snap or buckle. The pages, though yellowed and stiff, were not stuck together.

"The spring of 1936," he breathed. "That's . . ." He looked up, and fixed his gaze on Heaven's Rock as if someone or something was up there. He closed the book.

"What is it?" I questioned impatiently. But he didn't respond. He looked thoughtful.

"Char, my dear," he finally said. "My dream is coming true." He drew in a deep breath. "It is time."

"Oh?"

"First I want you to know that your mom apologized a million times for throwing the book away. She even apologized on her death bed. I had long since forgiven her. Of course I forgave her. She hurt so bad, I thought she would buckle, or even die herself. The book didn't collapse our relationship—nothing could. And second, could you please spare three or four days? I would like you to read it to me."

Without hesitating, I said, "Of course. I'm retired, too, you know. I'll make a few calls. Surely your great-great-grandson won't be born for a couple weeks. I'll just stay at one of the hotels in Panguitch. I might need to buy an item of clothing or two, but . . . no problem."

"Okay, it's settled then. We will start reading the book here, today, and then continue reading until we get close to the end. At that point I'd like to return to this very spot. I have a surprise for you, a big surprise. I pray you'll understand it, and know that I'm happy and at peace. Will you remember my plan?"

"I'll remember. But I can't wait that long."

"Oh, you can my dear, and believe me, it will be worth it. It's a gift from your mom to me. I've added a little bit to it as well. I was planning on giving it to you anyway. I'll place it at the back of my book so it will read like one complete round. So, for you, well, let's just say, you'll have no further worries or concerns when I'm done giving you your gift. The book, and your mom's letter, and my writing will all be yours."

His words were troubling. What was he saying? But quickly my heart and mind began overflowing with anticipation, then joy, and then gratitude. I reached over and took my Dad in my arms, and held him. All I could think of was how deeply I loved him, knowing that the yearnings of my aching heart would soon be no more. My thirsting for answers was surpassed with a turn of events that I couldn't have imagined, and I would now come to know a part of Mom and Dad that I had never known.

I reached over and helped Dad fold back the cover. I shifted the book a little so it was still partially on his lap and began to read.

CHAPTER 3
KENT WILSON

April 1936

*B*ranches whipped at Kent's face as he ran through the orchard. One of them cut, and blood began to ooze. He didn't pay it any mind. He just had to get away. The orchard gave way to the fence at the back of his family farm. Placing a hand on the top log, he hopped the four-foot barrier and kept running. Now the terrain began sloping upward, ever steeper. He wouldn't stop.

Kent Wilson slumped into the soft sand at the top of the sliding hill. It was a two-hundred-foot hill covered with sagebrush and sand that was a favorite playground for him and his buddies. They'd slide all the way down, whooping and hollering. But this was anything but playtime. He wiped a hand across his cheek, still panting heavily. Only then did he realize the sting to his face. Blood was trickling downward onto the skin that was already reddened and swollen from planting his cheek on Old Daisy for their morning milk. "Figures," he muttered.

He flopped onto his back, and stared at the dark blue, early morning sky. "Why?" he hollered. He reviewed what had just happened. He'd stopped in the mud room near his parent's bedroom door with the morning milk and eggs, and heard crying.

"But Charlie, Kent's only thirteen," his mom was saying.

"We have no choice, Hanna. We're already three months behind on our mortgage. You know the school district has cut our wages. Uncle Jim's offered me work on his farm and I've got to take it. If I don't . . ." There was a long pause before his father continued. "If I don't, we'll lose everything."

"But you'll be gone all day at school, and all evening at the farm, and all day on Saturdays, and then all during the summer. We'll see you one day a week! What kind of life is that?"

"Hanna, my love, it's our life for now. It won't last forever. Kent, is sturdy and strong. He'll come through. Our parents carved this beautiful town out of what was then barren wasteland. It's in our blood to make it work. It's . . . it's in *his* blood. He's a southern Utah farmer and rancher through and through."

"Then why does he disappear for hours at a time? Why is he back talking us? He's fed up. All he's ever known is work, work, work, thanks to this dreadful depression." Again there was silence. "Do you really think that a thirteen-year-old can run our entire farm on his own? Charlie, it's hard enough for grown men! Three acres of orchard, garden plots, the barn, the stalls, the animals, all the equipment . . ." Her words broke off with a small sob.

Now Kent sat up and looked out over the valley. His hometown of Tropic, to him, was the perfect town. It got its name because the weather was so much better than up on the rim above. The population was maybe four hundred people. Two dusty side roads full of potholes ran through town; each one lined with cement and stone canals. On either side were farms dotted with trees, garden plots, and hay fields. Main Street had a hardware and grocery store with a gas pump, a restaurant, hotel, and a repair shop. Smack dab in the middle of town were the schools, park, and the church. Rodeo grounds and a swimming pond were at the end of town, above his family farm.

Good people lived there, good friends and neighbors. Hard workers, most of them with ancestors who carved the land into a haven where children could be raised, livelihoods could be established, and memories could be passed on.

His father's words echoed in his mind. He was right. The land was in Kent's blood. He couldn't imagine living anywhere else. Over his right shoulder to the west, majestic orange pinnacles sprinkled with green pine and juniper trees marked Bryce Canyon National Park. The top of the canyon rim, which rose two thousand feet above him, glistened a bright orange from the morning sun. He swung his head east, to Escalante Mountain. It towered over ten thousand feet, with walls of pink and orange, and flat on top with a carpet of trees. All around were lakes and streams full of fish, canyons to explore, and plenty of deer and rabbits to hunt.

When he was young, his dad would take him to the best fishing holes. They'd build a fire, cook the fish, and camp by the stream. They'd hunt deer and rabbits, and go on hikes. The peace, enjoyment, and the contentment filled him clear through.

But that life was gone. When he was about seven years old, the Depression began slithering into their lives. Now it had placed the last bar on the jail in which he would live.

He swung his eyes back to town—to the church. He attended every Sunday without fail. He'd never felt a reason not to. It was what was expected. Everyone learned they were children of God, and the Savior, Jesus Christ, had paved the only way for them to go back home. But where was Heavenly Father now? A feeling of panic rose up. It wasn't that Kent minded hard work or helping with his family. But year after year, no matter how hard he worked, there was always a new responsibility, and more to do than the hours of the day seemed to cover.

He looked down at their family farm. He couldn't do it. Without Dad there to lead, guide, and encourage him, it would be miserable, it would be . . . backbreaking . . . impossible.

Even as he thought this, he could picture his dad's face: steady, calm, but careworn and tired. How could he say no to his father? After all his dad had sacrificed? And his mother, too, who worked from sunup to sundown? Some warmth began to work its way into Kent's heart. Even at his young age, he appreciated that his parent's and his hard work provided the meals on the table. He liked watching the eager, contented expressions on the faces of his brother and sisters as they ate.

Dad was right. Kent wanted this life. A farm with horses, cows, sheep, pigs, and chickens; land for pasture, a hay field, and a nice garden. But then . . . well, it was awful hard work. It was springtime, and the weeds were already a foot high. They would torment him all summer. The barn, cellar, and fences always needed repairs. Caring for all the livestock, cleaning the chicken coop, the orchard, the watering . . . ugh!

Maybe he'd teach school someday, like Dad. He was good with numbers and letters. And he knew engines. He could teach mechanics. All the grind work he could do on the side. He'd have a car that would take him quickly up the mountain to fishing holes and hunting spots.

Sitting up again, he gave himself a swat on the cheek. "So what's your problem, Kent? It's not like you have a choice. You have to eat, and . . . it's true, all the family depends on you. Mom's got her hands full with the little ones. Gosh, all five of them; Marilyn, David, Jillian, Gretha, and Jessica."

He stood up, brushing the sand from his trousers. His heart was still heavy, the doubt and fear still ominous. If only Mom and Dad, if anybody, could see the real me, they'd know I'm not a bad person. I'm a good person; it's just that no one sees it. Well, maybe my parents, and I'm usually good with the little ones.

Kent knew he had to get home. Mom would have breakfast ready, and he'd have to wash up and get ready for school. He gritted his teeth. "Let's do this," he whispered silently. He'd prove himself to his parents, even if it killed him.

As Kent slowly walked home, he passed Anita Johnson's home. Six months younger than Kent, Anita lived right next door.

Anita and Kent had grown up together but had been brought up very differently. Anita's parents fought, and her father was often gone. Sometimes for weeks at a time. Anita had told Kent that she often cried herself to sleep, listening to their quarreling.

Back when Kent was little, about the time the depression began, Kent had heard people whisper that Anita's parents were getting a divorce. Kent didn't know exactly what that meant, but he knew it was bad.

But the struggle of the depression had changed Anita's father. It was as if he had repented of his ways and sought forgiveness from his wife and family. Kent knew that his own father had been involved in Mr. Johnson's change somehow. Some people had said that the one good thing the depression did for anyone, was that it brought the Johnsons back together.

The two sets of parents, who were close before, had become good friends lately. That tossed Kent and Anita together at family outings and games.

Anita had often asked why she liked Kent more than some of the other boys. She often said they were more like brother and sister, but sometimes she said that they were meant to be together.

She wasn't the only one that thought they were meant to be together. A lot of folks thought they would one day get married. Even some of the kids in school said so.

Once, when they were barely in elementary school, some of the kids dared them to kiss. During recess that day, she grabbed Kent by the hand, dragged him down behind some bushes, and planted a big first-grade kiss on him. It was supposed to be a secret, but it seemed every kid in school knew about it because they gathered on the school lawn and cheered as they emerged from the bushes.

After school that day she and Kent had gone to Kent's bedroom, grabbed paper and a pencil and planned their honeymoon to Canada. Kent must have had cold feet though, because he climbed to the top shelf of his closet, and she spent a good while coaxing him to come down.

Anita and Kent had their own problems, though. She really didn't like the backwoods country of southern Utah the way Kent did. Tropic was too small for her. She liked pretty dresses, fancy makeup, jewelry, reading, playing the piano, and was excited by the idea of city life.

When Anita was ten, she had spent the summer with an aunt in Salt Lake City. She came back and regaled her friends with stories of restaurants, movies, plays, and operas. She told everybody she was going to attend the big university in Salt Lake after high school.

Now that Anita and Kent were teenagers, Kent noticed that Anita had changed. She had become beautiful like her mother, with long flowing light brown hair, a dainty little figure, deep blue eyes, dark brown eyebrows, and plush eyelashes. She caught the attention of all the boys. That thrilled her, but Kent wasn't sure what to think of it.

Kent realized that Anita often used her beauty to get her own way. When she didn't get her way, she got angry or jealous. Sometimes, she even was conniving and manipulative.

But she was smart, and enjoyed her studies, and got good grades. She often won the lead in the school play, and sometimes she was asked to be the master of ceremonies for a social event.

But Anita wanted to leave Tropic. And Kent didn't.

CHAPTER 4
FAMILY COUNCIL

*T*hat evening, the chores done, the supper dishes cleaned and put away, Charlie Wilson grabbed a second kerosene lamp. "Gather round here in the living room," he called. "Grab a chair everyone. Let's form a circle."

"Do we have to?" seven-year-old Jillian yawned.

"It'll just last a few minutes, dear," Mom said, helping her with a chair.

"What's this about?" nine-year-old David asked. "I haven't finished tomorrow's math problems."

"Now hush," Mom scolded. "If this wasn't important, we wouldn't be doing it."

There were no more protests after that, just the scuffling of chairs being pulled closely in a circle. Jessica, age two, was on Mom's lap, with four-year-old Gretha leaning against them.

Kent looked at Marilyn, who was two years younger than he. She looked bewildered. "None of the kids knew what this is about," he concluded.

"This is called family council," Dad announced.

Kent knew what it was. They'd done it before, usually when a change was to be made. Sometimes though, they'd call everyone together to recognize a good deed or play a game. This was not going to be one of those times.

"My dear family," he began. "I want you to remember what I'm going to say forever. Are you ready?"

The kids all nodded. He'd managed to capture their attention. "The most important thing in this world is," he paused a moment for emphasis, "the family. Do you know why that is?"

No one answered. "It's where we learn and grow," Mom said. "It's where we learn to work, to love, to be kind, to forgive, to love our Father in Heaven. It's where we learn to be good people."

"Thank you, my dear," Dad said. "This great country that we live in is only as great as the families within it. Even if there's just a mom or a dad, or whatever the circumstance. Now, how important is that?"

"Mighty important," David said.

"It takes a lot of effort to make a family work," Dad continued. "Your mom and I want you to know we are pleased with the help you all give here in our home. We appreciate you with all our hearts. Now that you're getting so big, it's time to make assignments. To make our family work, your mom and I have listed the chores that need to be done. Are you ready? I'm going to read the chore, and if you think you can do it, raise your hand."

"What about our homework?" Marilyn asked.

"And what about playtime?" Jillian added.

"Now kids, those things are important too," Mom said, uneasiness hinting in her voice. "It's just that chores need to be done each day. There will be time to do homework and play—you'll see."

"Now, for the first chore," Dad announced. "It takes money to run our farm. Money for food, gas for the car, feed for the animals and so on. Eighty-five dollars a month should cover it. Who would like to do this chore?"

Not a sound was made. Kent's mind began churning as he realized how Dad was going to present the chores. He couldn't choose that job. He hadn't made that much money his whole life. He couldn't volunteer if he wanted to. But he knew, even as a heaviness was building inside of him, he knew his turn was coming. It was the only way.

After a good pause, Dad's voice penetrated the silence. "I'll do it," he said. A few sighs were heard around the room, but all eyes were on him anyhow. Everyone knew, even little Gretha, that Dad was the only one who could do that job.

He went on to explain what he'd have to do to earn that much money. For the first time, Kent thought of the work load his dad was willing to carry for his family—working six days a week from before sunup until after sundown.

He then outlined all the work it took to keep the house up, and care for the children. This job seemed never ending, but everyone knew there was only one person who could do it. She did it every day anyhow. Mom volunteered. This time there were a few muffled cheers from around the room. Everyone was catching on.

Next came the farm. "In order to run the farm, first and foremost is the garden. It provides the majority of our food. The ground needs to be cleared and weeded—tilled and raked flat—all seventy by one hundred feet of it. Furrowed, planted and watered, and of course . . . weeded continuously. The orchard is also part of this job, pruning, clearing dead limbs, and keeping the birds from eating the harvest."

Kent focused on shooting the birds out of the fruit trees. That was one chore he didn't mind. But slowly, a heavy weight started pressing down on him. It was gloomy and depressing. He remembered his feelings to rebel—to say no, to start drinking alcohol and distance himself from his family. But that wasn't who he was. And in fact, he couldn't rebel if he wanted to. He had to eat. His family needed to eat—he was trapped.

Dad continued. "The animals need to be fed, and watered, the pigs slopped, and . . ." The job seemed to go on forever. Kent distantly heard Dad's relentless words: the cleaning, the tidying, the upkeep, and more, much more.

Kent shook himself out of his trance. Dad had stopped speaking. A change had settled over the room. The air was heavy, anxious, and silent. Kent looked around. All eyes were on him. But their eyes were speaking. They emanated bewilderment and worry. Each of them knew they couldn't do it. Could it possibly be done by big brother?

Knowing that he'd come to grips that morning with what his life would now entail, he calmly turned his head toward his parents. "I'll do it." This time there were no cheers. The air was too heavy. Kent felt Jillian's little arms, hugging him around his waist. More arms . . . every child had come over and wrapped their arms around him.

Someone was sniffling. Kent peeked between the shuddering children. Mom and Dad still sat in their seats. They didn't know Kent had heard their morning discussion. But their eyes were moist, their countenances full of hope and relief.

The night ended with more chores being handed out and accepted by each of the little ones. Kent was relieved that as much of his chores as possible were assigned to Marilyn and David—even the milking of old Daisy.

The lamps had faded and the room was now dim. They all knelt in prayer except Mom, who stayed sitting with little Jessica asleep on her lap. Dad's prayer was one of gratitude for his family, and a petition of help for each of them as their lives expanded to their new roles. There was a sensation of hope, of resolve, and of unity. Maybe it was reassurance from God. At any rate, the next day April 24th, 1936, life would be different for the Charlie Wilson family.

CHAPTER 5
STRENGTH IN THE FAMILY

*P*igweeds are the worst! If you let them grow, they'll run you out of house and home. They'll reach the height of a man, they set their red roots deep, and they'll choke any garden vegetable. These words resonated in Kent's mind as the sweat from his forehead trickled into his eyes. The stinging was irritating, but he wouldn't take time to wipe off the sweat. Not unless it blurred his vision so he couldn't see the weeds.

He found that scooping at the weeds with a shovel was quickest. But it was an art. If the shovel blade glanced off a root, he'd have to scoop again. The more tired and bleary-eyed he got, the more weeds he missed. It was a tedious and arduous.

He had a deadline to meet. Old man Stevenson was scheduled to bring his tractor over and till the garden Saturday around noon. That was tomorrow.

Kent had just finished his week of school, changed clothes, and then dived into the garden weeds. Now, two hours into it, he calculated the work he had left. One sixth done and two hours of daylight left. If he was correct, even if he started tomorrow at daylight, he wouldn't finish until about three in the afternoon. It couldn't be done.

As he worked, Kent daydreamed about the things he'd rather be doing than digging pigweed. Of course, he'd rather be hunting or fishing. That only made sense. Then he thought of the big sheep shearing in Cannonville. He'd like to see that someday. For about five weeks each year, Sam Griffin's shearing operation was the biggest employer around. In addition to his regular workers, Sam employed about twenty-five workers just during the shearing each year. The shearing of Sam Griffin's sheep would be an inspiring sight for a young boy to behold.

He kept at his work. His hands were starting to blister. They weren't bad yet, thanks to his work gloves, but they were forming. His mind began to wander again. Sometimes before at about this time he'd sneak off for just some type of relief from his work. But there would be no leaving now. There would be no shirking of his work ever again. His mind drifted to the rest of the evening chores. And he was getting hungry. His role in the family was impossible.

Kent hit his pillow that night totally spent—exhausted physically, mentally, and even emotionally. And this was just the beginning! Sleep quickly overcame him. Dad woke him up well before sunup. "Mr. Stevenson is scheduled to be here at noon. You can do it, son. It may take a miracle, but I know you'll be ready for him."

Kent turned over in his bed, his face now buried in the cushion. Already he could feel the ache in his muscles, the rawness in his hands and the despair in his heart. There was no way. Did Dad face similar challenges? He gritted his teeth. He had to try. Maybe he calculated wrong.

The darkness of night had retreated to where he could make out the shapes of the barn and stables. Kent stumbled past them to the garden plot, shovel in one hand and rake in the other. Something was moving right in the middle of it.

Instinctively, he thought of running back for the gun. But there was a rhythm to the movement. It was unlike a deer or any other animal. He moved closer. It was a person. "Dad," he yelled.

"Over here, son. Thought I'd help you a bit before I headed out to Uncle Jim's."

"Wow, Dad, really?"

They worked together for an hour. Then, tossing his shovel aside and wiping his brow with his shirt sleeve, Charlie slipped over to his boy and squeezed him tightly. "I love you, my boy. Thank you, thank you, thank you." He slipped away. Kent tossed a look at him over his shoulder. He would return home at dark. He felt more respect for him at that moment, than ever before in his life. He turned, shovel slashing through weeds.

The sun was hot in the cloudless sky. Sweat was dripping from Kent's face. He'd skipped breakfast. He felt a tug on his back pant pocket. It was little Gretha.

"Mom says to come to breakfast."

Kent turned to face her. "Tell her I can't. I'll eat at noon when Mr. Stevenson starts tilling." He turned back to the weeds.

Another tug at his pant pocket, Kent turned again. "Mom said you'd say that. She says to come now, and not to worry."

"I just ca- . . ." Kent's jaw dropped. He fixed his eyes on the three figures walking toward him.

"You've got to eat, son," Mom called out. "You need your strength. You'll make better time. Just look in on Jillian and Jessica, and take Gretha back with you. When you come back, Marilyn will go in and care for them, and the three of us will work at it until it's done." There would be no arguing. Kent did as he was told.

Maybe it was a miracle. At five minutes to noon, they finished. The weeds were piled ten feet high and thirty feet around near the canal for burning. Kent heard a tractor in the distance. Soon the tilling would be done, and the real work would begin: raking all seven thousand square feet of it flat, hoeing straight furrows, planting the early seed and the potatoes; waiting three weeks for the first major planting, and then staggering future plantings after that so the vegetables wouldn't all come on at the same time. Then there was clearing all the irrigation ditches.

It was time for a breather. Each of them could sense it as they looked each other over. The sweat was pouring off Mom, and even some off David, and it was only about eighty degrees. Kent was a mess. He'd done the lion's share. Hands calloused, shirt drenched, all his muscles crying out. His hat could probably be wrung out. "You knew all along that you'd help me today, didn't you, Mom?" Kent asked, puffing heavily.

"Yes, I've helped your dad for about fifteen years now. Don't you remember?"

"Come to think of it, I do. I just wasn't sure because of how we divvied up our jobs in family council."

"Our family, as long as we stay united, can do just about anything, son."

Kent bowed his head, pondering her words. "I believe you."

CHAPTER 6
THE RELIEF PLAN

*K*ent's days started well before sunup with the morning chores. Then he'd grab breakfast, go to school, and then come home and work until after dark. Each night he'd fall head-first into his pillow, exhausted—spent. He felt he couldn't make it another day. A week had passed. The ditches were all cleared, and the second watering was currently underway. The garden was raked flat, furrowed, and the early crops of peas, carrots, potatoes, and onions had been planted.

It was Saturday night. He'd planted potatoes nearly the whole day. He reflected on his undertaking. He had dug six rows—trenches a foot deep and a hundred feet long. Then he had cut the seed potatoes, which included cutting a finger twice. He placed them about five inches apart, with the eyes facing upward and shoveled a couple inches of dirt over them. Then added a little fer-tilizer mixed with manure, covered them the rest of the way, raked them flat, and then hoed a furrow to water them.

He looked at his hands. He'd covered the cuts on his fingers with cloth tape. Many calluses had formed on his palms that were cracked and leaking clear liquid. A couple of them had a tinge of blood. Their stinging was incessant, and it kept sleep from over-taking him. It was over. He'd have to tell Mom and Dad he had nothing left.

There was, however, one day a week he didn't mind—Sundays. He wasn't allowed to do more than the necessary chores even if he wanted to. It was a day of rest. They'd all just arrived home from church. "Mom, Dad," Kent asked. "Would you mind if I went up to the sliding hill for a little while?"

They looked at each other. "Not at all, son," Dad said, "but would it be okay if I came up and joined you?"

"Are you serious, Dad?"

"Sure am."

"Okay."

"You run along, son. I suppose you want to get up there in case Anita comes over. I'll be up in fifteen minutes or so."

Kent chuckled. Dad was right. He needed time alone, time to unwind. Entertaining Anita would wind him up more than he already was, and he didn't need that.

He sat atop the hill looking down at their farm. Kent began to see things he'd never noticed before. Their three horses and Daisy were contentedly crunching on the hay he'd carried over. He carried two bales a week for each of them. Every time, the hay and dust would get in his eyes. He tried mightily not to rub them, but he'd give in, and his eyes would swell up and redden more than if he had left them alone. Their water troughs were full from the two buckets he carried fifty yards from the canal. This had to be done several times a day. Kent smiled. Where would they be without me? He looked at the two pigs he slopped every day. They were content. The fridge out back was nice and cool, thanks to the burlap bags that he'd dowse with cold water and spread over the top twice a day. The garden . . . well, the garden looked fantastic. He smiled again with satisfaction.

Dad flopped down next to him, puffing heavily. They sat in silence, gazing over the valley. Not much was happening in town. A few riders on horseback meandered up the road, an occasional car puttered along, and beside that, just the beautiful valley that was deeply engrained in each of them.

"How are you, my boy? You've done a fine job. Are you pretty well given out?"

Sometimes Kent felt like his parents could read his mind, and this was one of those times. "Well, if you'd asked me that last night, I'd have said I can't do it anymore—it's impossible. But thanks to a day of rest I feel a little better. How are you holding up, Dad?"

32

He held out his hands. They compared. They were both in bad shape. "No one can accuse us of not being hard workers," he grinned.

Kent looked over at his dad. He didn't feel like his little boy any more. He felt like he was being treated as an equal, and it felt good. Nonetheless, he was worried and unsure if he could keep it up much longer.

"Son, would you like me to paint a huge picture of what I expect will happen for us as the days and weeks roll on?"

Kent was taken aback. All he could see was a wall of never ending work. He thought of it as a ball and chain. He doubted his dad could change that, or even give him a glimmer of hope, but . . . why not. "Sure, Dad."

"I know you're exhausted, tired, and worn out. You've worked your tail off. So, do you want the good news, or the . . . good news?"

"No bad news?"

"Nope, just good news—the hardest work is over. What did you think of the potatoes?"

"Let's see. I got blisters on top of blisters, cut myself twice, and I felt so muggy in the hot sun that I figured you could wring me out as well as my shirt."

Dad laughed. "Well, son, the corn, beans, squash, melons, and all the rest are a piece of cake compared to that, and we can't plant them for three more weeks, anyhow. Just thought you might like to know that as soon as I get done teaching school—that's four more weeks right?—I'll have Saturday's off. What do you think about having weekends off?"

Kent felt the clouds of doubt and despair recede from his heart. "For real?"

"For real, son. We're going to lick this depression yet. Maybe even fit in a fishing trip or two."

"Wow, Dad!"

"So, son, what do you think you'd like to do? I've got some projects to do, but . . ."

Kent interrupted. "I've already given that question some thought, but I thought it wouldn't be possible."

"Oh?"

"I'd like to see Sam Griffin's sheep shearing operation. I hear he's starting as soon as school is out."

"Sounds right interesting, but how are you going to get down there? Promise Rock is eight miles from here."

"Anita's big brother is working for him. I'll just hop in the back of their truck."

Dad rubbed his chin and wrinkled his brow. He looked up at the puffy white clouds drifting by. "You know, it just might work. Robbie and Henry will be responsible for you, though. You'd need to always let them know what you're up to."

"I would. I think I've gone over it a thousand times while I've worked in the garden."

"I'm sure you have. I'm real proud of you, son."

They sat a while longer in silence—Dad's words echoing through Kent's being. He noticed he had more confidence that things would work out. He could handle four more weeks.

CHAPTER 7
I'M THROUGH WITH HIM

*A*nita awoke early. It was the last day of school. No lessons or lectures, just cleaning out desks, receiving report cards, signing yearbooks, and socializing—right up her alley.

Her heart would soar as she beheld A after A. She'd try hard not to brag, but it would feel good. Signing yearbooks was a favorite event for her. She could pen her feelings for her friends in a way they'd know her true heart; especially for that neighbor of hers—Kent Wilson.

She thought of the day they'd planned their honeymoon together, and relived their kiss in the bushes. It was real to her. But for him, she didn't know. Sometimes she'd catch a look or a glance. She knew her beauty and grace caught his eye. If only he'd come to his senses. He was always so busy. The only time he would give her was on Sundays, and most of that was her doing. She'd finagle a way to sit next to him in Sunday school, or afterward when their families got together she'd try to get him to reveal his true feelings for her . . . but it never happened . . . well, not since first grade.

At least today, she could sign his yearbook. She'd put her heart on the line. That would make him come around. He could review it over and over, and glean its true feeling.

* * *

35

Kent woke up that last day of school, his confidence shaken. Dad's pep talk had helped him over the past four weeks, but the work never got easier, nor was it less.

This day should be a jubilant day; a day to sit back and reflect on a job well done. But Kent felt despair and emptiness. All he'd done for five weeks was work the farm.

Right now, his worst concern was his grades. They'd taken a real dive. He was amazed that neither Mom nor Dad mentioned his school work. They had always hovered over him, Marilyn, and David before. It seemed as though it wasn't important to them anymore; at least, not as important as his work on the farm.

He'd get his report card today, but he'd made up his mind not to open it. If he failed, life would be over—he'd have to repeat seventh grade. He'd be with those younger rascals, Tommy and Glenn and . . . Miranda. The kids his age would make fun of him. No sir, he'd just quit school all together if that happened!

It was also yearbook signing day, and he didn't feel up to it. His feelings for his friends ran deep. Normally, he'd reflect and ponder his yearbook signings—more so than the other boys. It was just that he had hardly had time to say hello to anyone, and if he did, it was just to be cordial. He sighed. He was spent in every way.

The day unfolded with laughter and chatter. Students eagerly compared report cards, and outlined plans for a fun-filled summer. Others searched the meaning of words written in their yearbooks.

Anita gleefully jumped from yearbook to yearbook. She was having the time of her life. Kent signed the yearbooks as best he could, offered good-byes and congratulations, then tucked his unopened report card under his arm, and plodded toward home with Anita.

"Let's stop for a moment," Anita said, jabbing him in the ribs. "Come on, I've never seen you so . . . what's that word we learned in the spelling bee? Oh yeah, despondent."

"Sure, why not."

"Let's go over to the clearing by the stream with the little bridge and the bench."

They sat down. The cottonwoods covered with green, the brook gurgling along at their side, the bridge in a curved shape arching over the sparkling water—it charmed Anita clear through.

"So, what are you so gloomy about?" Anita probed. "I never see you anymore. You're always too busy. What's happened?"

"Just work on the farm. No fun, no friends . . . no nothing."

"Now, wait a minute," Anita scoffed, becoming a little irritated. "I'm your friend. I've always been your friend. Even when you're down and out, which just happens to be about all the time."

"Well, how would you like it if you had to work yourself to the bone every day? No time for yourself? No time to read books, do your make-up . . . " Kent stopped. He didn't want to make her mad.

Anita wasn't mad, but she was getting that way. She was frustrated for sure. She admired his hard work. But at the same time she hated it. That wasn't the life she imagined. "You're right." She looked down. "I would hate it. I couldn't do it."

"Sure, you say that, but what if you were forced to do it?"

"I don't know. I like to work, but not that kind of work."

"Yeah, your hands are soft as silk. Your work is school projects, paper chains, and poster contests."

Now Anita was mad. She stood up and glared at him. "Now listen here. There's nothing the matter with me. I don't know why I've tried to be your friend all these years." With that, she stomped off.

He jumped up and ran after her. "Anita stop! I'm sorry!"

She didn't stop. She'd reached the road, where other kids were on their way home.

He hesitated and then ran and caught up to her. "Anita, please forgive me."

"Well, next time, since you're so miserable, don't take it out on me."

"You're right. That was rude of me. I won't do it again—I promise."

The promise softened her a little, but she had nothing more to say to him. They walked in silence. Kent lugging his ball and chain, Anita thinking of another visit to her aunt in Salt Lake. Or she could flirt with the high school boys at the July Fourth celebration, check out the summer park service employees when they'd come down to the school gym for dances—she'd have a fun-filled summer at any rate...and she was through with Kent Wilson.

CHAPTER 8
THE TRUE GRADING SYSTEM

"I didn't have time to study," Kent said to his little sister Marilyn.

"I know, so let me open it. I let you see mine."

"I know sis, but . . . but I may have flunked."

"Of course you didn't flunk."

"So how would you know?"

"What's going on, kids?" Mom came into the room

"Oh, nothing," Kent said, turning to ascend the stairs to his room.

He didn't make the first step before he heard, "Kent won't open his report card."

"Is that true, Kent?"

"Yes."

Kent felt a hand on his shoulder. "Son, it just may be that I know something you don't. Mary, could you excuse us please?"

"But Mom, he . . ." She left quickly when she noticed Mom's stern expression.

"Come, sit down. Son, you did the best you could with the time you had. Go ahead and open it. There's a letter inside."

Kent's eyes widened. His mother did know something he didn't. He opened it and together they read,

> Math B
> English A
> Social Studies C
> Geography C

Science C
History C
PE B

Then they read the letter:

Dear Kent,

You gave 100% of your available effort to your education during your seventh-grade year, and for that I am very proud of you. You may think these grades are a little high, but I grade my students on who they have become. When it's all said and done, that is what's important in life. Hard work is the key to becoming that fine person, and hard work is what defines you. I have no doubt you'll be successful in whatever undertaking you choose, and that you'll spread works of goodness wherever you go. You're a fine young man. You deserve good grades. Enjoy your summer, and we'll see you in eighth grade this fall.

Sincerely,
Mrs. Shawl

Kent folded the card, eyes still wide in disbelief.
"How about that, Kent? You sure are good in English."
"You talked to Mrs. Shawl, didn't you, Mom."
"I talk to all your teachers, my boy, but mostly to Mrs. Shawl, because she teaches four of your classes."
"She raised each of my grades two letters, didn't she?"
"Does it matter?"
"I guess not."
"Yes, each of your grades was raised a letter or two."
"Would I have failed?"
"If you and the others who had to run farms had more time to dedicate to their studies, you would have passed. We agreed to just make it fair."

Kent hesitated a few moments. "You were always right there—thank you."

"Both your dad and I were. And thank you. You did your job well. Our family is truly blessed because of you." She remained quiet a moment longer. "So, Kent, are you really going to go see Mr. Griffin's sheep shearing operation? Dad says you're going on opening day Monday, and then working with him on Saturday."

"No, actually I . . . He really said that?"

"Yes."

"Yeah, sure."

"Well, we'd better plan your day. You don't want to be unprepared."

Kent placed a hand on his forehead. What he thought would be the worst day of his life had become one of the best.

CHAPTER 9
I'M OUT OF TROPIC!

 he old Ford bounced and clanked down the dirt road toward Promise Rock. "It's chuck full of chuck holes," Kent laughed out loud. The morning was beautiful, the air still a little crisp. The sun was glowing behind Escalante Mountain.

He'd waited half an hour for Henry and Robbie to come out. There would be no chance of getting left behind. He stood up on the truck's flat bed and breathed in the fresh morning air. He tipped his head back and let the relief sweep clear through him. From deep inside he shouted the words he'd mulled over in his heart a million times. "Hooray! I'm out of Tropic!"

The road wound along the river, rolling hills looming on either side. It was tough going. It was a good thing Henry slowed down for the washes. Some of them had eroded the road away nearly a foot, and others had good sized rocks washed down from the spring rains. After a good seven miles they passed Cannonville. They crossed the bridge over the Paria River, and they were there.

Promise Rock loomed above his head. It must be a couple hundred feet high.

The boys pulled up behind a few other trucks and a wagon. Kent jumped out and scurried over to the rock to behold the scene. He scrambled up its steep face until he found a good overlook. "Wow, look at all those sheep!" They stretched out as far as he could see. Those that were far away looked like puffy marshmallows swaying back and forth. Lots of sheep dogs darted busily about, men on horseback keeping the sheep together, and dust was everywhere.

A huge corral with a funnel chute caught his attention. The sheep would enter the chute to be sheared, and then exit on the far side. He saw a big machine with a rubber belt on it and figured they must use electricity to shear faster.

Men gathered in the stalls, and still others worked on a big bin next to the rock that already had a bunch of big cushy wool sacks in it. Another truck arrived full of sacks. A man got out and surveyed the valley. He lifted his arms and stretched. Seeing Kent he called out. "Come on over here, young man. Help us carry these sacks and ties."

They loaded him up with as much as he could carry. As he rounded the rock, struggling with the load, he nearly bumped into a horse. Stepping back, he looked up. The man sitting on the horse was peering down at him. He wore a large black cowboy hat, and clothes that were well worn and made for the trail. His features were soft, yet seasoned. He sat his saddle with ease and comfort.

The horseman turned back to the men in the shearing stalls. "Are you ready?"

"Ready as we'll ever be, boss," one called back.

Kent swallowed hard. *It's Mr. Griffin himself. Hope he doesn't want me out of here.* He tried to stand a little taller. Sweat began running down between his shoulder blades. *He's going to make me leave. My plan is doomed!*

Mr. Griffin let out a shrill whistle, then waving his hat yelled, "Bring 'em in!" Turning to Kent he said softly, "Son, take those sacks up on Promise Rock and drop them next to the bin. Watch your step."

"Yes sir." Kent turned. *Whew, that was close.*

He carried several more loads of sacks, and then, sensing that was enough, scampered up Promise Rock to his lookout spot. He looked for Mr. Griffin amongst the shearers, but he wasn't there. He saw him out in the sea of sheep assisting other horseman. It seemed he was more comfortable out there than near the shearing.

Kent watched for over an hour, dazzled at the process. Through the noise and the dust, he could see the workers. Two used the electric shears, and two others used manual ones. It seemed like they were racing, but the electric shearers beat them every time, and appeared to do a better job. A sheep could be sheared in a matter of minutes, and it didn't take them too long to fill up the big sacks. The men would toss them over the fence into a bin, where they bounced off the rock or landed with a gentle thud. The pile grew quickly.

Kent mulled over the thought of working for Mr. Griffin next year. He'd be a year older, fourteen, and he hoped he would be bigger. He could make some real money. "Not a chance," he breathed. "I could never get away from the farm."

He heard another thud, but this one was heavier, and no sack had been tossed over the fence. Looking down he was surprised to see a girl picking herself up, and scurrying over to a place where the rock wasn't as steep. She climbed the rock, her two long pigtails bouncing back and forth, and then ambled over to the ledge above the pile of wool sacks. She was preparing for another jump when Kent called out with his high-pitched, squeaky voice; "Hi . . . that looks fun! Can I have a try?"

Startled, she looked toward the voice. She stared for a moment. "Sure, come on over."

Kent worked his way over next to her and looked down. "It must be a ten-foot jump."

"Yup. Watch this!" She jumped straight out, did a half turn and landed on her back, looking up at Kent. "Okay, your turn."

Kent waited until she was out of the way, but hesitated. It was scary jumping from that high. Mustering all his courage, he jumped from the secure rock ledge. He landed on his feet, then fell sideways. It was really soft. He scampered out of the sacks and went up for another jump. He made his way to the jump-off point and placed his hands on his knees to catch his breath. He could feel this girl's eye on him. She'd been studying him.

"That was pretty good," she said. "But you ought to try to land on your back. It's plenty soft. Just try to land smack dab on a sack so you don't slip through."

"I'll try, but I'm afraid I'll go too far or not far enough and get hurt."

"Well, it takes a lot of practice. This time I'm going to do something a little different. Watch this." She jumped straight out as before, but this time tucked her head and landed again on her back.

"That was swell! You did a flip."

"Yep."

Kent watched her run toward the gradual incline of rock. He'd never seen a girl like her. She was certainly nothing like Anita. Before he took his turn, he asked, "Now, which jump is easier to land on my back?" She surprised him by asking him a question.

"Aren't you upset that a girl is doing things you can't do?"

Startled, Kent stayed silent for a moment. He wasn't sure what to think, but he'd have to sound grown up. "Well, my mom taught me that I'd be a fool to not accept help from someone who knows more than I do about something."

"Unbelievable! Every boy I've ever known gets upset when I best them at sports or games or something." She paused a moment. "It's easiest to just stand here and allow yourself to fall straight out, and do a half twist and land on your back."

"Would you do it one more time?"

"Sure," she said, giving him a grin of either bewilderment or admiration. "Here goes." She did exactly as she said.

As she scrambled out of the sacks, Kent marveled. Dang, that's mighty good. He watched her make her way up the rock. She wasn't like skinny, but yet she was. And she was solid—strong, and maybe even a little taller than he, and she looked older. She wasn't beautiful like Anita. No makeup, perfume, jewelry, or pretty dress. But she could probably be pretty if she wanted to—maybe. Her clothes were made for the backwoods—for work like his.

Kent braced himself, gathering his courage to jump before she got to his side. He let himself fall kind of sideways. He gave out a yell. It was real scary, but gratefully, he landed mostly on his back. He lay there a second just checking to see if he was still alive. Just then there was another shout.

"Watch out!"

Kent had just enough time to shield his face as a sack came over the fence and landed on top of him. He could hear the girl laughing. Pushing it off, he worked his way through the bags, and back to the girl.

"I'm sorry. I should have warned you that the men like to toss the sacks at you when they get a chance."

"Oh, that's fine," Kent said, breathing heavily. "It was neat." Trying to catch his breath, he panted, "I don't even know your name?"

"And I don't know yours. My name is Betty," she announced, holding out her hand.

Kent took her hand in his. It was rough. "And I'm Kent. What's your last name, Betty?"

She leaped up, and in midair called out, "Griffin!"

Of course, she'd have to be. She's Mr. Griffin's daughter! Kent waited for her to get back up. "Do you mean Sam Griffin with all the sheep's daughter?"

"Yep."

"No wonder you're so good at jumping on the wool sacks."

"I guess so," she said, still puffing hard. "I started when I was pretty small. So what's your last name?"

Kent hesitated, then hurled himself off the rock and shouted, "Wilson!" Neither the shout nor the jump was especially good. He climbed up next to her, panting heavily.

She waited a few moments then said. "I didn't hear you. What's your last name again?"

"Wilson."

"So where are you from, and what brings you to Promise Rock?"

"I'm from Tropic, and, uh, well, I'm just tired. I'm the oldest of six kids, and I'm expected to work from dawn to dusk every day. I feel like I'm in jail with heavy steel balls chained to my ankles. I'm tired of it!"

"Figures," she whispered.

"What?"

"Well, Kent Wilson. It's nice to meet you, but I have to be getting back home." She gave him a distasteful look and turned to leave.

"Why so early? It's not even noon."

She took a few steps up the rock then turned. "I'm the oldest of six kids too. My family depends on me. But I enjoy helping." With that, she turned and scampered up the rock.

"Betty!" he called, but she kept on going. Where in the heck is she going? Oh well, who cares? He turned and began kicking at a rock sticking up between a crack. She's just a dumb girl anyhow.

Just then he heard a voice from high up on the rock. "Hey, Kent, want to come up?"

He looked toward the voice, flabbergasted. She must be crazy! What in the world is she doing up there? She had plenty of grit. "Okay," he yelled.

He made his way up the steep incline, topped out, and looked around. Betty was sitting on a little ledge like a natural seat in the rock. "Isn't it beautiful? From this point you can see my hometown of Cannonville, the red rocks behind, about a mile of the road going to Tropic, and all of my dad's sheep."

"So you live in Cannonville?" Kent panted.

"Yep."

"So that's what you're doing up here. You're going home."

"Yep."

Kent wrinkled his forehead, bewildered. "I thought you were crazy coming up here."

"I don't think I'm crazy," her face coloring. "You don't even know me."

"Well, you don't know me either. Fact is, I worked very, very hard around our house so my mom would let me come down here." It felt good saying that because he felt she was judging him.

"Sorry if you thought I was judging you."

Kent was taken back. Stepping back, he widened his eyes. *She's reading my thoughts!*

She spoke again. "I'm sure you do a lot of work at home. But why do you do it?"

"Well that's easy. I'm the oldest. I'm the only one that can carry the water buckets, and the hay bales. The little ones can't mend the fences and . . ."

"Yes, but why?"

He looked away. She had her eyes fixed on his; and they were narrow. She was studying. Kent didn't like it. It made him feel like Dad was reprimanding him for skipping out on chores.

Now his eyes narrowed. "So why do you have to know? Who cares?"

"Well, I care." She crossed her arms still peering into his. "I thought you were different, but you're the same as all the other boys." She paused a moment. Kent just stood there with his mouth open. "So why do *you* work?"

He remained silent, with his stomach turning and his mind reeling. He couldn't figure what she was getting at, and he darned well wasn't going to satisfy her with a response like *because I love my mommy and daddy*.

She held her gaze for a good moment, then shrugged her shoulders and scoffed, "I must be going."

"So you're going to judge me and run off are you?"

She stopped, still looking away. Kent was afraid she was going to come back and they were going to tussle.

After a good moment she turned, but her face wasn't one of readying for a fight. Rather, it was sincere. "You know, I help my family day in and day out because I love them. It feels good to see them get the care that only I can give. I know this is the right way to feel. I was hoping you were the same." She hesitated a brief moment. "You really do have a ball and chain around your ankle. Too bad *you* put it there." She turned and broke into a steady run down the rocky decline.

Kent watched Betty run the whole half mile to Cannonville without stopping, her pig tails tossing back and forth with each stride. "She's so weird," he said out loud. "Why should she care why I do my chores? They have to be done so I do them. And . . . she doesn't know what she's talking about. Life put the ball and chain on me, I didn't. Girls."

He sat in the natural seat, leaned back against the rock, and closed his eyes, hoping to rid this Betty from his mind. Several minutes went by. Betty kept popping back in like wasps after spilled honey. The only good thing she had was straight teeth, and the one time she smiled she had little dimples and a curl to her lips. Finally he got up, and made his way back to the noise and bustle of Mr. Griffin and his sheep.

CHAPTER 10
WORK YOUR HARDEST AND LOVE IT

The days that followed were full, in spite of not spending eight hours a day in school. It seemed like everything needed to be repaired. Early on Friday, Kent was mending and cleaning the trays in the chicken coop. He had to keep them clean so germs wouldn't infect the chickens. Also, rodents kept getting inside, so their holes had to be filled. The only good part of it all was Kent was allowed to shoot them with the .22 if he got the chance.

Kent chuckled as he remembered his arrival home from his day at Promise Rock. His brother and sisters had met him at the front door. Mom came in, too.

"How was your day?" she asked.

Knowing that all eyes were on him, Kent figured to paint a real nice picture. "Well, let's see . . . the ride down there just about shook me to death. I thought it might rattle my head clear off. But I think it's still on okay." He shook his head around for emphasis.

"It's still on," Gretha giggled amongst the laughter.

"When I got to Promise Rock, the whole valley was covered with marshmallows, only they moved around like dandelions seeding in the gentle breeze."

"You mean the sheep?" cried Jillian.

"Oh yea, that was the sheep. So, anyway, I watched the wranglers and the sheep dogs herd them into the chute, then the shearers went to work. They had a generator that made electricity so they could shear with a vibrating blade rather than clippers."

"Wow," David exclaimed, wide eyed.

"Then they put all the wool into big sacks and threw them into a bin under a cliff. Pretty soon there was a huge pile. I found a friend and we jumped into the bin. It was soooo soft."

"Wow wee," Marilyn exclaimed.

"Was your friend real neat?" David asked.

"Oh yeah, sh- . . . he was okay."

"It was a girl?" Marilyn asked.

Worried, Kent answered. "I guess he was a little strange. I gather he thought I was real strange too. But, wow, he could sure jump off that cliff onto the sacks. He even did a flip."

Kent's mind reverted to the present, but now he was thinking of Betty. The words she'd told him nagged him like mosquitoes. I didn't put the ball and chain there, he pondered. What was she getting at anyhow? Is it possible she works as hard as I do? Her being the oldest and all, and her dad being gone a lot? And is she really happy doing all that work, and does she really love it? No way! The work is awful, and life is no fun without some balance like fishing and exploring.

"How are you, Kent?"

Kent twirled, his thought process vanishing. "Fine, Mom."

She was looking at him with narrowed eyes. "Are you deep in thought?"

"Oh, uh, yeah, I guess."

"Are you thinking of the fine man you've turned out to be?"

"Oh, Mom, stop it. Any oldest child would do the same."

"Son, where would our family be without you?"

Kent stood there silently, grateful for the appreciation of his family, but still thinking of what Betty had said. "Ah, Mom, I enjoy helping out, and, well . . . I do it because I love you and our family."

Several quiet moments went by. He looked up and was startled. A tear was trickling down Mom's cheek.

"Finally," she whispered. "I've been so worried that you may feel life is unkind and unfair. That you have to drag yourself out of bed every day and work your hands to the bone because if you don't we'll all starve. That you were consigned to a life of misery until this . . . idiotic depression ended."

Kent was shocked. That was exactly how he felt . . . at least until he ran into that weird girl. "Ah, Mom, I'm fine. Maybe going to Promise Rock helped me get some jitters out."

"Maybe you should go back again."

"What! Are you sure?"

"I'm sure. You're shouldering your workload for the right reasons. You've learned how God wants us to live, and . . . with work like this you deserve it. We all need some balance, right?"

"Yes."

"Why don't you go next week? If you don't mind, for tomorrow . . ." She listed out a bunch of jobs that were out of the ordinary.

"Sure, Mom."

Alone again, he busied himself with the trays, but now his mind was in full commotion. He had said what Betty had said, and it made his mother cry. How strange is that? Maybe a trip to Promise Rock would be good. That weird girl Betty might be there, though. You've never hung out with just one girl, he told himself. Well, maybe with Anita but she's . . .

In the next breath he was telling himself—this one is different. She can probably best me in any sport. And it looks like she can run faster and farther. Just the kind of friend I'd like to pal around with. Only problem is . . . she's a girl.

CHAPTER 11
NOT WEIRD ... AMAZING

$\mathscr{B}$ack at Promise Rock, Kent surveyed the sheep. About one half were still left. He looked up toward the top of the rock. "What am I thinking?" he said out loud. "She doesn't like me and I, well, if she doesn't like me, then I don't like her either." But he climbed the rock toward the natural seat anyhow. Just as he arrived, he could see Betty racing through the sagebrush covered valley. But there were no pigtails. Her long dark hair tossed back and forth. He gave a hesitant wave, and noticed that she waved back. She made it to the seat and sat down hard, out of breath.

"Glad you could make it."

"Is that so? I thought you'd never want to see me again," she puffed, standing up and placing her hands on her knees. "I can't believe you came."

"Well, for a while I thought we had a fight brewing, but ... I could never fight with a girl."

"Why not?" she snapped. "I'd probably whip you too."

Kent's blood immediately began to boil—his face beet red, but no matter. He didn't like being challenged or threatened. Summoning all his courage he squared his shoulders to her and glared back. "That's not what I meant."

"What did you mean then?"

He noticed her eyes were a hint less narrow. "I meant ... well, the 'never could fight with a girl' wasn't what I wanted to say. I'm sorry about that."

"What did you want to say?"

"Good golly, are you always so full of questions? I don't know what you want. Are you mad? Do you want to fight? So yeah; you make me mad. You always want the truth, but you never give me a chance."

"You're right," she stated, bowing her head.

"What?"

"I said you're right, and I'm sorry. Very, very sorry."

"Sorry for what?"

"For judging you."

"Well, I'm sorry, too. I don't know how to act around girls."

She burst out laughing.

Kent stood there, not believing what was happening. They weren't mad at each other, at least, not for the moment. "So what I meant to say at first was that I had a good time jumping on the sacks . . . so . . . why not come back?"

She gave a rather skeptical look, and shook her head.

"I'm sorry," Kent said again. "I just don't know how to talk to girls."

"Oh heck, you're just fine. It's just me anyhow. You probably think that anything you say to me will make me mad—which, come to think of it . . . it does." But as she said it, she wore a broad smile. "I was hoping you would come back, because . . ." She looked away, then straightened up and slowed her breathing. She turned and squared her eyes to Kent's, but they weren't those narrow mean-looking eyes, they were soft . . . searching. "I've been really feeling bad about how I treated you. I hope you can forgive me."

Puzzled, Kent stepped back, placing a hand on his forehead. Deep inside he felt that just maybe she was hoping he was different, better than other boys she knew. "Why did you judge me then?"

For the first time, Betty looked uncertain. She looked down at her feet and began shuffling. "The boys I know help their family because they have to—like if they don't they'll get in trouble. They go to church because their mom and dad make them. I was hoping you were the kind that helped because you loved them."

Kent looked at her in disbelief. "Wow, you sound like my mother." He quickly caught himself. "And I mean that in a good way. I think she's been trying to teach me that for about thirteen years now."

Betty grinned.

"Are you like sixteen or something? Why are you so wise?"

This time she laughed. "No, silly, I just turned thirteen in April. So you're thirteen too?"

"Yeah, I'll be fourteen in November. So I'm six months older, and you're like six years wiser. Why is that?"

"No, no," she laughed. "I was the one judging, remember?"

Kent couldn't believe the difference between now and a moment ago. He stood there bewildered. What brought about the change?

Betty's voice shook him out of his thoughts. "By the way, you probably noticed the bin is clear full of sacks."

"Yup, I noticed."

"Don't worry. The people that buy the wool are coming today. Want to help me roll the bags to the loading dock?"

"Sure."

They made their way down to the bin. Opening the gate, Betty shouted above the noise. "It's best to just roll the sacks rather than try to carry them."

They each grabbed a sack, shoved it to the ground outside the bin, and began rolling it to the loading dock. On the second trip Betty yelled, "Watch this."

"What?" Her sack caught him square in the face, knocking him backward over his sack. His feet came up, and he landed headfirst in the brush and sand. His arms were scraped from the brush, and he had sand in his eyes, but no matter. Laughing, he stood up and brushed himself off. "Okay, you got me back."

They rolled the sacks for an hour, all the while trying to catch the other off guard, and knock each other over. Kent succeeded. Just as Betty gave her sack a shove, he heaved his sideways. It caught her foot, toppling her forward over his sack. She bounced off her own, her legs came up, and she went headfirst into the sand. She ended up on her back with her sack over her face.

Kent rushed around the wool sacks, and lifted the bag off her face and found Betty, covered with sand, coughing and spitting the dirt out of her mouth. He was horrified. He'd gone too far. He knelt down trying to help clear some of the sand from her eyes and forehead. She sat up making it easier to wipe some of the sand off, her eyes still closed. With one last gasp she was able to clear her throat. Kent was about to panic.

She burst into laughter. "Way to go!"

Kent couldn't believe it. He just stared at her. Even his friends Joe or Sam would have been up for a fight about that one.

She got up and dusted herself off, but it didn't help much. Sand and little pieces of sagebrush and sticks were all through her hair.

"Here, let me see if I can get some of the sticks out of your hair." She looked at him briefly, then bent her head toward him. He could see this would really take some doing. "Why didn't you braid your hair today?"

"Can't say." She couldn't say she wanted to look pretty in case he came back.

"Well, you should have braided it. It'll be hard getting all that out."

"You don't mind the braids?"

"Of course not. Not out here."

"Oh." She waited another moment. "Don't worry about it. I look like one of the workers now."

"Believe me, you look a lot better than your dad's workers." They both broke into laughter again.

"Hey, the sacks are down far enough we can do some jumps," she shouted. They rolled their sacks to the dock and ran to the ledge above the bin. Betty jumped first and let out a yell, landing on her back looking up. Kent did the same without the yell.

On their next jump, Betty was acting a little different. "Okay you first this time," she said. Kent jumped and landed on his back, but a sack came flying over the fence and landed right on top of him. He tried shoving it off, but it pressed down heavily upon him, pinning him down. Betty must have jumped and was on top of the sack. He couldn't see and could hardly move. He heaved with all his might but his hands just indented into the wool sack. He was pinned. He began thinking about panicking, but not with Betty there. She'd think him a wimp. He checked to see if he could breathe—no problem, although the air was choked with sand.

"Give up?" a voice asked.

"Never."

"Okay then."

Several moments went by. Kent could see she had him. "All right, I give up." The pressure was removed and then the light of the sun poured over him. Betty bent over looking down.

"So you give?" she said, sticking a hand out. Kent took it and she hoisted him up. "Took you a long time, I thought you were figuring a way out."

"There is no way out."

"I'm sorry to say it," Betty countered, "but there just might be a way." Kent stood there perplexed.

"No, there isn't."

"I panicked the first time they did it to me, but the next time, instead of pushing up, I wriggled my way down and sideways. Pretty soon I was out from under the weight. I had some bags over me by then, but it was no problem to get them off."

"You don't say, down instead of up." Kent breathed just thinking about the genius of it. "Well, let's not try it again; how about if I just take your word for it?"

She giggled. "Deal."

The lunch bell rang.

"Great, let's eat," Betty said.

They made their way over to the shade of the rock, where the hands were gathering in kind of a semicircle. A horse pulled up outside of the circle they had formed. It was Mr. Griffin. He strode over to her and knelt down. "How are you, my dear?"

"Never better, Daddy."

"And who is this youngster next to you?"

"This is Kent Wilson."

"Oh, Charlie's boy," he said, but at the same time gave Kent a hard glance. Kent read it clearly. Something like, "this is my beautiful daughter. You'd better treat her like a queen, or there'll be heck to pay."

He then glanced back at Betty with kind of a bewildered look. Probably wondering why she was covered with sand, and had hair full of brush. There was even some dirt on her lower lip. He got up to get some food then turned back to Betty. "Thank you for helping us out here and at home. You're a blessing from God for us all. And thanks for the prayers too."

Sam Griffin got his food, and then slipped away.

After lunch, Betty said she'd better be getting back home.

"Mind if I go with you? I just have to be back at five." He slipped over to Henry, who was just finishing his lunch. "Mind if I slip over to Betty Griffin's place? I'll be back at five."

A look of recognition swept over Henry's face as he realized who this young girl was that Kent was palling around with. "Sure, but we're working until six."

"I'll be back before six then."

Henry laughed and waved a hand at him.

Kent went back to Betty, barely believing what he was doing. But there wasn't anything more he could do at Promise Rock, and . . . well, Betty didn't seem weird at all anymore. She was fun to be around, at least, as long as she didn't get mad. But Betty was taken back a little, and it worried him. She narrowed her eyebrows and probed as if she was asking if that's what he really wanted to do.

"Well, are we going?" Kent asked again.

"Okay, let's go," she said finally, with a little hesitation in her voice.

"Whew," Kent breathed.

They walked over Promise Rock, passed the natural seat, and made their way down to the flat. Kent was quite nervous about it. They walked without speaking.

At the bottom of Promise Rock, Betty said "That was more fun than I've had in a long time. You really got me good."

Kent's mind was in high gear. He'd really had fun too. But more than that, she was . . . fun to be with. She was nothing like Anita. Anita wouldn't have stood for such rough housing for one instant, and she was too proper to jump onto the wool sacks.

"How come you're so quiet? You couldn't stop talking before."

"Uh, I don't know. I guess I'm a little nervous."

"About me being a girl? Or is it the five pounds of dirt in my hair?"

Kent burst out laughing. "No, no, silly. I . . . I've just never palled around with a girl."

"And I've never palled around with a boy. What type of things do you like to do?"

"Well, I like to climb the sliding hill behind my house. It's nothing like the red sand and rocks here. Just black sand, but its real fun to run and jump and land in the soft dirt. You can jump a long ways 'cause it's real steep. Then you can slide all the way down." Kent was quiet a moment. He wanted to mention things that sounded more grown up instead of playing kick the can, run sheep run, or racing homemade boats down the ditch. And then there was his squeaky voice and his short stature. Oh well, there was nothing he could do but grow up.

Betty broke his train of thought. "What else?"

"Uh, I like to work on machines. My dad got a windmill, and I was able to generate electricity to kind of light our house. Of course it only works when it's windy, and even then it sort of flickers. Dad said he's going to buy a generator. It's supposed to provide good lighting, and we can also hook up a radio."

"That sounds grand," Betty said with what he thought was some admiration. "Anything else?"

"Yeah, I've worked on my dad's car a little. I'm learning how they work so maybe next year I can get one of my own." Kent paused. That pretty much summed him up. "Oh yes, and I like to work on our farm."

She laughed. "Glad you found that one out."

"So what things do you like to do?"

"Promise you won't laugh?"

"I promise."

"Okay . . . I like playing games like kick the can or run sheep run."

Kent gave himself a rap on the side of his head. Betty didn't see.

She continued, "I love a warm cozy fire in the fireplace, rainbows, dandelions on the ditch bank, and babies' smiles. I like fields of corn shucks and pumpkins, and I just love the town of Cannonville when I look at it from up there," she said, pointing at the high wall of red rock behind the scattered houses and barns. "It reminds me of my grandma's patchwork quilt."

She was so different. Such little things meant the world to her. It was as if she saw things with her heart rather than her eyes. Here he was trying to push the little things away, and those were the very things that made her happy.

"And I like to roughhouse. You know, like knock my friends down with a wool sack or get knocked down. I like playing with and caring for my family. I love to sing to them, and calm them with a lullaby. My father taught me how to sing." A brief pause, "I like to write."

"Really? What do you write about?"

"Oh, about anything that touches my heart."

"So you keep a journal?"

"Yep, I also write poetry."

"Wow, I could never begin to figure out poetry."

"Well, here's my home town of Cannonville." They started up the road. "Do you mind if we try to steer clear of people? I'd like them to meet you, but I'm afraid I'd scare them off."

Kent chuckled. "Hey, there're some kids playing in the park. Let's go meet them."

"You're such a tease," she said, pushing Kent on the arm.

They made it without meeting a soul. Betty breathed a sigh of relief as they entered the gate to her front yard. She opened the door and two little girls leapt into her arms.

"Is that you, Betty?" a voice called from a back room.

"Yes, Mother."

"Could you please take the dirty diapers and clothes out to the wash?"

Just then the high-pitched voice of a girl of perhaps seven or eight said, "But mother, she has a boy with her."

"Oh my," there was silence, then a patter of feet. Martha Griffin came out, carrying a baby of perhaps eight or ten months in her arms. "You must be Kent. Betty told me all about you."

"Yes, ma'am. I'm Kent Wilson."

"Did you get to eat lunch?"

"Yes, we did. Thank you."

"What do you think of the shearing?"

"I think it's the most amazing thing I've ever seen. It must take forever to shear them all."

"Oh, they'll be all done in about five weeks. Well, Kent, make yourself at home. And Betty, don't worry about the wash, I'll take care of it." She returned to the back room.

Kent was relieved that Mrs. Griffin was so pleasant toward him. He could see some of that same warmth in Betty.

There was a rustle at his feet. Kent looked down and noticed three sets of eyes glued on him. He knelt down to be at eye level with the littlest one. "What's your name?"

An older sister answered for her, "Judy. She just turned three."

"You sure are pretty." She squealed and looked away. "And what's your name?" Kent asked, looking at the next oldest, who must have been about five or six.

"I'm Sara," she announced gleefully. "And that's Mary, she's nine, and Pamela isn't here—she's eleven."

It seemed they were instant friends. Betty excused herself and did the wash anyhow. Kent played with the kids and ended up answering question after question, all the while with both Judy and Sara on his lap.

"It's too bad Pamela isn't here," Mary stated. "She watches us when Betty and Mom aren't here."

"I can't wait to meet her if she's anything like all of you." They all giggled their pleasure.

"Would you like to see our horses, and our cow, and the chickens?" Mary asked.

"I'd love to," Kent said, getting up, and at the same time lifting Judy and Sara off the floor.

They showed him around their whole place. It was a lot like the Wilson farm in Tropic, only it wasn't kept up quite as well. He guessed Betty and her mom did the lion's share of the work.

They ended up in the front of the house, with Kent twirling the little ones and setting them down when they were dizzy. They rocked back and forth, and sometimes fell down. Kent caught them so they wouldn't get hurt. Pretty soon he got dizzy as well, and went down. They all piled on top of him, laughing.

Kent hadn't noticed, but Betty had emerged from the front door. The dirty hair had been replaced with long, dark brown, glowing hair. Her whole face spread into a beautiful smile.

"We're playing with Kent," Sara announced.

Kent lay there, reflecting on the moment. He felt acceptance, even love, and he'd only met them a short time ago.

"I was thinking I'd like to take you somewhere—a new place; a place that's very special to me," Betty said.

Kent looked at her. She seemed to be struggling.

"Kent, this place is very close to my heart. I've only shared it with one other person besides my family."

Then it hit him. *She's starting to think of me as a friend. She approves of me! She likes me.*

They left the house. The little ones put up a fuss, but a stern look from big sister gave them the sense they'd better let them alone. "You have a few hours left, don't you?"

"Yes."

"Okay then."

She led him toward a stand of cottonwood trees. On the other side was a little clearing like a small meadow, and behind it was the huge rock wall Kent had seen from Promise Rock.

As they neared the rock wall, he said, "There's no way up."

"Are you sure about that?" she asked with a grin.

"Since you figured a way out from under the wool sack, no I'm not sure."

Arriving at the wall, Kent observed a thin opening that wasn't noticeable from further back. They entered and walked about thirty yards on the sandy bottom. Then the floor became rock and gradually ascended until they were on top. Kent was amazed. He felt Betty's eyes upon him. He could tell she was delighted to see his reactions to this new experience.

They turned, faced the town again, and walked up to the edge. She led him north about fifty yards to an incline with a little plateau on top. Just beneath it was a patch of sand about eight feet across.

They stood at the plateau and looked out over the valley. It was just as Betty had said. You could see Promise Rock, her dad's sheep, and the patchwork quilt of roads and farms below. They stepped down to the sandy area.

"This is my piece of heaven on earth," Betty said. "Do you remember what my dad said about my prayers?"

"Yes."

"This is where I pray, on this little patch of sand. Even on the hottest days," she dropped to her knees and wriggled them into the sand, "you can work your knees down a few inches, and it's nice and cool."

Kent dropped to his knees and worked them into the sand. Sure enough, it was cool.

"So . . . I can't be seen from Cannonville here," ceasing to speak for a moment as she made her way upon the flat rock, "but I can see the entire valley. As far as I know, I'm the only one that comes up here, at least often. I don't think too many people even know about it."

"It's a perfect place, Betty. I have a place like this in Tropic. There are times when I just want to get away from everything and be by myself."

"You sound like me," Betty grinned.

"It's true. I go up there to think and to figure out how to solve my problems."

"That's just the way I feel. I also try to get on top of my weaknesses and faults. I ask the Lord for help."

"Why would you do that? You don't have any faults."

Betty smiled. "You know better than that. I'm going to work on not being judgmental, and . . . to not be quick to be angry with boys."

Kent laughed at that one. "Wish I had such small faults to work on."

"Oh, gosh, it's you that don't have any faults." She looked down at her feet for a good while. "Kent, I don't know why but I want to give this place a name today. Since I pray to God in Heaven here, I'm going to name it . . . Yeah, I'm completely sure of it," she said, perhaps making sure she was thoroughly convinced of the name herself. "I'm going to name it Heaven's Rock."

Kent didn't say anything. He knew this place meant the world to her, and he was going to respect that. "I think that's the perfect name. I feel something special up here too. Maybe it's because we're so high up we're closer to God." Betty smiled warmly.

"What are you thinking about?"

"Uh, I was . . . I was thinking that . . . I should be more like you."

"Oh, you want to step down the ladder several rungs. Not a good idea."

"Oh shush, I'm serious. I help my family because it has to be done. And, just like you said, I'm miserable because there's no way out of it. You help yours because you love it and enjoy it."

"I don't believe you."

"What? You don't?"

"I know you love your family. I think you work so hard because you love them."

"Do you want the truth again?"

"Nothing but . . ."

"I only came back to Promise Rock because I copied what you said to my mom. She started to cry and said because I'd changed so much I should come back."

"You don't know yourself very well. You just need some time. So . . . I want to show you one more thing."

"Right here?"

"Yes."

Kent looked around. "But there's nothing else here."

"Always so sure, aren't you?"

"You're right. I'm sorry."

She walked over to the rocky ledge, picked up a stick, and probed it inside a crack in the rock that he hadn't noticed before, then reached in and brought out a book wrapped in a sheet.

Kent jumped to his feet, placing a hand on his forehead. "I never would have known there was a crack there."

Opening the book, she announced, "I'll read it out loud."

I am Thankful

Dear God, for the blessings you give me,
The moon and the stars and the deep blue sea.
The fun and love and things to do,
Father In Heaven, I thank you

For my sisters and Mother and Dad,
The best that any girl ever had.
For this comfortable home and food to eat.
And for my many clothes to keep me neat.

For all these things I can truthfully say,
I'm thankful for more, every day.

Kent was impressed. "That's fantastic! You have a gift."

"Oh, I . . . you're very kind."

They were silent for a few moments. Kent pulled his watch out of his pocket. "I need to start heading back in about an hour and a half."

"Yes, I know. Come on then."

"Where are we going?"

"There are some more things up here that I haven't shown you."

"It never ends."

Betty grinned at him. "It's a little more adventurous if you're up to it?"

"Yeah, sure, or maybe I'm not sure when it comes to you. Are we going cliff jumping?"

"No, silly."

"Oh, now I'm silly."

"Well, okay you're not too silly, and the cliffs aren't so high. There's another way down."

They skirted north for a few hundred yards where Kent could see another indentation in the rock.

"Now, this one," Betty said, "is a little tricky. You have to climb down in some places, and there's one place where you have to put your back on the rock wall and your feet on the other side and shimmy down. I'll go first because I know the footholds."

Arriving to the first one, she put her back toward the decline. It was a good ten feet down to the next ledge—plenty scary. She placed her feet in places Kent couldn't see, and made it down with ease. He knelt down, and then turned like Betty did, placed his hands on the same hand holds and lowered himself; only, he couldn't find any footing. He felt Betty's hand take his foot and push it toward the cliff. Sure enough, it was a good foothold. Dropping down next to her, he wiped his forehead. "Yup, I was right, cliff jumping."

"You're such a tease."

Next there was a more gradual incline, but still plenty steep with no visible handholds.

"Here, I'll help you with this one," Kent said taking her hand.

She stopped, then turned and looked at him. It was frightening, but he didn't let go. She backed down the incline, not letting go of his hand until she was near the bottom. Kent followed, and found himself at the spot where they'd have to shimmy down between the rocks.

"Do you want to go first?" Betty asked.

"Oh no, I'd rather see how the teacher does it."

She placed her back on the wall, put one foot on the other side, and gradually eased into the crevice. It looked to be about a fifteen-foot drop. Kent copied exactly what she'd done. Arriving near the bottom, he jumped, landing in soft sand. Looking up at the sliver in the rock he yelled. "We conquered you!"

He heard Betty laughing behind him. "You're talking to a rock. Have you lost your marbles?"

"I think I have. I think that was the coolest thing I've ever done. Betty you're . . . you're . . . I like being with you."

She just looked at him, saying nothing. He immediately became flushed. It was the wrong thing to say. He began searching for a way out "Betty, I . . . "

"I really like being with you too," she interrupted. "I always wished I had a best friend. I've never really had one."

"I can't believe that. Everyone must lo- . . . like you."

"Actually, there aren't too many other kids my age here."

They began making their way down the gentle slope to town. "Kent?"

"Yes."

"Are you still worried about me being a girl?"

"I don't know what to think. I'd rather be with you than anybody. I mean any of my friends—you're more fun." He hesitated a moment, "What do you think? Should we stop being friends?"

"I think it would be wrong for us not to be friends."

"For real?"

"Yeah."

"My mom said she and Dad became best friends at age sixteen. Should we wait and be friends when we're sixteen?"

"That would be stupid." They arrived at the town park. It had some grass, a swing set, teeter totters, and a slide. "Kent, this is what I think. Of course we learned from Mom and Dad, and at church, the wrong things boys and girls can do with their bodies, so . . . how about we just stay good friends?"

"Yeah, that sounds perfect! Do you know what I really want to do?"

"What."

"I'm the Tropic champ in the swing set jump. Are you up for trying my thing now?"

"What happens if I'm the Cannonville champ?"

"Oh, I never thought of that. You probably are."

"Well, don't worry, I've never tried, but let's see what you've got."

"Okay."

They ran to the swings, hopped next to each other, and pumped higher and higher—each of them getting as high as they dared before taking the jump. Just as Kent was getting ready to jump, Betty yelled, "Look at us, we're married." Sure enough, the swings were side by side.

Kent lost his focus—the jump was horrible. He landed in the sand, and rolled. Coming up, he yelled back at her. "You really got me. By the way, I don't think the marriage is uh . . ."

"Binding," she yelled back.

"Yeah, binding."

Betty let go of the chains and flew through the air landing a good three feet past him. She rolled in the sand, but before she could get up he pinned her down. "That's foul play, no fair."

Betty was laughing so hard she couldn't speak. At least she didn't wrestle back.

"Okay, I'm sorry; I won't bother you on your next jump."

Kent grabbed her hands, and helped her up, then ran to the swings. "We each get one more jump," he called. "Then I have to go back."

"Okay."

Kent pumped as high as the swing set allowed. At the highest point the chains actually slacked as he rose above the support bar. He swung forward and let go just at the right time, landing a good two feet past Betty's mark.

"I can't believe you didn't try distracting me," he called as she ran to the swing.

"I gave you my word, didn't I?"

"I suppose."

Betty did just as Kent had done and flew through the air. They both jumped to look at the indentations in the sand. It was close. "You still beat me," Betty exclaimed.

"No, we tied."

"No, you won by two inches."

"No, we tied."

"Say what you want. You still won," she said.

"You're impossible," Kent muttered back, each of them still facing each other in the sand. "Betty, I have to get going."

"Yeah, I know."

As they neared the house they were greeted by the welcoming party. Even a taller girl was there, holding the baby. That must be Pamela.

All the girls wanted to know about the hike to the rocks.

"It was just grand," Kent said tauntingly.

"Yea, but what did you do?" Mary asked.

"We climbed."

"But what else?" Sara pleaded.

"We talked."

"About what?" Mary persisted.

"About how wonderful all you kids are," Kent said, scooping Judy up in my arms. She laughed and kicked.

"Now I've got to go," he said, "or I'm going to miss my ride. I'll have to walk all the way back to Tropic."

"No you won't, silly," Mary said, pointing with her finger. Kent whirled around, and there were Robbie and Henry, waiting in their truck out on the road.

"Oh my!" Kent gasped. He hurried to the truck. There was a roar of laughter.

As the truck pulled away, they all waved and shouted. He took one last look over his shoulder, hoping to see Betty. She was still there, waving, holding Judy's hand. He turned and faced forward, letting the wind sink the events of the day into his heart. He was absolutely sure of one thing now—a thing that he would never have dreamt before this day. Betty was anything but weird. She was amazing!

CHAPTER 12
IS THIS LOVE?

*B*etty Griffin lay in her bed. It was late, and everyone else was asleep. She reviewed the events of the day over and over. She'd had fun—a lot of fun. And it was all because of Kent Wilson. "I think I know him better than he knows himself," she thought. "He's a good boy. He's going to grow into a fine man some day. I like him. He's kind to me, and respectful of the things I hold most dear. And he likes to roughhouse, and he enjoys my little sisters."

She lay silent a while longer, and then sat up with a start. "He held my hand," she whispered softly. "Does he like . . . love me? Oh, stop it, Betty. But he's impressed with me. He admires me for who I am. So . . . it's not love. We're just good friends who like to be together—that's it."

She lay back down, and continued her pondering. She wanted to see him again. But how? Maybe he wouldn't come again. She bolted to a sitting position again. "I know," she thought, "I'll send a letter to him. I'll send it with Henry. He could give it to him. I'll . . . I'll invite him on a horse ride. He could send a letter back with Henry telling me which day he could come."

Again she lay back. She liked these feelings. She liked having a friend. Sleep began to overtake her. Somewhere about the time she was drifting off, she whispered from deep down, "I like that he's a boy."

* * *

Kent worked the hoe around the corn stalks, making sure to get only weeds and not the thin stalks. The evening sun was low. He stopped a moment and wiped his brow. Hoeing was hard, and there was plenty of it. But the summer days weren't near as bad as during the school year. Dad accomplished a lot on Saturdays, and Kent had more time because school was out.

His mind drifted to a familiar place, a place that he enjoyed reviewing again and again. It made his work enjoyable. He repeatedly relived the day he had spent with Betty. She had completely captivated him. He'd mulled over a million times. He couldn't believe a girl like Betty existed, so strong, able, fun-loving, and not afraid of getting dirty.

He knew that he enjoyed being with Betty. He'd roughhoused with her. He'd taken her hand—why? It was like enjoying adventures with his best friends, but different. She was . . . well, she was a girl, and that made all the difference. Did he enjoy her as a friend or was this . . . no, it couldn't be. It couldn't be love.

He felt a tap on his shoulder and turned. It was Henry.

"What? Oh, hi, Henry. You startled me."

"Sorry, but I have something for you that I'll bet you'll really like."

"Swell, where is it?"

"Right here." He pulled a letter from his pocket. "It's from a girl named Betty."

Kent dropped the hoe, and grabbed the letter. Then, he realized that Henry was Anita's big brother. What would he think?

As if reading his mind Henry said, "You know, Kent, Anita really cares for you, but you don't seem to like her. There's not a boy in town that doesn't drool over her. I can't figure you." He stood there a moment longer. "You two are more like quarreling kids anyway." With that he turned and left for his home.

Kent ripped open the letter and read. He knew he lacked experience and understanding of grown-up things like romance and affection, but he figured there was a word for what he was feeling. Only one word could fit: love.

CHAPTER 13
HONEST WITH PARENTS

*I*t was Sunday—hooray! As the Bible said, "A day of rest from your labors." It was a perfect sunny day. Kent walked with his family the half mile to church. Often they'd meet Anita's family and walk together.

Kent arrived to his Sunday school class eager to see his friends, and even learn from their teacher. They were all thirteen-year-olds—all seven of them. They'd grown up together; participated in Fourth of July sack races, school plays, chasing the greased pig at the rodeo, and a host of other activity.

Anita sat away from Kent. "Figures," he shrugged. "She must still be mad at me."

The teacher started the lesson with a question. "Did anyone do anything exciting this week?" Kent's mind reverted to a pleasant scene—Betty. But there was no way he was going to mention her.

He scarcely heard the soft voice from across the room. "The only thing I can think of is Kent went to Cannonville. He met a girl. Did you jump on the wool sacks with her?"

Kent flashed Anita an angry glance. The room erupted into chatter.

Quickly the teacher silenced the room. "My, my, you kids are chatty today. That's enough!" But her expression showed surprise as well. She struggled to regain her composure. "Okay, so a friend showed Kent around Cannonville—end of story. Now, let's get started on the lesson."

Kent sat in his seat, his mind in a frenzy. As hard as he tried, he couldn't concentrate on the lesson on the Beatitudes. He could only focus on two things—he was furious with Anita, and he prayed that his friends wouldn't make a big deal of him and Betty. He was wrong.

After the prayer was offered his friends caught him in the foyer and swarmed around him like bees. Anita led the charge. "Her name is Betty Griffin, and now she's sending him letters. What's next?"

"Did you hold hands?" asked Joe.

"Yeah, did you kiss her?" asked another.

"It's not like that," Kent barked. He had nothing to say. His face was beet red. He was confused and frustrated. He just wanted out. "Just leave me alone." He pushed through them, and headed for the door. He skipped the part of Sunday school where everyone, young and old, gathered to hear the teachings of the Lord. He ran all the way home, ascended the stairs, and tossed himself face first on his bed. "Some friends I have," he muttered, "and I'll never forgive Anita."

About an hour later, the front door opened, and clamor erupted downstairs. The little ones would be pouring through the front door. Next, there was the beat of footsteps on the stairs. The kids would be going to their rooms and, as always, making a mess of the house.

Instead, the door opened. Kent looked up, and was surprised to see his parents in the doorway. Had they heard what had happened? They didn't seem upset.

"Mom, Dad, maybe I should have talked to you before. Did you hear about Sunday school?"

Dad pulled the hall chair into the room, and mom sat at the foot of the bed. "We heard that you and your friends were unruly in class, that you had a girlfriend named Betty Griffin from Cannonville, and that you left class very upset," Dad said.

"Now tell us what's really going on, son," Mom said.

"Mom, Dad, honest . . . I wasn't unruly in class. It's just that that darned Anita mentioned I was seeing Betty Griffin down in Cannonville, and the whole class erupted."

"That's Sam's oldest daughter, right?"

"Yes."

"So, you've been to Cannonville twice, son," Mom stated. "Tell us about Betty Griffin."

"Mom, Dad, I don't know. On the first trip, we nearly got in a fight. On the second trip, we got along great. We jumped on the wool sacks and rolled them to the loading dock. I met her family, played with her little sisters, and then she took me up on the red rocks above Cannonville. It was really fun!"

"Is that it, son?"

"Yes, Mom."

"So all the kids your age think you're dating at age thirteen, and they're upset about it."

"That's the size of it."

"What do you think?" Mom asked.

"I don't know. When I'm with her, I feel like I'm with Joe or Sam. But, with her it's different. I feel like I'm a better person when I'm around her. She knows why she does things."

"Oh?" Dad exclaimed.

"Yeah, she helps her family for hours and hours every day, and you know why she does it? Because she loves them; because it feels good to see them receive the nourishment that only she can give."

Mom and Dad looked at each other with eyes wide. "Could she be part of the reason you've changed your attitude so much, son?" Mom asked. "I think you work so hard out of love for your family as well."

"If I do, it's because of her. Well, I'm sorry. I shouldn't say that. It's mostly because of you. I'm one of the luckiest kids that ever lived."

Mom and Dad again looked at each other with wide eyes, their foreheads wrinkled. No one spoke for a good while.

"Do you think it's wrong to associate with her, son?" Dad asked.

"Dad, I've asked myself that. It doesn't feel wrong."

"Are you in love with her, son?" mom asked.

"Oh, Mom, certainly not. I'm more worried about getting in a tussle with her. She's real strong."

Yet again, Mom and Dad looked at each other. "Would you please excuse us, son," Dad said. "We'll be right back."

"Okay."

They were back in a few minutes.

Dad began. "Son, you know what happens when a boy and a girl get too close. The two together have God-given power to bring children to earth."

"Yes, Dad."

"A man and woman need to be older and married to do that. The Bible teaches that a man should leave his father and mother, and cleave to his wife. And they also need to be able to care for and raise those children."

"Sure, Dad."

"Are you ready for that, son?"

"Not by a long shot. I've never even thought of it."

"Well, son, when a boy and girl bring a child to earth, and they're not ready, a million problems result. No money to feed them, often poor skills to care for them, no roof over their heads, the kids' parents have to get involved, more problems result there, and so on. Can you see where this is going?"

"Yes."

"So what do you think you should do, son?" mom asked.

"I don't know. I just know that it doesn't feel wrong when I'm around her."

"Well, you're going to have to make a decision. Sam's only got a couple weeks of employment left for Robbie and Henry. It may be a long time until you see her again. So . . . I guess the decision is made for you."

Kent puzzled about that for a moment. "Mom, Dad, I'd like to see her again. I think I'll be the better for it." There was no response. "She sent a letter with Henry inviting me on a horse ride . . . this Friday."

They looked at each other again. "Excuse us a moment," Mom said.

Soon they were back. "Can we trust you'll be appropriate with a daughter of God?" Dad asked.

"Sure, wow! Especially when you put it like that."

Mom couldn't help but start chuckling. "So what's Betty like? I expect she's as fine as her mother?"

"Oh yes. But . . . fun. We had a swing jumping contest."

"Oh, you did. That's interesting. Who won?"

"We tied. We agreed we are just friends."

72

Mom chuckled again and nodded her head. "I can picture that conversation."

"Yeah, but I'm finding out she's different than any boy."

"Oh?"

"Yeah, she feels things instead of seeing them. Little things mean so much to her. You know, the things I skip over, like dandelions on a ditch bank, or a baby's smiles."

"Son, there's no reason you can't have friends that are girls. I'm glad you talked to us, I hope you see that you can learn a lot from us."

"I've always learned from you, Mom."

"So, we'll let you go, son," Dad said, "but always remember who you are."

Sometimes that phrase was bothersome, but this time was different. He would need to remember who he was. He would be with a daughter of God!

CHAPTER 14
MORE THAN FRIENDS

*I*t was nearing sundown. Betty quickly finished drying the last of the dishes and placed them in the cupboard.

Betty ran all the way to her piece of heaven on earth. The real mystery, the majesty of her piece of heaven on earth, was only known by her and her parents, as far as she knew. At the perfect moment, when the sun prepared to sink behind the painted cliffs above, her shadow would cast itself as if jumping off the rocks, and, ever so slowly at first, would slink across the meadow as the sun prepared for its disappearance. Just as her shadow began to climb the cottonwood trees on the far side, it would vanish, and the whole valley would retreat to the soft dimness of evening in Cannonville. It was the rocky pinnacle that made the jump occur. To Betty, this was her own natural phenomenon, her best kept secret.

She looked down at her hands. She held an envelope—a letter from Kent Wilson. Tomorrow they would go for a horse ride. "I just know my heart is going to leap right out of my chest," she said out loud.

* * *

The next morning, Kent was waiting in the back of Henry's truck when they came out. He was afraid they'd leave him because of his treatment of their little sister.

"Fancy seeing you here," Robbie teased. "Any idea why you'd be so anxious to come all the way to Promise Rock with us?" Kent managed a grin.

As they passed Cannonville, Kent swore he saw a figure up on Heaven's Rock darting away. Could it have been Betty? Was she watching to see if he'd come?

Kent nearly lost his grip on the truck cab as it lurched to the side of the road. "Maybe you should just get out here," Henry yelled.

Kent jumped out; "Yeah, thanks!"

As they pulled back onto the road Robbie patted the hood of his truck. "Don't be late!"

Two horses were tethered in front of Betty's home. Betty emerged from the front door. "Hi, Kent. Come on inside. Just one thing we need to do."

"Good morning." It was Martha Griffin. Betty went out the back door—Kent was alone with her mom. She resembled a grown-up Betty—very pretty, with that same long dark brown hair. Only, she seemed a little more serious—more solemn.

"So, Kent. Sam is gone a lot this time of year. I have a question for you. Come in here." They entered one of the children's rooms. "What do you make of this bunk bed? I'm afraid it's going to collapse. I don't know if I should get a new one or if it can be fixed."

Kent was dumbfounded. Surely they could figure something out, but he looked it over anyhow. "You're right, Mrs. Griffin. With some weight on this outside corner, it'll come down. The support beam is good; it's this crossbeam that's come loose."

"So what do you suggest?"

"It needs a bracket."

"Hum, I don't think we have one."

"Well, if you have a piece of wood about an inch thick, three inches wide, and six inches long it could be fixed. The only problem is you could see it if you stooped down."

"I'm not worried about how it looks. I've got a piece of wood that could be cut to those dimensions."

Martha gathered the tools Kent needed. He went to work, preparing the piece of wood.

"Betty says you're good with kids," Martha stated while she held the end of the wood Kent was sawing.

"Oh, she's very kind. But it helps having five little kids in my own family."

"It's a good trait to have. Heaven knows they require patience, guidance, and . . . love."

"They sure do."

"Kent, what do you think about Betty?"

He stopped. "Betty is the finest person I've ever met. It feels good to be her friend. I feel like I'm a better person when I'm around her."

"She's happy to have a friend like you, and . . . she feels the same way about you." They went back to the room so Kent could nail the wood into place.

Kent couldn't help wondering why Betty would think so highly of him—no one else did except his family. He stopped at the bedside and turned. "Mrs. Griffin, Betty is changing me. She's helped me see things completely different."

"Oh?"

"She works day in and day out because she loves. I wish I could be like her."

"So what's your motivation to give and to serve?"

"My what?"

"Betty says you work hard for your family. Why do you do it? Why don't you run off and get into mischief like so many other boys?"

"Well, ma'am. I guess I love my family. Maybe I just didn't know it."

The crossbeam finished, they stepped back and checked their work. It was sturdy.

"Thank you, Kent. You do fine work." They stepped out the front door where Betty was waiting with the horses. "Have a great time in Georgetown, you two. And, by the way, your horse's name is Smoky. He's as gentle as a kitten."

Betty handed Kent the reins, and he mounted. As he did so, Martha mouthed the words, "I trust him," to Betty. Kent didn't see, but Betty was smiling from ear to ear.

The horses walked the road south of Cannonville eagerly. It was perfect; just two paths with weeds a foot high in the middle. There wasn't a cloud in the sky, and it was already getting hot. "Was that you I saw up on Heaven's Rock?" Kent asked.

76

"Yep. I couldn't wait for you to arrive. I . . . I guess life down here gets a little dull. I mean, not much happens around here."

Kent considered that a moment. Truly Tropic was the "happening town," with the high school and more than double the people. "Betty, I have to ask you. Why is your dad so grateful for your prayers, and why did he say that your prayers are helping real good?"

"You're full of questions," she said, raising her eyebrows. "Well, there's a lot of things. As you know, we're hurting from the depression. We don't notice much clear out here, but my dad said he wasn't getting too good a price for wool this year. Just last week, though, Dad's buyers got competing with each other, and must have bid each other up. He's quite pleased with the price now."

Kent remained silent. He sensed there was much more. After a moment Betty spoke. She seemed a little reluctant, but continued. "Dad is very concerned for Mom. He's afraid he's going to lose her, and he could never live without her."

"Why would he ever think that?"

"I'm not sure. It's true that she doesn't have much strength, but I can't imagine anyone being too strong with six kids and one on the way."

"One on the way? Oh my gosh! That's fantastic! Another like you would be just dandy."

She smiled broadly.

"Anyway, he spends so much time in the saddle. He does it because it's the only way he feels at peace. He still makes it home almost every night. He sings us lullabies, and tells us bedtime stories."

They rode, saying nothing. Only the clip clop of the horse's hooves could be heard. Betty took a deep breath and continued. "There's quite a story behind him."

"I can't wait."

"It's not what you think." She paused a moment. "My dad's family moved to Cannonville in the early 1890s. His mom died in childbirth with her ninth child in 1901. Dad was about two and a half at that time. The baby survived, but my grandpa was fit to be tied. There was no way he could make a living and care for nine kids. His oldest child was a daughter of fifteen—she could take care of the baby. The problem was Dad. He needed lots of care, and there was no one that could give him what he needed. That spring, a caravan of sheep herders came through town on their way to the Paria River. Grandpa stopped them and told them the situation. They offered to take him, and teach him to be a good sheep herder."

"It was said that when the people took him, his screams could be heard clear out of town. The people treated him well. He obviously became a sheep herder, and a real good one at that."

"Wow," Kent breathed. "What a story."

They cleared the end of the red rock wall, rounded a bend and there was Georgetown; four houses, a few barns, lots of livestock, fields, and gardens—not a single car or tractor. Kent wondered if they'd pick up on new inventions or try to stay the way they were.

"I think we should walk the horses up to where the creek crosses the road so they can have a drink."

"Sounds good."

They rode in silence for a few moments. "Are you out of questions?" Betty asked chidingly.

"Well, actually not."

"Too bad. I have one for you."

"Okay."

"What do you want to do when you grow up? I mean, do you want to get out and see the world, go to the big cities?"

"That's funny, that's what I was going to ask you."

"Oh, no you weren't."

"Yes, I was, and I'm not going to arm wrestle you for it."

"Okay then, you win."

"Betty, I don't want to leave here. This is my home. It's, it's like heaven to me. I don't care about all the cities. I love the mountains, lakes, and streams. I want to hunt and fish and explore. You know, my dad once shot a deer from our back porch. You sure couldn't do that in the city."

"How would you make a living?"

"I think I would teach school like my dad. Maybe make extra money fixing cars. I'm good with engines. I'd have a garden and fruit trees, and some livestock, and I'd have . . . I'd have a beautiful wife, and raise a family."

"That sounds just heavenly, all right. Too bad the beautiful wife counts me out."

"Oh, stop it. You are beautiful."

Betty looked away.

Arriving at the stream, the horses walked into the water and drank freely. Kent dismounted. He circled around to Betty's horse, in water about a couple feet deep.

Swinging one leg over, she said, "So, kind gentleman, you're going to help me down, are you?"

"Sure." He held up his hand, but she never took it. Instead, she jumped off her horse, knocking him backward into the water. He went in, totally submerged, and came up dizzy and pawing at his eyes. Betty was laughing hysterically.

"Thought you needed to cool off."

"You're right. I was mighty hot. It's slippery, help me up." She reached out her hand. That was a mistake. Kent grabbed it and pulled hard. She went into the water headfirst and came up splashing and coughing—her hair completely covering her face. Kent scooted over in the water, worried about what was coming next. Instead, after a couple of coughs, she burst out laughing. Kent quickly joined her.

Betty cleared the hair from her face. They caught each other's eyes and stared intently—both still neck deep in the water. Her eyes were sparkling, and the twist on the edges of her lips curled upward.

"I figured you were a little hot too," Kent said at last.

"You did, huh. Well, now I can't trust you. I'll just have to get up myself." She got to her feet, stating, "By the way, smarty, it isn't slippery."

Kent held out his hand.

"Oh no, I'm not falling for that again."

They made their way to the horses and started the walk to Georgetown, the horses on either side of them.

"Are we still friends?" Kent asked.

"I thought we were, but I'm not sure now. A friend, you can trust."

"Now wait a minute. Who pushed who in the water first?"

Betty tried to hold it in but burst into laughter again.

Arriving at Georgetown, they tethered the horses.

"I have the perfect spot in mind," Betty said as she pulled a good sized cloth tied at the ends out of the saddle bag.

"Fantastic!" Kent exclaimed, "Food!"

"Yep."

They made the fairly steep climb to a flat place on the side of the hill surrounded with juniper trees. It was quite high. Kent turned around and drew in the beautiful valley. "It looks like your grandma's patchwork quilt."

"You remembered."

Kent turned around and immediately noticed a change in Betty. She didn't look at all like the bright fun-loving girl she was just moments before.

"What are you thinking about?" Kent asked. She remained quiet as she spread the blanket out and set the food on some flat rocks. "Is it the friend deal?"

"Yeah, it's the friend deal. I've never had a best friend. You know the kind I could always trust."

"Sorry."

"Kent, what are you going to do after my dad finishes shearing? This is probably your last trip down here."

"Yes, I know. I've thought about that a lot. I think about it every day. I have an idea, though. Betty, I . . ."

She interrupted, "I think I should say it."

"Okay."

"I don't think I'm a very good friend to you."

"What?"

"I mean, I don't think I'm keeping our agreement. You know the one where we just stay friends."

"Betty, I should say it. I'm the one that's messed up. I can't play with you, I can't arm wrestle you, I can't dunk you in the water . . . I just can't do it. It doesn't work to just be your friend." Kent turned, looking out over the valley again. "And what's worse, I think I lied to my Mom."

A few moments went by, then Betty said softly, "Kent, I can't watch you play with my little sisters any more. I can't jump on the wool sacks or climb on the rocks."

"So where does that leave us?" Kent stammered.

"Is it so bad? Have you done anything with me that's wrong? Do we have to say our friendship won't work?"

"Well, if my mom knew how I really felt, she wouldn't have let me come down today."

"You mean . . ."

Kent interrupted this time, but didn't turn around. "Yes. I mean, no matter what we do together, I just can't do it, I just can't help it, I just can't help . . ." he turned around and faced her. She was looking at him, eyes wide—wondering. "I just can't help . . . falling in love with you."

Her face took on a rosy color, her eyes reddened, and then she turned her back to him. He walked over and put a hand on her shoulder. She shrugged, as if to say, get it off. He stepped back bewildered. Kent knew deep down she had to feel the same about him—she had to. "Betty?"

All of a sudden she turned, half crying and half shouting. "And I love you." Her arms wrapped around him, and she almost knocked him over the steep embankment. They hugged each other for a long time and parted reluctantly. "What are we going to do?" Betty whispered. "Is this what our parents said would happen?"

"I don't know what happened. I tried to just have fun with you as I do my friends. But it doesn't work."

"I guess our plan wasn't going to ever work," Betty sighed.

"Nope, it wasn't. So what do we do now?"

They both just stood there, studying, longing—questioning.

"Well, I don't have any idea, but how about we eat? I'm starving," Betty said at last.

They sat next to each other on the blanket, since they hadn't dried off completely and didn't want their clothes to be dirtier than they already were. They ate for a while in silence. The only sounds were the birds chirping and an occasional "moo" from the cattle below.

"Want to hear my plan?" Kent asked.

"Sure."

Taking in a deep breath, "I'll be fourteen next year. Hopefully, by some miracle, things will improve and my family could do without me for five weeks. If your dad could hire me, I think I could do a real good job for him. I could earn enough money to buy a car. That way I could see you at least a couple times a week after work."

Betty bowed her head a bit, thinking. Lifting her head, "It just might work. But the work you'd have to do is stinky and awful. You'd have to come down at least a month before he starts, to make sure he'll give you the job."

"Sounds perfect to me. And just think, the next fall you'll come up on the bus to high school so we will be together five days a week."

"And you'll be almost fifteen. Do you think it's lying to tell our parents that we're just friends?"

"Well, I know what I told my mom yesterday didn't sit well with me. But we can't tell them we're boy and girlfriend."

"About the girl and boyfriend deal," Betty said. "I have something that I think you'll like. It proves that I'm the one that messed up." She reached underneath the cloth and pulled out another cloth that looked like it was covering a book and un-wrapped it.

"Your journal!"

She laid it between them, parted her hair and began to read.

"Today was another miracle day. Kent came over to my house. He was kind and thoughtful to my little sisters. We went to my cliff that I now call Heaven's Rock. We read my poems, climbed rocks, and swung on the swings. He is so respectful and nice to me. I wish all my friends would treat me as he does. I think I started giving a piece of my heart to him today."

Kent's mind went wild. He looked at her, sitting there so sincere. *This is what love is*, he thought. *I know what it feels like. I want to kiss her. But that would go against everything we said we wouldn't do. Our parents would string us up if they found out.* Still, he felt like he couldn't help it. He kept looking at her; he knew he was in love.

"Betty?"

"Yes."

He scooted in front of her, and drew in a deep breath, and whispered. "Betty, may . . . may I kiss you?"

She stayed silent, eyes wide. Kent inched a little closer, heart pounding, waiting for her to close her eyes and bend her lips toward him. Instead, she turned away.

Kent knew he'd done wrong. "I'm sorry, Betty . . ." She looked back, and there it was. That little twitch as her lips curled upward. After what seemed forever she said, "No."

Kent's mouth dropped open. He couldn't believe it. She just told him she'd given him a piece of her heart, and now she said no to their first kiss. Maybe she was stronger than he was, and would be able to stay just friends.

"No," she said again, "not here."

"Not here?" His mind raced, but he waited, knowing now that she had something different in mind.

"Not here," she said again as if she was convincing herself. "I would like it to be on Heaven's Rock."

Kent was silent for a moment. He didn't think Heaven's Rock would make that much of a difference, and this was such a special moment. He remained silent, trying to get hold of his thoughts.

"Well, then let's get to Heaven's Rock now."

Betty giggled, and then without warning reached over and touched his hand. Kent kept still. "Kent, I know it seems strange, but it means so much to me."

"I know it does, Betty. I know."

They got up and made their way down the hill to the horses. Kent glanced at his pocket watch. It was three thirty. There was no way they could make it to Heaven's Rock, and then to Promise Rock. Still, he hoped there would be time.

They swung upon the horses and started back. The horses could smell the water in the ditch nearby, and were persistent for another drink. They took them over to the stream. It was extra time lost.

They neared Cannonville at a good canter, but each could see that Heaven's Rock would have to wait for another day. They continued toward Promise Rock. Just as they arrived at the Johnson's truck, Henry and Robbie strode up. "Hi, you two!" Henry said. "I'll bet you've had quite a day."

Kent glanced at Betty and gave her a wink. "We sure did, quite a day."

"Betty, could you please lead the other horse back to your place?" Robbie asked. "We need to get back to Tropic."

"Of course I can. Thanks for bringing Kent down with you."

"Don't mention it." Henry said. "Maybe we can bring him again next year—your dad hired us already."

Kent got off the horse and handed the reins to Betty.

"Thank you Betty," he said tenderly. "I won't ever forget this day."

"Nor I. Hope to see you soon."

"On Heaven's Rock," Kent yelled back as Henry drove away.

CHAPTER 15
GROWING UP

The summer of 1936 faded away, and was replaced with the busy harvest season. The patchwork quilt of Cannonville exchanged its plush green color for orange, yellow, and brown.

Life for Betty was the same as years past—difficult but filled with small pleasures and simple joys as well: harvesting the garden and the fruit, preparing for winter, assisting with the little ones, reading them stories, singing them lullabies, helping them with homework, enjoying their smiles, and taking pleasure in school, community, and church.

This year, she had a new-found strength—strength in memories. Heartfelt thoughts of Kent Wilson, the only true boyfriend she'd ever known. She thought of him daily—reviewing each moment they'd spent together.

Next summer seemed so far away. She'd already explained to her dad about Kent's desire to work for him, and he'd promised to consider it.

The fall soon gave way to winter, and the winter to spring. Would she soon be receiving a visit from Kent? And . . . who were these people looking over the empty lot next to their house? More specifically, who was the tall young man who kept eyeing her with a sullen, distasteful look?

* * *

James Davis wasn't about to change his ways. He had gone through the motions of enjoying his family, but inwardly he was mad. It was completely unfair to drag him out of the only life he had ever known.

He had been the real star of the junior high basketball team, and he had been regarded highly by neighboring high schools. He had his ring of friends. Most of them had been rather unruly, but they had brought contentment and excitement to the cold winter days in Salt Lake City.

And now, with spring coming on, Mom and Dad had put the icing on the cake. The three of them traveled all the way down to this awful, backward, desolate, tiny town called Cannonville. And there he saw girl across the fence with two long pig tails. She looked like she was out of some nursery rhyme book with cows and pigs and a farm. This couldn't be happening!

He thought of staying with his Aunt Millie, back in Salt Lake, but he knew his parents would never consider such a request.

They would start building a new home that spring, and be ready to move in before his freshman year. "Very considerate of them," he growled under his breath. He was lost, confused . . . upset, and he had no cards to play.

* * *

Kent Wilson and his family had enjoyed a bountiful harvest in the fall of 1936. Two nice bucks from their hunting trip had added to their winter stores. Kent had still taken care of the farm, but he noticed Dad was working a few less hours with Uncle Jim, and relieving him of some of the workload.

He'd patched up his disagreement with his friends, mostly because there was no way he could see Betty again, but partly because they felt bad about it. Anita was the most reluctant of his friends, but she treated him kindly enough. She was so involved in school, activities, student council, and cheer leading that she didn't have much time for him anyhow.

Kent remembered the first Sunday in November, when Charlie Wilson had gathered his family in the living room to make an announcement. "Do you want the good news or the good news first?" While the little ones had struggled with the question, Kent had wondered if it would affect the work load he carried.

"Okay, the good news first," Charlie grinned. "The school district is returning us to full pay, effective immediately. How do you like them apples?"

There were plenty of ah's, even from the little ones who didn't understand, but knew whatever he said was worth joining in with ooh's and ah's.

"Next," he stated proudly, "the late payments on our mortgage are paid, and then some." That was great news, but Kent wondered where Dad was going with this.

"Now, the big question: Shall I continue to work for Uncle Jim? I've already cut my hours down, but shall I quit all together? If I stay on, I plan to save the money for an investment that just might catapult us into a life with plenty of money. Or, I could quit and spend more time with you." He grabbed little Jessica and swung her up on his lap.

"What do you say, son?"

Kent was startled. "Dad, I don't know. It's sure nice to have you around." He paused a moment. "And, I've started to play the trombone in school. I need to practice, and . . ." A light bulb switched on. "I know, Dad. I've already been thinking about this."

"Okay, son. Let's hear it."

"I'd like to work for Sam Griffin next summer. Over the five weeks I could earn nearly seventy dollars. If you could work that in, I know I can keep the farm up during the winter."

Mom and Dad gave each other a bewildered look before answering. "Son, that's a fine idea. But would he hire you at your age?"

"I think so. We'd have to pay him a visit at least a month before he starts."

They looked at each other again, this time with a nod. "Son, I believe that would work. I'll drive you down some time near the end of April."

Kent made good on his proposition all through the winter and into spring. He had new aspirations and goals. He enjoyed the little free time he had with his friends, excelled on the trombone, and even started practicing a guitar that Dad had given him.

Whenever he felt really down in the dumps, he'd think of his friend seven miles to the south. No, not his friend, his girlfriend.

Then, to add to the excitement, Dad showed up with a generator. Kent helped run wires all through the house and then hung the light bulbs and placed the switches. Having light during the darkest of nights seemed a miracle. And if that weren't enough, in early spring Dad brought home a radio. It was huge, but it fit neatly in the living room, and could be run off the generator. It was so thrilling to sit and listen that the whole family made every effort to set aside a half hour or so before bedtime to listen to stories or the latest news.

Spring finally rolled around. Butterflies started to mount in Kent's stomach. It had been nearly ten months since he'd seen Betty. Would she have a change of heart? Had she informed her dad of his desire to work for him?

One day after school, their neighbor walked over to talk to Kent. Paul Richards was a tall lanky fellow and somewhat hesitant. He was likely pushing sixty and had a bum arm. He kept it tight against his stomach.

"How are you, Kent?" he asked, reaching out his good arm.

"Just great, sir." They shook hands, and Mr. Richards stepped back and looked away as if he was embarrassed to share his message.

"Well," he said, turning his head back at Kent. "Times have been kind of hard for me and my family. This depression seems like it's never going to end. My old car sat out back all last winter. It's not doing me any good. It won't run right now, and I'm not good with engines because of this fool arm, but I know you're good with cars. My car is for sale for thirty dollars, if you want it. What do you think?"

It was all Kent could do to not jump up and down. "Sir, that'd be wonderful! Except all I have is fifteen dollars saved. But I'm going to work for Sam Griffin come the end of school. I could pay you the rest after just a couple weeks."

"That sounds like a right fine offer."

"Wow, Mr. Richards, that sounds real good." Kent could tell he was hurting for money. It was a great deal for the both of them. "I'll need to talk it over with my folks, but they'll say yes for sure. Could we come get it this weekend?"

"That will be fine."

Kent watched him walk away, hardly believing what had just happened. If he could get it running, he could stay and see Betty after work! A far cry better than going down with Henry and Robbie, and just seeing her amongst the dusty sheep. He could . . . he could . . . now his mind was in a frenzy. He could take Betty up to Heaven's Rock. They could finally kiss!

CHAPTER 16
WOULD LOVE ENDURE?

*T*he next day, Charlie and Kent made the bumpy, windy drive to Cannonville.

Charlie observed his boy, staring straight ahead, hands clenched on the seat. "Son, you're as restless as old Jumper was when that rattle snake crawled in his stall."

"Sorry, Dad. I just hope I get the job."

"Well, son, just look at you. You've grown about four inches, put on about thirty pounds, and look at those muscles. If he doesn't hire you, it's because he doesn't recognize you."

Kent managed a grin, but he felt his whole life hinged on this meeting, the job, rekindling the fire with Betty, the car . . .

After nearly an hour they arrived at the Griffin home. Lights glowed brightly inside. Kent gave the door several good raps, and after a moment the door opened and a tall, beautiful girl answered. She was shapely, with hips and . . . well, shapely. "Betty?"

"Oh my gosh, Kent!" She cupped her hand over her mouth. "Hi, Mr. Wilson," she said somewhat embarrassed. "I'm so happy to see you. Come in, please. Mom, Dad," Betty called, "we have visitors."

Betty's parents came in together, Sam carrying a little girl of about two—was her name Lola?—and Martha carrying a new baby boy.

"Your new baby," Kent exclaimed. "What's his name?"

"This is Kenneth," Sam said proudly. "We're going to call him Kenny."

There was another rush of feet as every one of Betty's sisters came rushing in. Sara hesitated for just a moment, then ran over and hugged Kent around the waist. Judy, not to be outdone, did the same.

Kent knelt down and put his arms around them. "My goodness, look how big you are! You're all grown up now." They laughed and giggled.

Kent wondered what his dad would think of their affection for him. They acted just like his own little brothers and sisters.

"Hi, Sam," Dad said. "Do you remember me?"

"Sure do, Charlie. Good to see you."

There was silence for a moment, and then Mr. Griffin stated. "Well, as you know I'm going to start shearing as soon as school's out. I could sure use a good hand."

Kent couldn't contain a smile. The relief spread all through him. Betty must have already taken care of it. "Thank you very much, Mr. Griffin," Kent said, taking extra effort to take his eyes off Betty. "My dad has taught me that if a job is worth doing, it's worth doing my best. I'll give you my very best, sir."

"I have no doubt of that." There was a moment of silence, then Sam turned to Betty. "Your mom, and Charlie, and I have some catching up to do. Don't suppose you and . . ."

". . . would want to go for a walk? We'd be delighted," Betty said, answering her own question. She grabbed Kent's arm and they were out the door, and walking down the street before their parents could change their minds.

"Betty, that was, that was . . . great thinking," Kent said. "It's wonderful to see you. You've changed."

"Oh really? I hope it's not a bad change."

"Oh no, gosh no, it's a great change. I mean . . . you're all grown up."

"And what'd you do with your voice?" she challenged coolly. "And look at those muscles; seems like you've changed a bit too."

They both laughed.

"We haven't seen each other since our horse ride nearly ten months ago," Kent said. "Are we still friends? Best friends?"

"Hmm . . . I'm not sure; seems I recall some devious behavior from you."

"Wow, what have you done with your vocabulary? Betty, we have so much catching up to do. Start first. Tell me everything that's happened since our horse ride."

"Okay, let's see. I'm getting better at cooking. Mom's letting me cook a lot lately. I've grown closer and closer to my family. I'm sure you know that I still go up to my favorite place—Heaven's Rock—whenever I can. I feel I'm getting closer to God."

"Come on. Are you a thirteen-year-old girl or a grown-up lady? Sorry, please go on."

"Well, to answer your question, no. But I do believe more than ever that God hears my prayers, because last August I was playing in the ditch with four of my little sisters. It was sunny here in Cannonville, but up on the mountain there was a huge thunder storm. I had a feeling to go down and gather them and get up on top. Just as we were nearing the top of the wash, a wall of water came crashing down."

"Wow! I've been praying too, but I think I'll have to step it up a bit. Sorry for interrupting."

"I've written some more poems."

Kent remained silent, wondering if she might say something like, *I missed you*, or *I thought a lot about you*.

"Well, that's enough about me, what about you?"

"I'd rather hear about you some more. What about, well, uh, did you . . ."

"Oh all right," she exclaimed, obviously reading his thoughts. "Kent, I did think about you, and the special moments we shared together. I still think of you as my best friend. That special piece of my heart is still yours. After all this time, is there still a special place for me in your heart?"

"Betty, not a day has gone by that I haven't thought about you— best friends for sure."

They stood there a moment looking at each other. Finally, Kent broke the silence. "We will make it up to Heaven's Rock together, real soon. Won't we?"

"Hum, I'm not sure. What would you want to do up there?"

"Maybe I'm planning on collecting on an old debt."

"I don't see it as a debt, I see it as . . ."

"Long overdue."

"You're the one that's impossible, you know that?" she muttered.

"You know, I'm not sure about collecting this debt anyhow. I mean, you're, you're . . ."

"I'm what?"

"You're different."

"What's that supposed to mean?"

"It means that . . . you're so grown up and beautiful, I'm scared to be with you."

She blushed. "You had me worried there, but you might be right. Maybe we should try the friend deal again."

"You're right. That's just what we should do, but, I already tried—it didn't work, and I suspect . . . it will never work."

Betty burst into laughter, and Kent joined in.

"Seeing you today has made this one of the best and happiest," she paused to let the words sink in, "birthdays of my life."

"Your birthday? April 23rd? You're fourteen today? I can't believe I never asked you." Without thinking, he took her hands in his. They were still rough, strong, and sturdy. His hands felt comfortable—at home. She gripped his hands, too. She quickly released them, but not before Kent felt love—the same love he'd felt for her those many months ago.

"Now, Kent, tell me how you've been all this time."

"Well, I bought a car. I haven't even picked it up yet, but I'm sure I'll have it running by the end of school. I could drive it down here, and we could go up to Heaven's Rock and . . ."

"Betty, Kent, come back in. You're going to catch cold out there." It was Martha Griffin.

"Oh no!" Betty sighed.

"I'll get a letter to you. I promise. They're starting to carry mail on the grocery delivery truck. I'll tell you everything and throw in a few thoughts for the summer when I get to come down."

They turned and started walking back to her house.

"Kent," she said, and then paused. "There's a way you'll always know that a piece of my heart is yours."

"Betty, what could you possibly do more than you already do?"

"I will stand on Heaven's Rock and hold my right arm high, pointing toward Heaven. I'll point to Heaven! Then you will know that a piece of my heart is in heaven . . . you."

"Who are you?" Kent reached for her hand. She took it. "My Sunday school teacher says that you're a daughter of Almighty God. I'm learning what that is."

"And I'm learning what it means that you're a son of God."

They stopped in the front yard, peering into each other's eyes. Betty broke the silence. "Heaven's Rock just gets more holy all the time doesn't it?"

"It sure does."

"And just think. There's more to it that I haven't showed you."

"There couldn't be more. You've showed me every inch of it."

"So sure are you?"

"You're right. The miracle of Heaven's Rock just keeps going on and on. So . . . what is it?"

"Can't tell you. But I can show you."

"Please?"

"Well, it has something to do with your shadow when the sun . . ." The door burst open with a swarm of little sisters. Kent lost his grip on Betty's hand just in time to catch Judy stumbling into his legs. Even little Lola was there, tugging on his trousers, and Mary and Sara began hounding him with questions. Unsure of what to do with all four of them, he reached out and grabbed them all and gave them a tight squeeze.

"Oh, I've missed you all."

"Now, everyone, get back inside before you get a chill," Martha scolded from the doorway. Kent quickly let them go, and they all scampered inside.

"We thought maybe you got lost out there," Mr. Griffin teased. "It's been darn near an hour."

"Sorry, daddy. We had a lot of catching up to do."

"Thanks again for the job, Mr. Griffin. And thank you for your hospitality, Mrs. Griffin."

"You're welcome," Sam returned.

"We'd better be on our way, son."

"Yes, Dad." Kent looked again at Betty as he entered the doorway. Her long brown hair was nestled softly over her left shoulder, and the light of the kerosene lamp shone behind her, burning her image deep into Kent's heart and mind. There was no doubt. He was still in love.

CHAPTER 17
WISE COUNCIL

*K*ent settled into the seat cushions, a smile spread upon his face. He'd got the job, but even far more exhilarating, he was still in love! And Betty still loved him, too! And . . . she was so beautiful and grown up.

"Congratulations on your new job, son." The words shook Kent from his reverie.

"Thanks, Dad."

"It was nice catching up with the Griffins. They're mighty fine folks. Seems they think highly of you. That tells me that you've been an honorable young man around them."

"I've tried, Dad."

"It's quite obvious your feelings for each other haven't diminished after all this time. I'm not sure what to make of it." Charlie drove on, scratching his whiskers. "Kent, what attracts you to her? That she's so tall and pretty?"

"Gosh no, Dad. Well . . . of course it's nice she's pretty, but . . . she's so much more than that. I mean, what she does, the life she lives day in and day out is always for others. Giving, caring, helping . . . finding happiness in just about everything."

"I'm proud of you for recognizing those qualities in her, son. It would be shallow to just see a tall, pretty lady, wouldn't it?"

"That wouldn't happen with Betty, Dad."

Charlie drove for a while, looking straight ahead. At last he turned toward Kent. "Son, I wish to counsel you on three things. First, don't let your feelings for her hamper the effort you put forth on your job. Give a hundred percent to your work. You will appreciate her more, and knowing of her as I think I do, she will only have greater respect and admiration for you. Now I understand she'll be coming up to high school this fall. You know, they bus students in from all around from ninth grade on up. You'll be able to see a lot more of each other. Don't let your feelings for her get in the way of your studies either."

"Yes, Dad."

"Next, be the kind of person in your own home as she is in hers. Have you found out that she wouldn't be attracted to a boy that shirked his responsibilities, and did his work for the wrong reasons?"

"Yes, on the day I met her." Charlie laughed.

"Finally, I can't believe I'm saying this, but seeing the change that's come over you, and knowing what's ahead of you, I'm not going to say stop. But I will say this. As a teacher, I've watched many girls and boys take a liking to each other. Many of them blossomed into deep relationships, even courtship and marriage. Some didn't. Some got in serious trouble. Your mom and I agree that around age sixteen is the age when youth are mature enough to handle these relationships appropriately." Charlie looked at his son. Kent seemed somewhat confused, so Charlie clarified "You know, like kissing—not a good idea. Even holding hands refers to a bond, a union of love and oneness."

"Now, having said that, please trust your mother and me. Come to us with any concerns, and always remember who you are. You respect her body. Don't do anything you know to be wrong. If you slip up, son, it will destroy your relationship."

"What do you mean, Dad?"

"Can you imagine how you'd feel about each other if you used your God-given power wrongly? Too early? You'd end up despising each other, being repulsed by one another. If you truly care for her, you'll respect her, you'll do only what's good for her. Do you understand everything I've told you?"

"Yes, Dad, I do. And . . . I think if you have any doubts about me, you can rest assured that Betty will handle things just right."

Charlie pulled to an abrupt stop on the sandy street near their home. He turned and peered at Kent with narrow eyes. "That may be true, but never forget: You are responsible for your own actions. You will be held accountable, and your actions could hurt her as well. It's wonderful to be able to trust Betty, but there's no getting around your own behavior."

"I promise I'll never forget that."

Kent reached for the door handle as they pulled up to their home. He felt his dad's hand on his shoulder.

"Son, before we go inside, I feel impressed to share one more matter with you. You're going to hear it soon enough so I think now is the right time." He took in a deep breath, and then his face spread into a warm smile. "Your mom is expecting again."

Kent was speechless. He often was when he heard big news. But with the thoughts of a new baby, just sent from Heavenly Father to their home, he reached over and hugged his dad. "You and Mom are the best parents in the world. It's a lucky child that's born into our home."

Dad appeared to be struggling to keep tears back. "Thank you, my boy. I love you."

CHAPTER 18
FRIENDS AND A CAR

Charlie Wilson helped his son tow the car to their home that Saturday. It was a 1929 Model A Shay Roadster. It had originally been black, but it was now quite rusty. It had a convertible top with two handles, and only one bench seat. It would fit two, three if you didn't mind shoulder to shoulder, and four if one stood on the step outside the door. It would cruise at thirty or so miles an hour, and top out at forty—probably more if there was a decent road.

It's astounding how all kinds of friends show up when you have a car. Kent's good buddies Joe, Sam, and Bob magically appeared when the news got out.

The four of them spent their precious spare time in it for two weeks. None of Kent's friends were in a position to get a car, but this was their ticket to ride in one without their parents.

They had good success in getting it running, but with limited means of obtaining new parts and hoses, had a rough time fixing the water leaks. At last Kent determined it could run for about forty-five minutes. Then he'd need to stop, let the engine cool, and add water.

The car's big debut was the night of graduation. The ceremony was over, but a huge gathering of people were still at the high school. All four boys crammed in, and started buzzing by the school and city park, honking the horn and yelling out the window at their friends. The other kids waved and ran after them.

After a good half hour of buzzing around the school, laughing and hollering, they pulled up on the street in front of Kent's house to let the engine cool and add water.

"Wow," Bob shouted jubilantly, as he jumped out, giving the car some pats on the hood.

"What's next, Kent?" Sam asked. "Shall we go for a ride up to Mossy Cave?"

"We're going to have the greatest summer," Joe piped in. "We ought to go fishing up on the mountain. We could go up to Bryce Lodge and have ice cream, heck, we could go all the way to Panguitch and check out the city girls."

Kent chuckled. "We'll have to see. The most important thing is for this car to get me to and from work."

"You know what you should do," Joe said excitedly, "is go down with Robbie and Henry. You're all working for Mr. Griffin, right? You save on wear and tear on the car. You save on gas, and your car will just be waiting for fun times for all of us."

"That's a good idea, but I want to go to work in my own car."

"You're not making sense," Joe said.

"Well, there are things I want to do when I get off. You know, like leave when I want to."

"Yeah, we know, like come home and enjoy your best buddies."

Kent gently released the radiator cap, then walked into his yard and retrieved a bucket of water.

"Kent, you're acting strange," Joe clamored. "What's the deal? Aren't we your best friends?"

"Of course you are." He set the bucket down. "I, uh, just want to stop and see someone in Cannonville before I come home."

There was silence. Kent could tell their minds were churning. Finally, Joe spoke up. "Kent, are you telling us you have a better friend than us down there? I mean, how can that be? You've only been down there a few times."

"No, you're my best friends." Kent felt he was getting caught like a cutthroat trout at the reservoir. There was no way he could explain his feelings—no way to tell them the difference in his heart—they'd never understand.

"Kent, something's wrong with you. You're not coming clean." Joe walked over and placed his hands on Kent's shoulders. "We're your friends. What are you hiding from us?"

Kent had had it. Not telling them about Betty was like carrying that heavy weight around again. "Well, sometimes I'd like to stop and see Betty again."

"What?" Joe barked, letting go of his shoulders, his eyes shocked with surprise. "You haven't seen her in like a year. You may not even recognize her."

"So," Bob piped up. "You haven't seen Betty for a year, and you want to see her more than us?"

"Of course I want to be with you too. Come on, fellows."

"Come on," Joe clamored, his jaw tightening. "You're willing to drive all the way down there to see her, but not us? Are we piles of dung now?"

"Don't be ridiculous."

Sam, being the bookworm among them, and steadier of thought, spoke up. "Kent, have you seen her since last year?"

Kent grabbed a funnel and started filling the radiator. "Shall we make some more passes by the high school?" He looked up, Sam was still in the passenger seat, Bob was still leaning on the car, and Joe hadn't moved.

"So have you seen her?" Joe asked.

"Yeah, I saw her when I went down last month to ask about the job."

"One time, for probably a few minutes," Joe scoffed, shaking his head. "And in case you've forgotten, you're only fourteen. A little young, don't you think?"

"Come on guys. It's not like that."

"So, you just treat her like one of the guys?" Joe snapped.

"Yeah, you could say that."

"How does that work?" Sam interjected. "I mean, you can't wrestle her. You might touch her in the wrong place."

"Oh, she'd wrestle any boy, and probably win too."

"So, you're not attracted to her physically?" Sam persisted.

"Guys, I need a break here. You were just saying we could drive to Panguitch and check out the city girls."

"Yeah, but not date them steadily!" They all responded in unison.

Kent looked at his friends. They were planning on all kinds of fun with his car and he'd just dropped a bomb on them. "I'm sorry, but that's what I want to do some of the time. We'll still get to have fun. The car is ready. Let's go buzz around the high school."

None of them appeared to buy it. They didn't move, either.

"So, are we going or not?"

"Okay, but just answer one question?" Joe asked.

"Fair enough."

He squared his shoulders and looked Kent in the eyes. "Are you in love with her?"

The words landed like a brick on his head. He hadn't been expecting that. His mind raced, searching for a response. If he spent more time with Betty and not much with them, he'd be lying, and being with Betty was all he could think of—all he could dream of. All the pros and cons of his answer swirled aimlessly like feathers in the wind. But the word still escaped his lips. "Yes."

CHAPTER 19
ONLY THREE WORDS FIT

They all went their separate ways that night—the mood was gone. Kent went to bed and looked up at the ceiling. His mind sought for something soothing—Betty. Only four more days until he'd see her again, and this time with his own car.

He reflected on the letter he'd written to her the night he came home from their visit. He could still remember it word for word . . .

Dear Betty,

Seeing you today was . . . I don't think there are words to describe it except a word our Sunday school teacher uses: miraculous. Knowing that a piece of your heart is right here in mine makes me want to jump up and down all the time. I decided that if I see you with your arm held high as I go by Heaven's Rock on my way to work, I'll hold my arm out the window, and honk the horn. I'm sure that when I see you I'll probably want to jump out of the car, but I guess I might get hurt. But, just know that I'd feel like jumping out of the car.

It's black, has just one seat, and is a convertible. You can't miss it because it's the only one like it around here. Do you think, after I'm done with work on that first day, I could drop by? It will be Monday, May 31?

I've dreamt of going to Heaven's Rock with you for almost a year now. I try to picture how it will be, but one thing I know is that you'll make it far better than I could ever imagine. Hope I can be patient.

I Love you,
Kent

He remembered being hesitant on how to close the letter. His dad's counsel kept flooding his mind about how sixteen was an appropriate age. He also knew that if his mom and dad knew how deeply he loved Betty, they'd be very concerned.

Oh well, he decided. *When it comes to Betty there are only three words that fit—I LOVE YOU.*

CHAPTER 20
A FIRST KISS?

*S*pringtime in Tropic was the busiest time of the year, and there were just as many demands on his time as the year before. The only difference this year was Dad. Thank goodness he was able to help out more around the farm.

With the first crow of the rooster, Kent was up preparing for the day he'd dreamt of for nearly a year. Mom must have known of his excitement. In spite of not feeling well, she made a nice breakfast of boiled wheat with milk and sugar.

"Now, remember what your dad said. You can take the car twice a week, but that's it. You've worked it out with Henry, right?"

"Yes, Mom."

"We need your help here too, son."

"I know, Mom. I love you."

Kent left for Promise Rock shortly after first light. He was well prepared with buckets of water, and tools if he needed them.

As he neared Cannonville he found himself yearning for Betty to be on Heaven's Rock. "Please be there," he whispered. He stopped once and filled the radiator with water, and let the engine cool a bit, just to be on the safe side, but soon he was rounding the final bend into Cannonville.

He craned his neck, looking out the far window to see Heaven's Rock. There, tall and straight, bright in the morning sun, was Betty, arm held high, waving and pointing heavenward.

He ran off the road, bouncing and lurching back and forth, tearing out sagebrush with the front bumper, but was able to negotiate the car back on the road. Now that he was practically at a standstill, he leaned out the side window, and waved and waved. He sat back down and honked several times. He could feel a piece of Betty's heart in his. His dream had come true.

When he arrived at Promise Rock, many workers were already there. He was put to work immediately carrying sacks and securing the fences. To the south was an endless flow of sheep. Several men on horseback herded them toward the stalls with the help of sheep dogs.

The rattle of the generator broke the mood of the scene. It took fire and then faded. Again and again the engine did the same. Kent worked his way toward a group of men and called out. "I know engines! Can I help?"

A burly older man sighed, "Young man I don't know much about these things, but if you can start 'er, I can shear like none other."

Kent went right to work. He had it purring like a kitten within minutes. All he did was adjust the idle and the gas mixture a bit. The older man and several others cheered. Kent was an instant hero.

The shearing began. They worked three shearers at a time, and were getting ready to start a fourth. Kent was assigned to separate twigs, leaves, wool fragments, and even poop from the fleece before it was packed into burlap bags. It was exhausting, relentless work.

Finally, the clanking of the lunch bell echoed around the rock. They finished the sheep that were currently on the boards, and herded them into the "out corral." Kent was grateful for the rest as much as the food. Mr. Griffin even showed up. He wasn't much for words. He just picked a spot and ate, then slipped away.

When they'd all had their fill, they were back at it again. The hours dragged by, and Kent couldn't wait to see Betty. When the shift drew to a close, they formed a line and received their wages for the day—two dollars. It used to take Kent weeks of odd jobs to earn that much money.

"Good work," Kent heard as he accepted his pay.

He tilted his work hat back and looked up. "Thank you very much, Mr. Griffin."

"Now men. The next pay day is a week from today. Good work, all of you!"

Kent felt like a lion let out of a cage. He ran to his car and set-tled back in the seat, only to realize that he stank to high heaven.

There was nothing he could do. He'd have to go to Betty's house and ask if he could wash. He parked in front of their home, sur-prised at the construction of a new home next to Betty's. It was huge. Betty's little sisters came bursting out of the house, eager to give him a hug, until they caught scent of him. After that, the hugs were a little ginger. He looked toward the doorway, then around the house. No Betty. Sensing his concern, Pamela said. "Betty's not here. We don't know where she went. She's been gone about half an hour."

Kent's heart sank. What on earth could she be up to?

"Is that Kent?" It was Martha's voice.

"Yes, mother," Pamela called.

"Kent, won't you come in and wash up? Betty will be along soon."

That Betty; she'd know he'd need a good washing before they got together. He eagerly washed up. "Thank you, Mrs. Griffin. I'm pretty sure I know where Betty is. May I please be excused to find her?"

"Certainly. I'm sure you two have a lot of catching up to do."

Kent took off at a good run toward Heaven's Rock. He could now concentrate on the one thing he'd looked forward to for nearly a year—Betty, and their first kiss!

"What's your hurry?" He thought he'd heard that right. Kent stopped and turned to the voice. Betty was just stepping out from behind one of the huge cottonwoods.

"Oh, I uh, wanted to see the shadow you told me about."

"That will be in about an hour," she giggled.

"Is that so? Well actually, I was looking for a friend of mine."

"What does he look like?"

"She ... happens to be the finest girl I've ever met," Kent said, get-ting a feel that Betty was in a jovial mood. "Maybe you've seen her?"

They began walking slowly through the trees. "She has beautiful dark brown hair that reaches well past her shoulders. Hum, let me see, yours is kind of the same. She had pretty hazel eyes and high cheek bones, and a smile that curved up at the edges that would just make me melt. Why ... you have those same features."

Kent placed a hand on his chin so as to look deep in thought. "You know, I don't think you're the one. This young lady was about four inches shorter, and didn't look all . . . womanly."

"So you're looking for someone younger?"

"Well, that's a problem. She would have grown some over the past year, like I did. Yeah, I gained about forty pounds."

"Well good luck finding this girl," she announced skeptically. "I doubt she gained forty pounds."

"You're right." They started walking across the clearing. "Well, this girl can climb rocks like none other. Hum, probably not in a delightful dress like that one."

They entered the crevice. "Hum, you seem to have the same grit as this gal. You know, there's only one way to really know if you could be this fine lady."

"Oh? What on earth could that be?"

"She had large, strong, rough hands that were used to hard work. Oh, they're beautiful hands for sure. Ones that lift, and serve, and . . ."

Betty stopped walking. Kent stopped as well. They faced each other. "So you think if you like, test my hands you'd know for sure?"

"Yeah . . . that's it."

They stood there, the rock walls on either side extending two hundred feet above, searching each other's eyes. Several moments passed. Betty didn't move. Suddenly it hit. Holding hands wasn't something happy-go-lucky. It, like a kiss, would speak a thousand words of acceptance, of trust, of oneness, and . . . of love like Dad had taught. Kent held his breath.

Slowly Betty lifted up both hands. He gently took them in his. He started running his fingers over her palms, and then clutched them tightly. "Oh my gosh! Your hands. It's you!"

"And you remind me of a fine gentleman I knew long ago." The jovial moment was gone—replaced with sincerity and affection. They held their grip, and hand in hand, continued up the incline.

"Kent, where did you get so crafty?"

"To be honest, that whole deal was total luck."

They walked on. "So Betty, did you get my letter?"

"I certainly did. Thank you very much!"

"I have lots more to tell you as well."

107

"Then let's hear every word."

"My mom is expecting her seventh child come November."

"What wonderful news."

"Yeah, maybe I'll get a baby brother and even things up a bit."

"Oh, go on please."

"My dad bought a generator. We wired our house and now have lights throughout—it's absolutely wonderful. We also got a radio. Sometimes we all gather around it and listen to stories. We get the news clear from Denver and even Los Angeles. They often speak of things going on clear around the world."

Betty stopped, placing a hand over her mouth. "This world is getting to be such a small place. Imagine out here in the rocks and learning about China, and Russia, and . . ." she paused, "did you happen to get my letter?"

"You wrote me a letter?"

"I kind of thought you didn't get it because you haven't mentioned it."

"What did it say?" Kent asked.

"No, you first, I told you my story on my birthday."

"My mom and dad are okay with it . . . with us. I mean, of course they cautioned me about not respecting you, but they're okay, and I believe it's mostly because of you, because of who you are."

"That's interesting, because that's what my parents said about you."

"You shouldn't kid about something like that."

Betty stopped. They were nearing their piece of heaven on earth. Putting her free hand on his arm, she said, "I am completely serious. My parents see you as a fine person, one who loves children and treats his mother kindly. A hard worker, someone who gives of himself without asking for anything in return—they see that you respect me, and they . . . trust you with me."

Kent felt warmth sweeping through him. These fine people saw him as a good person, a trustworthy person. At the same time he was taken aback. Was he doing wrong, then? A first kiss at fourteen? Dad said to wait until sixteen. Would he ruin the trust with a kiss? But, oh how he wanted to kiss her. He'd dreamed of it for ten months! Surely it couldn't be that wrong.

She let go of his arm, but their eyes stayed fixed on each other. Her eyes were soft, gentle, loving—kind. He couldn't help it, he had to say it. "Betty, it isn't possible to just be your friend. You know, like a friend you just pal around with."

"I know." She turned and looked over toward the patch of red sand. To the kiss that just had to be. They walked in silence.

Betty broke their silence. "Kent," she said softly. "I've thought a lot about this moment—about us. What I have for you in my heart is real. It fills my whole being. It's as if we haven't been apart for the last ten months, because you're always right here," she said patting her chest. They reached the sand.

"Betty, I didn't know how to close my letter, only with these words: I love you." When Kent said those three words, the truth of them burned in his heart, and at the same moment, a voice spoke in his mind, *"This is not the time for that kiss."* He heard the words in his heart. *"I promise you that when the time comes, you will know it."*

He stepped back, almost off balance, torn between his emotions and the spiritual confirmation he had just received.

Betty said, "Kent, I had no doubt of how I wished to close my letter. Only with the words, I love you, too."

Breathing hard, he took her other hand and stepped closer. Her eyes conveyed acceptance, love, and trust. He knew that whatever he chose to do, she would reciprocate with all her heart. His mind, filled with emotion, was clear. "Betty, I love you. And because of that love, I feel that now is not the time for our first kiss." There, he'd said it, but he couldn't believe it.

Betty's expression, already thoughtful, loving, and tender, deepened still; he knew that she knew that this was not the time. She squeezed his hand. "We'll know when the time is right . . . we'll know."

Finally, Kent whispered back. "You're right, we'll know."

Still holding his hand, Betty turned toward the cliff. "It's time for the shadow!"

They made their way to the ledge. Almost instantly, their shadow jumped off the rock, made its way across the meadow, started climbing the trees, then vanished. A gentle, cool dimness settled over them.

"I'll be doggoned," Kent could only muster. He lifted his eyes heavenward. "I think this is a direct pathway to Heaven."

Betty's eyes were deep, her expression sincere. "I named this place Heaven's Rock because you were here. It's you that makes it heavenly. If I'm ever lonely, I can come up here, and I'll be with you."

"Betty, it was heavenly before I got here, and it was because of you."

"Now Kent, you're not winning on this one. Just let it be. And . . . I've told you everything I know about it. But," She looked pensive, "do you think there's anything else about this place?"

"Undoubtedly," Kent answered with assurance. "If I'm certain about one thing, it's that there is always more."

They stood a moment longer, gazing out at Promise Rock, the thousands of sheep, and the patchwork quilt below, then they turned and started home.

"Now I know," Betty said, "why Mom and Dad trust you." Squeezing his hand she repeated, "Now I know."

CHAPTER 21
A METAMORPHOSIS

*I*t took over five weeks that year to shear all of Mr. Griffin's sheep. Kent drove his car to work twice a week. The highlight, always, was seeing Betty standing tall on Heaven's Rock, pointing to heaven. He'd honk the horn and wave, nearly running off the road every time. The other days he went with Henry and Robbie, then returned home to add his much needed help.

He had hoped to find time to be with his friends. An occasional joy ride around town or maybe a drive out to Mossy Cave, but there was never any spare time. They'd meet on Sundays, but it seemed strained, as if they weren't in agreement so it was better to stay apart.

Kent readily turned his attention to the love of his life. She came out to the shearing operation several times to help. She could carry a hundred pounds on her shoulders. Kent got a kick out of some of the workers when they tried to best her.

On many occasions, Kent and Betty played with her little brother and sisters. Kent was amazed at how she enjoyed each moment with them. She listened to their concerns and helped them with their problems—always lifting, always nurturing.

Sometimes they walked around Cannonville. Usually there was an errand where she delivered something or just helped and listened to neighbors. She found out things to do that they needed or that they would appreciate.

Other times they read over some of her writing—it was good, very good—and if Kent caught her at the right moment, she'd read from her journal.

When those five weeks with Betty were up, Kent had a new appreciation for life. He was gaining a new respect for women, girls, and children. He knew that giving was greater than receiving, and he began appreciating little things, like a baby's smiles or little acts of kindness.

If this was the way all women were, he was hooked, and he wanted to have similar qualities as well.

Kent worked hard to become a better person. He recognized this metamorphosis on the last day of work. Betty came out at lunchtime. They sat in the shade of the rock, with several of the other hands. Kent felt their eyes on him, but he was comfortable. He felt quite a bit stronger, and a couple inches taller . . . just better. He was happy and grateful for that first day that he'd come to Promise Rock, for he had met Betty; and his life would never be the same.

The shearing done, his wages and bonus received, Kent grabbed Betty's hand and ran toward his car.

"Don't forget the town get-together a week from Friday," Mr. Griffin yelled to all the hands as they dispersed toward their vehicles. Kent had been thinking about this get-together a lot. It was supposed to be the biggest event of the season. All four towns, if you count Georgetown, were invited to meet at the Cannonville park. There would be dancing to the band, plenty of food, and Mr. Griffin would provide the mutton. It had been a good year for sheep.

The real catch was that Kent's friends were planning on coming. He felt torn. He wished he could spend the whole time with Betty, but he knew deep-down it was a time for him and Betty to spend time with all of their friends. He had no idea how it would all pan out, but he figured to give it a go.

Instead of opening the door for Betty, he grabbed a bucket of water from the trunk and did his best to clean up.

"What do you have up your sleeve?" Betty asked.

"I have a question for you," he answered as he pulled on a clean shirt. "Betty, there's only about an hour of light left. I'd like to do something different." He walked up and leaned back on the hood of his car. Betty leaned back next to him. "But first, I have a question."

"Yes, you said that."

"I'd like to go to the get-together with you . . . only you."

"I'd love to go with only you too. But . . ."

"But all my friends will be there. I think we should spend some time with them. Maybe I can patch up a few things."

"I know. That will be fine. We just need to establish some rules."

"Rules? What rules?"

"For starters—no holding hands." Kent already had his hand in hers, resting it on the hood of the car. He clutched it tighter.

"I don't think so. I want to hold your hand in front of the whole world."

She smiled, and then breathed softly. "Well then . . . we won't have any rules. We'll just go have a grand time."

"So, I'd like to take you up to the natural seat on Promise Rock."

"A little different than when we first met."

"Uh-huh."

They walked hand in hand along the path where they once rolled the wool sacks. They ascended the rock and stood above the empty bin. He noticed the empty stalls, the generator, and all the other equipment—silent for another year. Kent glanced at her. She had a puzzled look on her face. Kent grinned. It was working. He had a million emotions inside that he wanted to let out, and he wanted the moment to be perfect. He wasn't particularly skilled with words, but he had to try. All he knew was he was a completely different person than he was a year ago, and he wanted to thank Betty for it.

They made their way up to the top, and took in the view. The vehicles were all gone. Only some dust on the road to Tropic remained.

Kent sat back in the natural seat. "Do you think God placed Promise Rock here in the valley so your dad could run his sheep up to it, and then have us meet?"

"I have no doubt. That's just what God did."

"Have you ever thought that when you judged me, you were right on target?"

"Sure, I've thought a lot about it . . . how wrong I was."

"Wrong? You were right."

113

"If I could go back to yesterday, I'd be scared to talk to you, now that I know who you really are."

"Betty, it was you, always you. You're the . . . miracle. When I'm with you, I'm a better person. Anyone around you becomes a better person."

"You should go look in the mirror. That's the way I feel about you."

Kent left the seat, and stood next to her. "I'll never win with you, will I?"

"Nope, not until you get yourself all figured out." Now she went and sat on the natural seat.

"Well, at the rate I'm going, it will be on my death bed."

"No, I think you're starting to understand yourself pretty well."

Kent took a couple steps toward the rim, all the thoughts and feelings that he felt for her during his every waking hour hammering at his heart. "Betty, do you think we're growing up too fast?"

"Funny you would ask that. I think this land demands that we grow up quickly."

"Yeah, that's true." He looked out over the valley and closed his eyes. His mind drifted to his family. He opened his eyes and breathed deeply, feeling something a little different this time.

Kent observed the valley of sagebrush beneath, the bends and curves of the river, and the warm touch of the sun on the scattered trees and brush. But there was more. The feeling was peace. Kent turned back around facing Betty, a smile spreading across his face.

He spun around and cupped his hands around his mouth shouting with all his might. "To all the holy angels listening! I want to thank you for leading me to the most beautiful person on this earth. A daughter of almighty God! A miracle! She is the most loving, kind, and thoughtful person ever born. She makes everyone around her better. I'm the luckiest man in this world. Thank you, thank you, thank you."

He faced Betty. She sat there speechless, eyes wide and soft— filling with tears. Several moments passed. Kent's heart overflowing as he witnessed his words settling in her heart with the same depth and feeling they held when they were cast from his soul.

"Betty," Kent broke the silence. He sat next to her on the natural seat and took her hand. "I finally got the words out."

114

Betty, her mind searching, her heart pounding, closed her eyes and let Kent's words sink in. All the passion and love she felt for life and for Kent filled her to overflowing. Turning on the natural seat to face him, reaching a hand to caress his cheek, she whispered. "Kent, there is no longer a piece of my heart with you; you have my whole heart. You have it always and forever, no matter what happens. No wonder I love to stand on Heaven's Rock and point to heaven when you drive by. To me, you're out of this world."

Her hand slipped further around his neck. He drew her close. The life that was theirs to carry, complete with its seemingly endless work and sacrifice fled from their beings. Perhaps they, unknowingly, were being rewarded from on high with a small degree of the joy and peace that awaits those who endure the tests of life, and grow to the heights God intended for his children.

CHAPTER 22
TAKE CARE OF YOUR CAR

*K*ent made his way toward Tropic. The euphoria of the past few hours hadn't faded. He relived the tender, sacred moments he had shared with Betty. What a difference a year could make.

The car lurched, and then began to sputter. Kent quickly turned off the engine and pulled to the side of the road. White steam was pouring out from under the hood. "Oh no!" he groaned. He'd forgotten to fill the radiator with water. He waited for the engine to cool, and then grabbed the bucket and filled it, but it was too late. He tried to crank it, but the engine wouldn't even turn over.

He still had about three miles to go, so he started off at a half run. He hadn't gone far when he noticed a pair of headlights coming his way. Who would be going to Cannonville this time of night?

The vehicle slowed and came to a stop. It was his dad. Kent hurried over and got in.

"Are you okay, my boy?"

"Oh, I'm fine, but I'm afraid my car is in bad shape. It broke down about a mile back. How did you know I was in trouble?"

"I didn't. But I knew that Mr. and Mrs. Griffin wouldn't keep you too late. What happened to your car?"

"I forgot to fill it with water."

"Well, let's not worry about it tonight. We'll borrow your grandpa's truck and tow it back tomorrow."

That Saturday, Charlie Wilson and Kent surveyed the damage to the car. The block was cracked. He needed a new engine.

Kent tarried by his car for a good while, letting the repercussions sink deep. How would he see Betty? At least he'd get to see her at the town get-together, and then every week day when school started. But that did little to ease the ache in his heart.

CHAPTER 23
GIRLFRIEND OR FRIENDS?

The town get-together was the biggest event Cannonville had ever seen. There must have been over three hundred people there. Kent went down with his family. They'd managed to fit all eight of them in their two-seater car. Kent told his parents that he would help watch Jessica so they could dance and see old friends. He figured they knew he didn't want to dance with anybody but Betty. They did seem grateful, however, and left hand in hand toward the crowd of people in the park.

Kent picked up Jessica and slowly walked toward the huge fire in the fire pit in front of the dance floor. His plan was to stay back behind the crowd so no one would see him. As soon as he could find Betty, he would get to her side so no other girl would talk to him or ask him to dance.

"Hi!" The soft feminine voice made him jump.

He turned. "Oh, hi, Anita, how are you tonight?"

"Just grand. Hi there, Jessica," she said, tugging on her hand.

A restlessness quickly began spreading over him. She'd want to dance for sure. Maybe all was forgiven, or perhaps she wanted to throw herself between him and Betty.

"Let's see if my mom will hold Jessica so we can go dance," she hollered above the noise of the music.

"Oh, uh . . . I'd better watch Jessica. Uh, yeah, she'd get scared if one of the family wasn't with her."

"Nonsense," Anita shouted, grabbing his arm and tugging. She pulled him toward her mom, who was busy talking to friends. Sure enough, her mom was only too happy to hold Jessica. They made their way to the dance floor.

Almost everyone was doing the jitterbug. Sweaty and nervous as he was, Kent did his best. He'd danced before and quite enjoyed it. When the music ended, Kent turned to retrieve little Jessie. Again he felt a tug on his arm. "Silly, we're not going to dance just half a dance."

"Oh yeah, I guess that was kind of short."

"Why are you so nervous?" The band started playing again. "This number will definitely loosen you up." It was a fast number. Kent joined Anita. She was graceful and quick, and danced in excellent time to the music, but none of that mattered. Where was Betty? At long last the dance ended.

"I'd better get Jessica," Kent said, turning quickly. He made it over to Anita's mom who, to his dismay, was talking to Kent's mom. She was resting Jessica on the little bulge in her tummy.

Anita's mom quickly said, "You see, she's just fine. Run along and enjoy the dance." Kent felt Anita's hand grabbing his, pulling him back to the dance floor. It was a slow dance. She placed an arm on his shoulder and grabbed his hand. Kent placed his other hand on her back. He felt her softness, her smile, and her pleasurable company. But was it a show? Was she genuine, or was she getting back at him for his affection for Betty? He couldn't figure her out.

Through the couples on the dance floor, Kent caught a glimpse of Betty. His heart froze. She was dancing with some tall kid he'd never seen before. Kent swayed sideways slightly to get a better angle to see her. Their eyes met. She wore a resigned look. What was happening? What did all this mean?

As the music ended, Kent thanked Anita for the dances, hoping the relief wasn't too obvious in his voice. She cupped her hand around her mouth. "Kent, don't be such a stranger. We're next-door neighbors, you know."

"Yeah, okay. Thanks." Kent left Anita hastily, hardly caring if he appeared rude. His only thought was Betty.

Betty had slipped over next to her dad. The tall lanky kid was there with other people Kent didn't know. Kent thought, "This guy's trying to make a move on my girl. He's in for a surprise."

Kent worked his way to an opening where Betty might notice him. Her face lit up when she did, and she said something to her dad before making her way through the crowd to him.

"Oh my gosh, Betty. I thought we'd never get a chance to be together."

"Me either. Dancing with that guy was like dancing with an icicle."

"Who is he?"

"He and his family are going to move into the house next to us. They live in Salt Lake and are just down for the weekend." She looked back at the lanky kid. "His dad suggested he dance with me. He gives me the creeps. Let's get out of here."

"Fantastic idea."

They made their way to the far side, away from the fire, where it was darker. Kent breathed a sigh of relief and reached for Betty's hand. Her hair rested gently over her shoulders. Her dress was simple, nothing like Anita's, but to Kent she was more beautiful.

"You look beautiful." Kent choked with emotion.

"And you look very handsome. Care to dance, kind sir?"

"I'd love to." They did the jitterbug and two other dances before there was a slow dance. Kent melted into her embrace, his anxieties fading away, but . . . there was a hint of concern on her face.

"What is it, Betty?"

"Kent, I'm sorry, but I have to go check on Mom and the baby. Mom isn't feeling well. Thank goodness for Pamela and Mary, but the baby is just four months old."

"I'll come with you, if you don't mind. Maybe I could help out a bit."

"Would you? But, what about the dance, and the food, and your friends?"

"Oh, Betty, I'd rather be with you. Here, I'd be as nervous as a lamb with a mountain lion lurking about."

"Well, I hope we can calm your nerves," she said as the slow dance ended. They found Kent's mother dancing with his dad, who was holding Jessica in his arms. They were trying the jitterbug, but were having a difficult time. Kent motioned to take Jessica. Dad willingly passed her over. Kent asked if he could accompany Betty to her house. Dad said that he knew Martha was not feeling well, and that that would be just fine.

"Hi there, young lady. You must be Jessica," Betty said.

Jessica buried her head in Kent's shoulder. Kent could tell she was playing and probably smiling.

As they made their way to the edge of the crowd, Anita was talking to some of his friends. Their eyes met.

"Hey, Kent and Betty, come join us," she called.

"Hi, everyone," Kent said and started in on the introductions. "This is Betty Griffin. And this is Joe, Bob, Sam, and Jane. We've grown up together."

"Yeah, and I got to see Anita when she'd visit her uncle," Betty said.

Kent could see the others were sizing Betty up.

"The same Griffin as the one with all the sheep?" Sam asked.

"Yep. I'm his oldest."

After a brief pause, then Joe said, "Well, take Jessica back to your folks and come join us. We've got a whole bunch of firecrackers left over from the Fourth. We're going to sneak away for a bit. No one will know we're gone."

"That sounds great," Kent said, "but we've got to check on Betty's mom."

"She's not feeling well," Betty quickly added. "Kent has been kind to accompany me."

They started walking again toward Betty's house, but Joe quickly said, "So, you promised us you'd still be our best buddy in spite of your girlfriend from Cannonville. For once, spend some time with us. We'll get to know Betty, too."

Kent stood there speechless. Even Betty waited to see what he'd say. Joe was baiting him, and he didn't like it. He also knew Joe and his other friends were probably still upset with him. Taking in a deep breath, he glanced at Betty, and then slowly turned around to face them. "You guys will always be my friends, but tonight I'm going with Betty to check on her mom."

"Some friend. You're never with us," Joe growled.

There was silence, but Kent felt something snap inside.

"Aren't you a little young?" Anita said coolly.

The snap turning to anger and Kent faced them. "I thought so too, but Betty is fourteen going on eighteen."

"Oh, I see," Anita said dryly. "How old are we?"

"I didn't mean anything by that," Kent snapped.

"I'm glad you have such wonderful friends," Betty said quickly.

"Had friends," Joe said. "We hardly see him anymore. Go on then," he snorted, kicking some dirt toward Kent. "You wouldn't be any fun to be around anyhow."

They quickly turned and left. When they were out of earshot, Kent tugged at Betty's hand. "I'm so sorry, Betty. I . . ."

"What's there to be sorry about? I'm more worried about you."

"What?"

"Those are your friends that grew up with you. It will be hard patching things up."

"Thanks, but I'm not worried about them. We'll work things out. Joe always speaks his mind then cools off later."

The house was unusually quiet. The baby was asleep, and Pamela was in the kids' bedroom reading a bedtime story. Betty excused herself to check on her mom. She returned shortly. "She's doing okay," she said. "She's had some stomach pain, and has been throwing up. She also says she feels weak and achy. This has been going on for a while. We're all worried about her. I'm going to get her a cool washcloth and sit with her for a few moments."

"That sounds like a good idea," Kent said, making himself comfortable on the sofa.

Jessica was drifting off to sleep. Kent put her next to him on the sofa and rested his head, savoring the moment to clear his mind. He heard snapping and popping in the distance. His friends were setting off the firecrackers.

What's happening to you? Why aren't you out there with your friends? Are you growing up too fast? As quickly as those thoughts entered his mind, they were replaced by a soothing, peaceful feeling. It was Betty. The moments passed. Kent settled deeply into the couch, and suddenly, a whole panorama lit up before him.

CHAPTER 24
THE DREAM

*T*he sun was bright and warm, shining down on Kent and Betty as they walked along the gently flowing river. Occasionally Kent skipped a rock across the quiet ripples. Betty assembled a bouquet of wildflowers. Kent felt as light-hearted as the summer breeze around them.

The river path led into a valley of fragrant sagebrush and sparsely scattered juniper trees. Red rocks lined the valley sides, creating a perimeter of protection and shelter. In the distance loomed majestic orange spires and peaks. A sense of homecoming swept over Kent. This was a place where hard work, passion, and love would result in fulfillment and happiness.

Kent remembered their life beneath the painted cliffs. The look on Betty's face mirrored the wonder he felt. He took her by the hand and they smiled. This was their dream, come true.

Their reverie was shattered by a sound so low and deep that at first they only felt it, but it soon became a roar. The earth shook violently. Kent tried to keep hold of Betty's hand, but the tremors shook them apart. A crack in the earth's crust surged toward them, endlessly deep. They jumped at the last second, ending up on different sides of the chasm.

Kent scanned the valley for any refuge. The cliff! Surely the crack would stop before it reached the cliff and they could at least get back together.

"Run toward the cliff!" Kent shouted. The sand dragged at their feet and a harsh wind threw tumbleweeds and debris across their path. Kent could see Betty fighting through thorns and thistles. He felt pierced by every cut and scratch she endured. Kent called to her, but his voice was drowned immediately by the roar of the quake and the wind.

The ground on Betty's side gave way and she was swallowed by the earth. Kent ran to the edge of the chasm, praying with all his might. Betty was clinging to a protruding limb, and below was an endless abyss. Kent could only pray and hope that God would grant him a miracle.

People appeared. They formed a line. Just as Betty could hold on no longer, the lead person grabbed her arm. "Pull," he yelled. The others pulled. Betty was pulled to safety.

Kent and Betty made their way toward the cliff. Kent could see the end of the crack and increased his pace, but . . . where was Betty? The tremors had stopped. The wind calmed. "Betty," he screamed. "Betty!"

He searched and searched. A calmness spread over the valley. It was again bright, warm, and soothing, but to Kent it was more horrifying now that Betty had disappeared.

For hours he ran and searched until the sun began to retreat to the West. He had one option left. He left the trees and walked into a clearing beneath the cliff, then dropped to his knees. "Oh God, please help me find her." He looked toward heaven, squinting in the sun. "Father, can you hear me?"

He felt assured that Betty would be on the cliff. He squinted into the sun, but could not see her. Despair smothered him and darkness overcame him.

CHAPTER 25
IF THERE'S A WILL THERE'S A WAY

"*W*ake up, Kent."

"What? Good grief, Betty!" He jumped up and threw his arms around her. "I thought I'd lost you."

"What are you talking about?" she gasped, stepping back in surprise. "I'm not going anywhere."

"I must have been dreaming." He was nearly out of breath. "It was so real!"

"Why don't you tell me while we head back to the dance? I've seen headlights through Mom's bedroom window. People must be leaving." Kent picked up Jessica and they started back.

"I'm not really sure how to explain it. I woke up before the dream was over. It doesn't matter, because the ending didn't seem too good."

"Then you'll just have to make up a real nice ending. All dreams have happy endings, you know."

"Right." Kent highlighted the dream. "Thank goodness I woke up to your beautiful face."

"Wow," Betty said, "when you dream, you don't mess around. Did you panic?"

"Well, maybe a little," he answered, jabbing her in the ribs.

The get-together was almost over. Cars were leaving, and the remaining people were just chatting and saying good-bye.

"By the way Betty, I have some bad news."

"What is it?"

"It's my car. After the most spectacular day of my life—the one with you—my car broke down. I was so happy and deep in thought I forgot to fill my radiator with water. Now we won't be able to see each other until school starts."

Betty stopped, letting it sink in. Kent could tell she was troubled. He stood there silently as well. Finally, he noticed the little curve in her lips. She smiled, "My mom always says, 'If there's a will, there's a way.' Uncle Howard goes to Panguitch about once a month during the summer. I'll see if he'll drop me off at your place when he leaves in the morning. He could pick me up when he comes home."

"That's a sensational idea."

"I'll send you a letter on the delivery truck so you'll know when I'll arrive."

"It's perfect! I'll watch for the delivery truck every day."

They started walking toward the dance again. "I have another idea," Kent blurted, "I could introduce you to my family right now."

"I was hoping to meet them. I hope I can make half the impression on your family as you've made on mine."

"I'm not worried."

"Glad to see you two," Kent's dad said.

"Thanks for watching Jessica," Mom added. "We had fun. Is this Betty? The last time I saw you, you were nine or ten. Kent said you were all grown up."

"He gives me more credit than I deserve."

"Let's round up the kids," Kent said.

"That won't be hard," Dad said. "This is Gretha." He held out her hand but it fell limp to her side. She was asleep. "David and Jillian are asleep in the car, and Marilyn went home with the Johnsons."

"Oh," Kent said, his plan ruined.

"Hope you all had a great time." It was Sam Griffin. Turning to Betty he added. "I know all is well at home because you're here."

"Thanks, Dad."

"Charlie, your boy is a fine worker. I hope he'll be able to work for me again next year."

"Sam, that means a lot to me. Kent works hard at home, too. There might be a problem next year, though."

Kent's heart stopped. What on earth was Dad talking about?

Dad continued. "I guess now is as good a time as any to let the news out. I've been preparing to buy the Tropic Cash Store. If the loan goes through, it'll be mine soon as I finish teaching school next spring." Turning to his boy he said, "I hoped you would be one of my clerks. It would require a lot of heavy lifting and communicating with customers, as well as help with the bookkeeping."

Kent flashed a quick look at Betty. She looked as bewildered as he felt. "I'm sorry, son. Perhaps this wasn't a good time."

"Oh no, Dad. It just took me off guard. You've talked about it before, but I never thought it would actually happen."

There was a brief moment of silence, then Sam said. "I'd best head home."

The grownups said their goodbyes. All Betty and Kent could do was take a quick look at each other, but Betty distinctly recognized him mouth, "delivery truck."

CHAPTER 26
A LOVE LETTER

 ent's Aunt Dorothy dropped off Betty's letter in early
August. He grabbed it, skirted by the little ones, and ran
up to his room to read it.

Dear Kent,

My Uncle Howard is going to Panguitch on August
6th. He will drop me off at your place for the day if
it's all right with your parents. I would enjoy meeting
your brother and sisters, and seeing your mom again.

We're all doing just fine, except Mom. She still isn't
well. In a couple weeks, Dad will take her to the hospital in Salt Lake City to find out how to help her
get better.

We've been busy while Dad has been moving the
sheep down on the Paria. The house next to us seems
almost finished—it's huge. Looks like the family is
going to move in soon. Their name is Davis. Hope
they're nice. That tall kid is unnerving.

I still find time to go up to Heaven's Rock, and . . . oh
yes, I think about you. I write a line about you in my
heart every day. I sure miss you. I miss pointing to

heaven as you drive by. I miss your kindness to me and my family. I miss holding your strong hands. I miss you!

I love you, Kent,
Betty

CHAPTER 27
BRYCE CANYON NATIONAL PARK

When August 6 arrived, Kent had every chore done by eight in the morning. He had the whole day planned. There was no question where to take her—Bryce Canyon National Park. The park boundary was only three miles from his home, and the lodge above the cliffs only three miles further. He had the horses ready, lunches prepared, and even an itinerary on where they would go. It was a fabulous day. Not a cloud in the sky. It would be hot in Tropic, but Bryce was two thousand feet higher.

His little sisters and brother eagerly waited for Betty. They'd heard plenty about her. It wasn't long until she arrived. Jessica, Gretha, and Jillian stormed out of the house to greet her. Betty stopped and knelt down on the path, and gave them each a cordial hand shake. She called them by name, which delighted them even more. At last she noticed Kent watching from the porch. She scooped Jessica up in her arms and stood up straight.

"Wow, you're tall," Jillian said.

"You have long hair," said Gretha.

Not to be outdone, Kent stammered. "Gosh, you're beautiful."

Marilyn and David burst out of the door. "Pleased to meet you," Marilyn said cordially, holding out a hand.

David just grinned. "So you're Kent's girlfriend. He said you were strong as any boy."

"Oh, he was just being kind," Betty countered. She asked Kent, "Is today going to work? I mean for me to stay a while?"

"Hmm, let me see. Well, it is a nice day, but there is quite a bit of work to do."

"Oh, you silly," Jillian blurted out; "Kent has the horses, and ..."

Marilyn kicked her in the knee. "You're not supposed to tell," she whispered through clenched teeth.

"Well, looks like the secret is out," Kent said.

Betty turned and waved to her Uncle.

"We'll all show you around," Kent said. "Come on in and say hello to Mom. Have you eaten breakfast yet?"

"Yes, thank you."

"Hello, Betty," Mom said, coming out of the kitchen, with a dish towel in her hand.

"Hi, Mrs. Wilson," Betty said politely.

"Looks like you have quite a following," Mom said, observing that all of her children were around Kent and Betty. "So, how is your mother? Kent mentioned she was sick."

Betty's countenance changed. "Not well. We're going to take her to Salt Lake next week."

"Our prayers will be with you."

"Thank you," Betty said. "But let's enjoy today." She looked at the little ones. "Do I get to see the light bulbs and listen to the radio?"

"Yes," the little ones answered in unison.

Kent felt like a proud father flipping on the light switches, and it appeared Betty could have spent the day just listening to the radio. Jillian and Gretha grabbed her hands and tugged her around the entire house. Then they toured the garden, the barnyard, the bee hives, the orchard, and even the cellar. It took over an hour before they were on their way.

They went out the back door and to the barn, where the horses were tethered. The whole procession stayed right with them. Even Mom came out and to wish them a pleasant and safe day.

As they mounted the horses and turned toward the road, the children yelled goodbye. It reminded Kent of a newly married couple setting off on their honeymoon.

As they cantered down the road, Betty was smiling ear to ear. The morning's events had surpassed Kent's grandest expectations. His family adored her, the day was beautiful, and so was Betty.

"So, Kent," Betty said as they passed the rodeo grounds. "Thank you for a wonderful morning. You have an amazing family, and your home is a piece of heaven."

"I've wanted them to meet you for a long time. I'm glad they like you." Betty was silent. "Would you like to hear my plans for today?"

"I certainly do."

Kent had done a little research on the park, and had prepared a little speech. He'd also ridden this trail before, so he felt prepared.

"Well," he said in his deepest voice, "Bryce Canyon was made a park in 1924, but wasn't actually named until 1928. It was just Utah National Park before, and before that it was just a monument."

"Wow, my own personal tour guide," Betty teased.

Kent continued. "They also built a lodge with a restaurant, rooms, and stage and ball room, and . . . ice cream."

Betty cupped her hand to her mouth. "I've never eaten ice cream at a restaurant before."

"I was hoping you hadn't."

They started up the trail, which gradually sloped upward through majestic ponderosa pines and oak trees. The horses could smell water and preferred to keep up the pace. They let them go. They arrived at a sparkling stream that wound its way over white and orange rock. The water was cold and fresh. They all drank freely.

"Betty, do you want to rest a bit?"

"No, let's keep going."

Kent grinned at Betty's transparency. She must be thinking about that ice-cream. He was hoping to "knock her socks off," as Dad would say, with the time of her life.

They climbed back on the horses, and rode at a good walk for about a mile. The trail became steeper and wound through spectacular rock formations. Pinnacles, arches, spires, and too many other incredible views to count were around each corner. Betty, for the moment, was completely immersed in the grandeur.

As they topped out on the rim of the canyon, Betty let out a yell. "Whoowee! That was, without doubt, the most amazing climb I've ever done." Below them stretched the vast hills and valleys that they called home. It was indeed, a view that likely would top any other in the world.

"The lodge is over that way," Kent said, as they made their way through stands of pines.

A travel coach was in front of the lodge, and several horses were tethered to the side. The parking way was separated from the lodge with gigantic logs. Picnic tables were arranged on a cement floor.

People hurried toward the main entrance. Wondering what was going on, Kent and Betty tethered their horses and followed them inside. An enormous fireplace was on the right, with comfortable chairs around it, and the crowd was gathered in front of large double doors. Suddenly, the doors opened and a cast of chefs, waitresses, and other staff began singing a song of Bryce Canyon. Kent glanced at Betty. She was humming the tune and tapping her feet. When the song was over, everyone went in and sat at beautiful dining tables.

Suddenly, the quiet setting was jolted by what sounded like a gun shot. Some of the guests moved to the windows to look out, but no one acted too concerned. Betty and Kent got up and tried to peek through to the main lobby.

More bangs were heard. They were now sure it was gun fire. The shots drew nearer. A group of horseman galloped up to the lobby door. Their faces were covered with handkerchiefs. They held their reins in one hand and a gun in the other. One of them burst through the door and rode his horse right into the lobby. His gun barked again. *Bang, bang!* Waving his pistol at the crowd he shouted, "This is a stick up!"

Kent was scared. He put an arm around Betty, waiting tensely to see what the bandit would do next. Other people were finally looking scared. Some appeared ready to run. Others had huge smiles on their faces. He couldn't figure it out.

The masked man growled again with an angry tone, "I said, this is a stick up." He reached for his saddle bag. A couple of the spectators took off running down the hall. Suddenly the crowd burst into laughter. The cowboy was holding up a stick.

Kent looked over at Betty who was also laughing. "What's so funny?" he asked.

"Well, the cowboy was right. It was a stick . . . up."

Kent gasped when it finally hit him. He laughed a bit, mostly at himself. "Well, Betty, now you know I'm a little slow."

"Oh shush," she said, squeezing his hand. They worked their way outside near the lobby doors where the cowboys were greeting some of the guests. Kent held his hand up high and one of the cowboys came over and tapped it.

"Hello there, young man." Then he noticed Betty. "And a right fine hello to you too, young lady," he stammered, as he reached down and gave her hand a kiss. "I'd ask you two your names, but we'd best get riding before either the law catches up with us or those thunder clouds."

With that he whirled his horse around and they all rode off toward the rim with the thundering of hooves, and a few more shots in the air. "What a show," one man stated above all the muffled voices.

But Kent's jovial mood had vanished. He slowly turned his head, a shiver quivering down his spine. Sure enough, thick dark clouds were heading their way. He glanced at Betty, and could see the worry in her eyes. Their ice cream and eating lunch on the log benches overlooking the canyon would have to wait for another day.

CHAPTER 28
GOD ANSWERS PRAYERS

*T*hey hurried to the horses and mounted, knowing that wet trails would be difficult for the horses to negotiate. If they could make it to the bottom, the gentle decent into Tropic wouldn't be too bad. As they descended, they could hear cracks of lightning and a purr that sounded like a distant waterfall. The wind picked up.

The rain came in like a wave just as they neared the bottom. Kent could hear Betty speaking softly to her horse in an effort to keep him calm. He did likewise, patting his mount on the neck. The horses didn't seem to be too alarmed.

Kent checked over his shoulder. Betty seemed to be doing well. The horses had no desire to stop, so they let them continue at a good pace. Already, little streams of water scurried across the trail.

They continued a mile or so until they arrived at the stream where they'd stopped on the way up. It was no longer a small stream, but was already a couple feet deep and maybe twelve feet across. The previously clear water had turned an ugly, rusty hue. Kent's horse crossed without hesitating. Betty's horse stopped for a moment and then gingerly made its way across. "Are you okay, Betty?" Kent shouted, hoping his voice would carry over the howl of the wind.

"Yeah," he heard faintly. They had a little over four miles to go. The sky seemed dark, but Kent figured it was about four o'clock. "We should be home before dark without a problem," he whispered to himself.

Soon they arrived at the park boundary, where the road began. "Only three miles left," Kent yelled.

"Sounds good!" Betty shouted as she brought her horse up next to Kent's. Kent hoped that she couldn't tell how unnerved he was. He had brought her into this. He was responsible for her, and he'd let her down.

"Don't worry," he heard through the pelting of the rain and the whir of the wind. "I needed a good washing anyhow."

"I'm so sorry," Kent called back.

"Sorry for what? I wouldn't mind it if you could calm the rain though. Maybe you should pray and ask God to stop it until we get home."

"Sounds like a good idea." They both laughed. Kent marveled at her aplomb. "I think you're an angel," he called over to her.

"What?"

He cupped his hands toward her and mouthed the words. "I think you're an angel."

"That's what I thought you said. I think your brain is waterlogged. How about praying?"

"I've been praying the whole time."

They had a mile to go. The rain calmed to just a steady pounding, and the winds slowed, but a new sound became evident. It sounded like a waterfall, but not muffled like a distant pounding rain.

Kent felt real fear sting down his spine. He knew the road would be washed out. It happened frequently where the wash crossed the road above his house. He and his friends had often run up to watch the torrent of water plummet down the wash. They thought they were lucky if they could arrive just before it arrived. They liked to see the wall of water come roaring down a dry wash and to get out of the way just in time. But this time, Kent and Betty were on the wrong side.

"Betty," Kent said, "do you hear the water?"

"I do," she answered. "Will it be bad?"

"It sounds pretty big. I've seen these flash floods lots of times."

"I'll bet you were never on this side."

"I was just thinking that. Are you reading my mind?"

"Well," Betty sighed, "as long as we're together, we'll be okay."

The flood was bigger than he'd ever seen. Muddy water cascaded down the wash. It was about thirty or forty feet across and maybe four feet deep. The water was swift and obviously dangerous. They could hear rocks clattering along the bottom.

Kent looked back toward Bryce, and his heart sank. All he could see was thick, black clouds. The storm wasn't going to end any time soon. The rain and wind started picking up again.

They dismounted. Kent took Betty's hand and held it tight.

"How about that prayer?" she asked.

They knelt down right there in the mud, and closed their eyes. Kent had prayed all his life, but this time seemed different. This time he was praying for their lives. He made every effort to feel the Spirit of God, and know of His will for them.

"Oh God, Betty and I have traveled as far as we can in this storm. The water is so high and fast. We can't travel to the bridge south of town. It will soon be dark and we can't make our way in darkness through the hills and gulches. We must cross or stay the night here. I don't know if we and the horses can cross safely. Please, please help us know what to do. We don't know if we should ride on the back of the horses, lead them ... or if help will arrive. Please bless us. We love you, and are grateful for all you have done for us and our families. We're thankful for each other and the strength we have together, in the name of Jesus Christ, Amen."

They continued to kneel silently, praying in their hearts for an answer.

After a while they stood up. Kent searched Betty's eyes. "Did you get an answer?"

"I think so."

"I think I did too. I think we should cross. What was your answer?"

"That we should cross," but she seemed a little hesitant. Betty peered back. "So how should we cross?"

"We'll just ride. I'll go first."

"Wait just a minute," she said. "My father has had to ford floods such as these. He told us how he did it down on the Paria. Your horse can't maintain his footing if you ride. Hold onto the mane and the saddle horn. Stay right at his side on the down side of the current. His strong legs and footing will take you across."

Kent reached over, grabbed her rain-soaked hand and kissed it. She flashed him a quick smile. His horse was getting restless. He wanted to cross, too.

Patting his horse on the neck, Kent spoke to him, and prayed again that they would make it across. The bank had been washed out, forcing the horse to lunge on the first step. Kent held on with all his might. By the time Kent felt the hooves hit the river bottom, the water was as high as the saddle. Kent's legs were swept up, his body floating on the surface. His horse whinnied loudly as he struggled to keep his footing. As he bunched his huge muscles to lunge up onto the bank, Kent let go and grabbed at the bank as well. He clawed his way up, and then turned to look back at Betty. She had her horse's mane tightly gripped in one hand, the other on the saddle horn. Her horse was preparing for that initial lunge. At that moment, the earth gave way under her horse's front two legs. He leaped, but was off balance and plunged head first into the filthy water. Betty, clinging with all her might, went headfirst into the water as well. The panicked horse lurched sideways. Betty's hands tore loose, and she sank beneath the current.

Without even thinking, Kent dove in, blindly thrashing at the water. He couldn't see anything. The current was sweeping him downstream. He could feel the bottom, but it was too swift to get footing. He couldn't see Betty. "Please God," Kent cried out, "let me find her."

Slipping again, he took in a mouthful of water and came up coughing and choking. He tried to take a breath, but again took in water. Everything started to go blurry, and coldness enveloped him. He was drowning!

He heard a voice. "I'm here." He felt arms wrap around him. "Grab on," he heard.

He felt the tremendous force of rushing water and pounding rain. He felt the stabbing of branches on his face and body. He groped for a handhold. He caught hold, and held on with the last of his strength. A hand grabbed his and pulled. He let go and felt ground. He pawed and scraped at it until the force of the water left. Then everything went black.

Kent awoke, fully expecting the serenity of angels to surround him. His head felt comfortable, and he could feel the warmth of a hand on his cheek.

"We made it," a distant voice said. "Your prayer was answered."

He opened his eyes to find Betty's face above his. At once, the ter-rifying ordeal came flooding back to him. He remembered jumping into the water to save Betty, struggling for footing, and wildly thrashing at the water, and then . . . nothing.

"Are you okay?"

She cradled him in her arms, his head in her lap. They were under a juniper tree, maybe the same one that saved them. It granted a little relief from the pounding rain.

"Can you sit up?"

He did so, but began coughing up mud and water. When it sub-sided, they stood.

"How long was I out?"

"About a half hour. It worried me, because you gurgled when you breathed. All I could think of was to keep your head up and to the side."

Kent embraced her with what strength he had left. "You saved my life!"

Betty's clothes were soaked, mud and sticks matted her hair, and water was dripping off her nose and hair. Kent knew he'd never seen anything so beautiful. She cupped his face in her hands. "I'll never forget what you did for me tonight. I know that you would give your life for me. I'll always love you, Kent. I promise I'll never let that love dim. Never, never, never."

They made their way back to the road, Kent so weak he could barely place one foot in front of the other—Betty supporting him. They were washed down nearly two hundred yards. The horses were gone, but they would find their way home. They stood there in amazement, looking across the deluge—this time full of gratitude to be on the right side.

"Can you make it back or . . ." Betty's words trailed off. Headlights were coming toward them.

Kent watched the blurry lights come closer. He leaned toward Betty. "You saved my life. I know more than ever . . . God answers prayers." Kent heard distant voices, felt the strong arms of his father, and everything went blank again.

CHAPTER 29
CHRIST'S TEACHINGS TAKE MEANING

*N*ews of Kent's near drowning, and Betty's rescue of him spread around the little towns under the painted cliffs. Many people wanted to hear the tale from Kent. He said it was worth a trip to Cannonville to meet the girl who saved him. Kent's friends started to warm back up to him. Sure, they were a little miffed that Kent wasn't around to take them joyriding, but thoughts of obtaining their own cars were becoming prevalent.

The only one who didn't warm up to Kent was Anita. She had always been able to get her way with boys—except for Kent, and that infuriated her. Betty's having saved him only drove the wedge between them even further.

Kent became sick. He coughed a lot. He was short of breath and didn't have much strength. Mom thought he had pneumonia. Even so, he worked as hard as he could. The storm had been one of the strongest in years. It had flooded the cellar and damaged much of the fruit and vegetables. The garden had to be re-furrowed, and the animals, pens, and shelters needed repairs.

Gradually he regained his strength and embraced work on the farm with greater fervor. It helped the days go by. Each day was one day closer to when he would see Betty five days a week.

He reenacted the trip to Bryce a thousand times, especially the flash flood in the wash. He also worried for the whole Griffin family as they took Martha to Salt Lake City. The storm had likely damaged those roads as well. It would be a difficult trip with all of their kids.

He developed better habits of prayer and found himself praying both morning and night for Betty's mom and the Griffin family's safe return. The principles he learned at church became more meaningful. He now understood how they applied to daily life.

He thought of Mr. Griffin and his gratitude for Betty's prayers. He thought of Sam's fear of losing his wife, soul mate, and friend— his all in all. Would that fear come true?

CHAPTER 30
A WRENCH IN THE PLANS

The day Kent and Betty had anticipated for fifteen months finally arrived. Kent was at the school bus stop well before it arrived.

The bus rounded the bend. He watched it approach, listening to the crunch of the gravel under its wheels. The students began streaming out, and finally Betty appeared, notebook and pencil in hand. He ran up to her. "Betty, you're safe! You're back home!" He looked around at the other students. "Aw, what the heck," he said, "I don't care what anyone thinks." He hugged her tightly. She hugged him back.

It was several moments. They stepped back to look at each other. Only then did they notice that a whole crowd had gathered around them.

"Are you guys a couple now?" someone asked.

"What's it like to drown?" asked another.

"Did you see a bright light? A tunnel?"

Kent and Betty parried the questions, saying they had an important matter to discuss. The other students seemed to understand, and began to disperse, most of them heading for the school, talking excitedly.

Kent and Betty walked over to a line of tall trees that sectioned the parking lot. " How is your mom?"

She didn't answer. She looked solemn—troubled. Kent tried to read her, wondering if she was thrilled like he was that their long awaited day had arrived. Perhaps she was just worn out from her trip. "Is your mom going to be okay?"

"Kent, I'm sorry. I guess I don't know where to begin. I'll start with . . . you can't imagine how good it is to see you." He smiled. "She's . . . she's . . ." She held her breath, and then burst into tears, and turned away.

Kent placed his hands on her shoulders. Her crying didn't let up. He slipped around, and hugged her trembling body. She turned away, and began pacing. Kent was bewildered . . . scared. He didn't want to press her, but he couldn't stand it. "Betty?"

"Kent, she's dying! My mother is dying!" She turned toward him and buried her head in his shoulder. The bell for the opening assembly rang. Neither of them moved.

At last she stepped back. "I'm so sorry." She dried her eyes the best she could, and took a deep breath. "Let's see. The hospital was a sight to behold. It looked to me like they could fix anyone there. They did blood tests and x-rays, and examined Mom until they knew everything about her since she was a baby. She has some type of cancer that may have started in her bowels and has now begun spreading through her body. There's no cure, and she's getting sicker and weaker each day. The doctors say she has between six months to a year."

Kent couldn't move. "No! She's young, she has little children." Now he felt the tears near the surface. They were silent for a good while. Finally he leaned over and took Betty in his arms. "I know that God has a plan for her—for all of us. As long as we're together, we can make it through anything." He held her, praying his words might soothe her aching soul.

Instead of calming, she jerked free of his arms, holding her face in her hands—tears leaking through her fingers. She began pacing again.

Kent watched her pace. What more could be wrong? At least they would be together. They could support each other. "Betty, we learned in the flood, that as long as we're together we can withstand anything. We'll see each other five days a week now. We'll get through this. We'll keep praying."

She began sobbing harder. What on earth? Kent's stomach was now churning. "Betty, I'll be right there with you."

She whirled. "Kent," she cried. "We won't be together! I won't be coming to school! I'm going to stay and care for Mom and little Kenny, and the others."

This couldn't be happening. He leaned against a tree, a blank nothingness enveloping him.

Betty, her heart now aching for Kent, slipped an arm around him. "I don't know what to do," she sobbed. "I don't know what's going to happen, but I do know this. We've said it many times. What we have together will never dim. Never, never, never."

Removing his face from his hands he said, "That's right, either you save me, or I come through for you—forever and ever."

They stood there for a while longer saying nothing—each lost in thought. At the sound of rustling inside the school they could tell the assembly was at an end. Hand in hand they made their way to school.

Tropic High had six class rooms and a gym. The hallway was bustling with students. "Hi there, Betty," a tall, blond, handsome boy yelled above the noise.

"Hi, James."

"Who's this?" James asked, gesturing toward Kent.

"He's my boyfriend through and through, Kent Wilson."

"Oh, hi. Well, got to go before the bell rings." James turned and hurried off.

"Who is James?," Kent asked. "Is he the icicle you danced with?"

"Yeah, he and his family moved in next to us last week."

By the last bell of the day, Betty had her home schooling prepared. Her teachers would prepare her assignments, and then Kent would gather them up and deliver them to Betty's friend Kindra. The following day, Kindra would return them to Kent, and he would distribute them to her teachers.

Kent watched Betty dart from class to class, meeting teachers and making friends. He ached for her. How long would it be until she could enjoy her precious high school years? As they parted at the bus stop, there was no sugar coating the sadness. Each of them fought with everything they had to keep away the tears.

"Betty," Kent called before she stepped up on the bus. "I'll slip notes in your homework. There's one under the front cover of your English book." She smiled and disappeared into the bus. Betty sat next to Kindra, her heart feeling the weight of the undertaking that lay ahead of her, but also feeling Kent's support. "Excuse me for just a moment, Kindra, Kent sneaked me a letter."

"I know. I think he spent his whole math class writing it."

Betty opened the front cover of her English book. Five small papers were placed on top of each other.

Please put your hand in front of you and touch a finger with each piece of paper if you believe what I say.

These five things I know.

#1 You are a beautiful daughter of God. (She touched her little finger.)

#2 Therefore he loves you far beyond what you can comprehend. (She touched her ring finger.)

#3 He will make you equal to any challenge that comes before you. (She hesitated thinking of the wool sacks and the wash, then slowly reached down and tapped her middle finger.)

#4 Like the angel that came to strengthen Jesus in Gethsemane; there are many that will love and support you, and pray for you; angels on this side of the veil and the other. (Again she hesitated, feeling mostly alone. Kent was nearly eight miles away. "I've got to have more faith," she thought to herself. She reached down and tapped her index finger.)

#5 Since the day we met, you started changing my life. I believe you're the best thing that's ever happened to me. If there's one thing I know, I'm truly, deeply, and profoundly in love with you. I pray you feel it when the days are tough. (She reached down and . . . grabbed her thumb, and then her whole hand.)

CHAPTER 31
TAKE ME, NOT MY DAUGHTER

The night was still and dark. With only a crescent moon to light his way, Sam Griffin rode down a familiar path. The clip clop of his horse's hooves was the only sound that pierced the night. He felt at home and at peace on his trusted mount.

He and his family had returned from Salt Lake City the day before. Betty had attended her first and only day of school. She arranged to have her homework delivered, so she wouldn't fall behind. And now, he had to get away. He couldn't last another minute without relief from the ache that filled his heart.

His mind settled on himself—his own simple upbringing. What could be simpler than being raised by people he didn't know? People who took him in because he was only two and could be raised to help them with their livelihood. They had become his family. Sure he'd met his father, and some of his brothers and sisters, but they weren't close. And now he was a loner—a man in a shell. But no, he was breaking that shell. He held the town get-together and it was a success. He was starting to be considered one of the prominent men of the area. Mostly because of his angel wife who now . . . now would be leaving.

Martha and their family had made all the difference. They had loved him, supported him, and . . . literally brought him from nothingness to more happiness than he ever thought possible. Of course he worried about his beloved companion. Life would be over without her. But not really. He still had his children. And now Betty! Betty . . .

He dismounted, and dropped to the sand. "Dear God, I can't let her do this. Betty has offered to stay home and care for Martha and the children, and our farm. I can't let her! It would tear her away from school, from her friends, from Kent, and all the dreams of her heart. But I can't keep a roof over our heads and care for Martha and the children. We could take her to the care center in St. George or Provo, but that's five hours away."

"Oh God, what's the answer? Is history repeating itself like my big sister?" He sat back in the sand. "King Lear," he said out loud. He'd read many of Shakespeare's stories. He held them dear. "Will I hold my precious daughter's head in my lap as she breathes her last breath, just because I want Martha with me until she passes? Will I lose them both?"

He knelt in the sand a good while, numb—his mind searching. He'd never been a real religious man. Only when he married Martha and began having children and made his house into a home did the feelings of having a Heavenly Father and a Savior begin resounding in his heart. And now, after all these years, he recognized the need for God. He was empty without Him, and without Him, he couldn't bear what lay before him. "Please Father; help me bear the pain of asking my daughter to do this. Please, please, please . . ."

Nearly an hour later he stood, mounted his horse, and started home. He'd received no lightning bolt answer nor loud voice, but he did feel a burning in his heart. It was a feeling to allow his daughter to do it and not to deprive her. How could that be? There was also a feeling that God would bless her and strengthen her to be equal to her trials, and that He would send her help.

But his own heart was breaking. Was this how God the Father felt when he sent His Son to be lifted up upon the cross? He arrived home, opened the door, and was met by Betty, who had waited for him. No words were said. He rushed over to her, and held her tight. He cried to an extent he didn't know possible. Thoughts of his first-born, from the moment she entered the world until the present, coursed through his mind.

At last the silence was broken. Sam said, "If only it could be me . . . not you."

CHAPTER 32
GRATEFUL FOR TRIALS

*N*ovember, the warm Indian summer days had retreated to a cold breeze, dark clouds, and an inch of snow. Betty's dad would be heading for the Paria tomorrow. He'd be gone at least a week. Two of his workers had come up missing. He was told they took off because they couldn't stand another cold lonely winter down there. Someone said they headed toward Page, Arizona.

Betty wondered if she'd be able to care for her family in her father's absence. Up until then, he had been gone good portions of the day, but he'd always been there in the evenings. He made a huge difference in those few hours he was home and during the night.

Betty had developed a routine that worked fairly well. She got up before anyone else, started the fire in the cook stove, and prepared breakfast. After getting the three older girls off to school, she could focus her energy on the three little ones and her mother, if Dad had to leave.

She worked hard with Judy, teaching her to entertain herself and Lola as well. Kenny never slept well. Betty figured it was colic and tried every remedy her mother had taught her. Nothing worked. After a month or so of struggling to help him, she noticed he was teething. He cried incessantly, and when he wasn't crying he was crawling. He got into everything. Betty could hardly take her eyes off him.

She instructed the older girls to come home right after school. She assigned Pamela and Mary to care for the little ones and watch Mom while she'd rush to care for all the animals, garden, and fruit trees before it got dark. Sometime during this frenzy, Betty would get dinner ready, and then instruct the older ones to get their homework done.

Dad would arrive home and gather everyone around him. They'd read a story from the Bible or talk about a parable. Sometimes he'd sing his favorite tunes of the trail.

As for mother's care, Betty knew it the best. Pain and vomiting were her biggest issues. If Betty didn't observe her closely, her pain would get so bad she'd curl up, clutch her stomach, and start to shake. Betty tried to figure which foods set better with her, and always tried to keep her well hydrated with plenty of water. Mom wasn't eating well, was losing weight rapidly, and was becoming weaker. The key was the morphine. They had a good supply. Betty worked hard to juggle the doses so Mom could be more comfortable and still be able to eat. It was more difficult when she was vomiting, because the morphine upset her stomach. It was like playing a game of chess.

Twice a day, Betty walked with her mother. Sometimes they went out in the yard and back, depending on whether she was able to get her dressed for the day.

Mom's mental faculties were clear. She was keenly aware of the effort her children and Sam made in her behalf. Martha expressed her gratitude about a hundred times each day.

Betty helped her wash and stay clean, and helped her look presentable if company showed up.

The night before Dad was to leave, she leaned back into the sofa. The day was over. It was her moment to call her own. She had started a new, one might say . . . ritual. She would look heavenward and pray, not look downward. Somewhere she'd heard that George Washington prayed while looking heavenward, and his prayers were answered miraculously—leading to her country's independence. She wouldn't know for some time that her dad had witnessed her prayer.

The story was written by Sam Griffin in his journal.

My Daughter, a Gift from God

It was late at night. I was sitting with my precious companion, watching her breathe. I heard something. I peered through the crack. It was my daughter Betty, praying.

"Oh God, my Father. Give me strength to care for my family while Dad is away. Bless him that he'll be safe. Comfort him as he watches our dear mother prepare to return to you. Bless my mother that she may be able to enjoy her children and home a little longer. Help me to know her needs. Help me with the children. Grant me patience and understanding."

She asked for a few more things, and then began crying. I readied myself to go comfort her. Surely she was buckling under the weight she carried. She missed the life of other teens. She missed school, and all the events of the world around her. She missed her friends. She missed boys—mostly Kent Wilson. She missed activities.

It was only natural. I stood up, but just before I pushed at the door, my eyes widened.

"Oh, my God," she prayed, with tears pouring down her cheeks, "I thank you for this opportunity to care for my beloved mother . . . to perhaps help her enjoy her family and home a little longer before she returns to you. I thank you for Dad, and all he does to provide us a home. I thank you for Kenny who you recently sent to us. I thank you for the privilege of caring for the rest of my family; to see their smiles, hear their laughter, and dry their tears. I'm learning the lessons of parenthood, love, and service."

"I thank you for our new neighbors. For Mrs. Davis who has agreed to help while Dad is gone. I thank you for the church and the help from its members. Oh Father, I love you! In the . . ."

I stepped backward and sat awkwardly in my chair, amazed at what I'd just witnessed. Was she real? I could think of only one thing. I knelt beside my bed, and thanked God for the gift of a daughter that he'd sent to me.

CHAPTER 33
SICKNESS: ROYALTY AND THE SERVANT

*K*ent did as he promised. Each day he gathered Betty's assignments and delivered them to Kindra, a pudgy, round-faced girl with thick glasses. Kindra was full of energy and had a bubbly personality. Kindra would return the finished work to him the next school day, and would giggle if there was a note inside. She became a close friend. Kent quickly found out why she was liked by all. She'd give you anything she could. She'd bake and bring you cookies if you were having a bad day. But Kent, though he would have enjoyed the cookies, was glad he wasn't a recipient.

After two months, Kent found himself growing empty. He needed to see Betty. He needed to know for himself that she was well. He devised a plan. He would borrow his dad's car on a Saturday. He could consider it a birthday present from him. That afternoon when he passed the homework to Kindra, he told her that there was a note inside the front cover of Betty's English book. She winked and smiled as she always did.

* * *

Betty finished her nightly prayer, still looking heavenward. Now she had another concern. Kent was coming that Saturday. She yearned to see him, but not in her current circumstance. She couldn't look pretty for him. She couldn't spend any time alone with him. He would witness the stress and struggle of the life that was now hers. She felt . . . helpless.

When Saturday arrived, Kent hopped in Dad's car and made his way to Cannonville. He was thrilled. The sky was deep blue and cloudless. "Here I come, Betty," he yelled out loud. "I'm on my way!"

When he approached Heaven's Rock, he leaned over the steering wheel to get a good look at it. He thought of the many times he'd driven by and seen Betty there standing straight and tall holding her arm toward heaven. He thought of their first kiss. Would it ever happen?

He turned into Cannonville and neared the Griffin home, taking note of the huge house next door. He pulled to a stop and took a deep breath. Somewhere deep down he knew this would not be a pleasant visit. He just needed to see her, and if she was busy, he could play with the little ones.

Arriving at the door, he reached up to knock. The door opened, but it wasn't the kids or Betty. It was that tall young man he'd met at school. He had little Lola in his arms.

"Hi," he said blandly. "I'm not so sure it's a good day for a visit. The baby is sick, and of course, you know about Betty's mom." Kent stood there speechless. The other boy paused a moment longer then said, as he started for his home, "Oh well, suit yourself."

Kent watched him walk away. He really didn't like him. He felt he was trespassing on his property. If there was help that Betty needed, he would provide it. But even as he thought about these new events, he knew he was in a pickle. He lived too far away.

He knocked, still anticipating a rush of little feet. None came. Finally he hollered through the door.

"Hello! It's Kent!"

Mary and Sara appeared. They looked a little disheveled but were glad to see him. Kent bent down and gave them a hug. "I'm soooo glad to see you two."

Sara wrapped her arms around him. Kent closed his eyes and hugged her back. After a moment, he looked up, and there was Betty, smiling broadly. But he was shocked. Her eyes were bloodshot, her hair a mess. She looked worn through and through.

He jumped up and ran over to her and hugged her. He looked into her eyes, noticing they were swollen.

"Betty, it's good to see you. How's your mom and Kenny?"

Her smile faded into a look of worry and stress. "Well, they're both real sick. I don't know if they got any sleep last night because they kept throwing up and little Kenny has a high fever. We've been keeping him cool the best we can."

"Betty, dear," a voice emanated from the back room. "Could you wet these towels again please?"

Betty scurried back into the room.

Kent bowed his head right there and offered a prayer. After a moment he looked up and noticed Sara and Mary quietly observing him. He felt helpless, confused, and angry, and then he got mad at himself because of his earlier selfish thoughts. He walked over to the kids. "What do you say we go to the park?" He thought they would jump for joy, but rather they stood, there not offering a single word.

Mary broke the silence. "I had a bad fever once. Mom says it caused me to have a seizure. I don't remember it, but I think that's why Mom and Betty are trying hard to keep Kenny's fever down."

"Wow, Mary," Kent answered. "You should be a doctor when you grow older." She giggled.

"If it's all the same to you," Mary said softly, "we'd just like to stay here. If we can keep Kenny cool he won't have a seizure like I did."

"Okay, what shall we do?"

A faint soft voice echoed from across the room. "Can you tell us a story?" It was Judy, peering out from behind the door, looking up rather pitifully.

"I sure can. The only problem is I have so many I just don't know where to start."

"Let's start on the couch," Mary said as she stepped backward a couple steps, and flopped down.

Kent went over and sat down between them. He could see that they too, were tired from a long night with their sick mom and little brother. Pamela also came in, not wanting to miss the story. "Now let's see." He paused, making sure he'd captured his audience. He had rehearsed it over and over, and now he felt he had it down pretty well. It reminded him of Betty. "Once there . . ."

But he was interrupted by Pamela.

"Tell us why you like Betty so much that you will come all the way here to Cannonville to see her. Surely you could like a girl in Tropic? And you can't even have fun with Betty anymore."

"Sure, in truth, that's my story. It will tell you why I came clear down here to see her." They all looked eager. He'd have to come through. He closed his eyes, drew in a deep breath, and started.

Royalty and the Servant

Once there was a servant to the Queen. He was lazy. He was unhappy, and he did very poor work. One day he ran into the beautiful princess. He thought she would look down on him and be hurtful. Instead, she was very kind. He saw that she was gracious to everyone. He watched her. She worked hard, and always with a smile.

One day the servant asked her, "Why do you work so hard? You're a princess. Why don't you have your servants wait on you?"

"I work out of love. Love for my family, my home, and my servants."

"But why?" he asked again.

"It's who I am," she answered.

The servant left. He didn't understand. But he did comprehend what she meant about work. He decided to follow her example. He started to work out of love—love for the Queen, the Princess, and everyone else—even the commoners.

Many years went by. He didn't notice before, but he found he'd changed. He enjoyed his work. He found he was happy. He had love in his heart. Love for the Queen, the other servants—everyone. Especially the Princess who he'd work alongside all that time—he was in love with her.

One day he was summoned by the Queen. He went to see her. He was a little scared. The Queen said, "I've noticed your good work."

"Thank you," he said.

"Young man, why do you work so hard? As I recall, you didn't at first."

"My Queen, it's because of what the Princess taught me. It's who I am now. I have love in my heart. Love for you, love for the Princess, love for . . . everyone."

155

"Oh, I see."

"My Queen, may I ask you a question?"

"You may."

"Why do you call me young man? I am but a servant."

"Are you now? Some years ago you did not know who you were, but I believe you know now. You are a Prince of Princes, destined to be King of Kings."

"But my Queen, I am not royalty. How can that be?"

"Now, my young Prince, are we not all children of Almighty God? Those who follow the example of His Son become filled with His love—the greatest gift that can ever be given. You see, young Prince, you have given yourself this gift—you've learned of Heaven."

The Princess, who was listening behind the curtain, stepped forward. She smiled at her mother, and then looked at the servant, or rather the young man with whom she had worked side by side for all those years. She ran and jumped into the outstretched arms of the mighty prince . . . And they lived happily ever after.

"Do you know who the Princess is?" Kent asked.

"Who is it?" cried Sara.

"It's got to be Betty," Pamela said.

"That's right. Since the day I met her I learned how to love, how to work, and how to enjoy life. She's helped me learn of Heaven. How could I not love her with everything I am? I'm the luckiest person in the world."

"We understand now," Pamela stated.

"You sure are lucky," Mary commented.

CHAPTER 34
I DON'T KNOW WHAT TO DO?

*S*ara answered a knock at the door. James stepped inside. "My mom has fixed lunch for you all. Get your sister." Betty parted the door, and stepped out as if she'd been listening. Had she?

"That's very kind of your mom," Betty said. "We're all famished, and we haven't been able to prepare any food. Surely she wouldn't mind Kent coming over as well?"

James's face twisted some. He seemed irritated. Finally, he said, "I'm supposed to stay here and watch Kenny and your mother while you all eat. I don't know what she'll say." Everyone was silent. James hesitated a moment longer, his countenance cold. "Oh well," he gestured at Kent. "Go on, then."

They all filed next door to the Davis home. It was elegant. Dark hardwood flooring, fancy lighting fixtures and no wires on the outside of the walls. Arriving at the dining area, Kent noticed a lady who had to be James's mom. When she saw him her eyes widened. "I was unaware of another mouth to feed at your residence," she said to Betty.

"Oh, I'm sorry," Kent interjected before Betty could respond. "I'm just visiting from Tropic. I'll see myself out." He moved quickly toward the door.

"Nonsense," she declared. "Come back in here, young man. Millie, set another plate at the table. We've planned this since early this morning. Now come back and sit down, and by all means, feel welcome. I'm Mrs. Davis. This sweet lady is my sister, Millie. You'll have to excuse my husband. He's detained with business in Salt Lake."

Kent made his way to a vacant chair.

"So are you going to introduce yourself?"

"Oh, excuse me. I'm Kent Wilson."

"Thank you," she said. "Now how are your mother and the baby?" she inquired, looking straight at Betty.

"They're both resting right now, and Kenny's temperature is down a little."

"Very well," she said as she turned and busied herself with a huge bowl of mashed potatoes.

Mrs. Davis and Millie served the meal on fancy china, and the table was big enough to fit all of them, plus a few more.

After a blessing on the food, they began passing the food around the table. There was plenty for everyone. Kent was surprised. He was raised in a home where supper was the main meal, sometimes quite late in the evening. Lunch was just a quick something or other to get enough energy to keep working.

"Is this meal surprising to you, young man?" James' mom questioned as if to hint that she knew this was far beyond any meal he was accustomed to. Kent hesitated a moment, struggling to find the right response.

"Well, then, don't worry about an answer, but answer this please. How are you related to the Griffins?"

"Uh, no, Betty and I are . . . best friends."

She gasped and choked on the piece of cucumber she'd gingerly placed in her mouth. "You talk like you're boyfriend and girlfriend, young man."

Kent felt his cheeks coloring, but tried to act casual. "We're just best friends."

She huffed. "Before marriage, best friends between a boy and a girl is called my boyfriend or my girlfriend. So how old are you, anyhow?"

"I'll be fifteen in a couple days."

This time she let out a sound like a muffled shriek. Her face wore a look of bewilderment laced with disdain. "Do they not teach you kids to wait until you're older to date? Oh, never mind that, but that's what we teach our children."

With that Kent dropped the silverware to the table. He was furious. Memories flooded his mind: Betty saving his life in the flood, the heartfelt moments they once shared, and what's more, they still hadn't kissed yet!

"I'll see myself out now." Kent scooted around the chairs as best he could. He shot a quick look at Betty. She looked pitiful. His heart went out to her but he didn't know what else to do. He just couldn't stay there.

He shut the outside door and ran for his dad's car. He stood next to the door for a moment; part of him afraid Mrs. Davis would come out and insist that he come back, but another part of him hoped Betty would come out.

The front door opened. Kent held his breath. It was Betty! She hurried over. "Oh, Kent, I'm so, so sorry."

Kent stood there, groping for some word to say. He knew it took great courage for her to get out of her seat and come out.

"The Davis family have helped us a lot. They're really not bad people once you get to know them. They're quite generous and ..."

Kent had had enough. "I don't think they're fine people at all. I've never been treated in such a manner. Betty, they have you brainwashed."

"Well, they are different. They kind of speak their mind first, and then soften up later."

"Well, I don't see anyone coming out to apologize."

"Kent, I've got to get back inside. They've gone to a lot of work."

"Yeah, a lot of work to run me out."

"That wasn't her intent."

"What do you mean it wasn't her intent? It was exactly her intent. Maybe she wants to hook James up with you."

"Of course she doesn't, Kent. Please, you've got to understand."

"You're the one that needs to understand."

That was the first time he ever saw Betty's cheeks color in anger. Her eyes were glaring. She looked at him until he turned away. After a moment she turned and walked away. Kent stood there silently, more bewildered than he'd ever been in his life.

Betty's voice broke the silence. She had stopped and turned around a few paces away. "I'm sorry this happened, Kent. I know this wasn't at all what you expected. Thank you for coming down." Then she turned and walked away.

The ride home was the longest trip of his life. His mind was in a frenzy. It seemed that all of his hopes and dreams had shattered. And Betty was so worn, so beaten down, and he'd snapped at her. He didn't notice the tears streaming down his face. "Why, why, why? Kent you were purposefully mean to her," he yelled out loud, slamming a fist on the dashboard. "What's the matter with you?"

That night he went to his room, exhausted from worry, so frustrated that he couldn't be comforted. He knelt beside his bed, looking up. "Dear Father, please, please, help me through this. Help Betty and her family, please . . ."

He remained on his knees for a good while—pondering, questioning . . . crying. At long last he looked up. "Father . . . I don't know what to do."

CHAPTER 35
THE DREAM IS FOR REAL

*T*he following Monday, Kent was waiting at the bus stop. He fidgeted nervously, waiting for Kindra to step out. She was the last one. She held Betty's books in both arms, with a dishtowel-covered plate on top. She handed the books to Kent and pulled back the towel to reveal a plate of cookies along with a note. She didn't say a word, just gave Kent a wink, and headed to class.

Kent read Betty's note and relief enveloped him like a warm blanket. Then he ate the cookies.

He and Betty continued exchanging homework and letters. All seemed to be forgiven. The only difference was that her letters were more informative—family situations, illnesses, and so on. He mentioned coming down again, but was quite nervous about it. She also seemed rather reluctant.

He settled into life as a high school student. A baby boy was born to the Wilsons the first day of December. They could not agree on a name until the name "Samuel" was mentioned. They all fell in love with that name.

Kent enjoyed his new baby brother. Their house was quite a scene. Grandma arrived from up north to help Mom. She was a fine cook. Their home always smelled yummy.

He found renewed comfort and strength with his friends. But, it's funny how life plays out. Now *they* were interested in girls, and spent a considerable amount of time with them. Kent was now the one without a girl, or better said, the one that couldn't be with his girl.

It was difficult for Kent to watch the juniors and seniors. Many of them were already paired up, and a few of them were engaged to be married.

Kent purposefully distracted himself with his musical instruments. He had been asked to play in the band. Their school was too small for a football team, but they had a good basketball team. Kent often traveled to neighboring schools to rally his team with the band.

Kent saw James every day, but they didn't talk. Kent thought about trying to break the ice, but there seemed to be a huge wall between them. James was new, and probably desperate for friends, but Kent didn't like him, even if he was helping Betty's family.

* * *

James was having a difficult time adjusting to life in a small town. It wasn't fair. Sure, he knew his dad was close to a nervous breakdown if he kept up the pace he was living in the city, but there should have been another way. He should have just retired, so they could stay in their home—not engage in all those stressful decisions.

Now James was trapped in a God-forsaken place where everyone was backward and uncivilized. No movies and college games to watch. Four more years of this nonsense. He wasn't making friends; he was just surviving—going through the motions. He had only one hope: the basketball team. He was amazed they even had one. He knew he'd do well. He'd easily make a name for himself, get any girl he wanted, and bully the kids that didn't kiss up to him. That Kent Wilson kid would be a good start.

As December drew near, the basketball team was assembled. James made the varsity team. The coaches immediately had high hopes for a freshman who stood six foot five.

The first big game, shortly before Christmas break, was played at Escalante, their biggest rivals. Kent was excited that the bus would go right by Cannonville. He'd be able to see Heaven's Rock and Betty's home. He would sit on the right side to get a good look.

The basketball team, cheer leaders, and pep band piled into the rickety old bus, and bounced toward Escalante. It was a two-hour drive. Kent couldn't help but notice that James was seated just behind and across the aisle from him. He didn't get the window seat but was on the right side of the bus.

The miles evaporated quickly and the bus rounded the last curve before Cannonville. He craned his neck to get a good look at Heaven's Rock, as a flood of warm and beautiful memories poured through him. Betty and their almost first kiss, the patchwork quilt, and . . .

A harsh tap on his shoulder broke the euphoria. He looked back around. It was James. "Just so you know, Betty and I see each other almost every day." Kent tuned back around hoping to get another glimpse of Heaven's Rock. He was trying to visualize Betty standing there straight and tall with her arm held high, letting him know her whole heart was his. There was another harsh tap. "So, I think Betty is coming on to me."

His focus lost, his blood instantly boiling, he swung around. "You have no idea what you're talking about. We've been in love for a long time, and no idiot like you is going to change that."

A rush of color flooded James' face. "If you're going to be calling names you better be able to back it up," he flared back.

Kent turned in his seat—firing mad. But he wasn't used to fighting. He'd been taught better than that. "You're right. Calling you an idiot was uncalled for, I'm sorry. You just don't know . . ."

"Don't know what?" James interrupted. "That you're chicken? That your old girlfriend is falling for me?" Kent was starting to fly into a rage. His breathing was heavy, and he could feel sweat trickling down his back. He took deeper, slower breaths, hoping to calm himself down.

"Chicken, buck, buck, buck, buuuck," James taunted. Kent sat there looking straight forward, his hands clenching the seat cushions. It took everything he had to not just jump up and swing away.

But, he knew this wouldn't bring him closer to Betty. He turned around and glared at James. "Go ahead with your stupid plan. You haven't a clue what you're doing, nor do you know Betty. But you're welcome to try."

"Okay, wise guy. You're on. And by the way, you're going down and going down hard. I can see her every day if I want to, and my mom is all for it. Our families are real close." He paused a moment.

"I can see our first kiss coming up soon," he gloated, taking in a deep breath. "I think I'll take her somewhere real romantic, say .. . my bedroom."

A lightning bolt burst inside. Kent had no thoughts of the bus lumbering down the road, the other kids, the bus driver—nothing. Only to pound James to a pulp. Leaping to his feet and swinging his body around he cocked his right arm to deliver the blow. James also was jumping to his feet. With all the power of a tough farm boy from Tropic, Kent let his fist fly. It was straight and true, but the blow barely skimmed the tall boy's nose. The exhilaration of a devastating thud had turned to panic. The bus driver slammed on the brakes and Kent flew backward.

The next thing Kent knew, he was lying flat on his back near the front of the bus looking up at the bus driver. He could feel all eyes on him. It was piercing and embarrassing. He saw James easing himself back into his seat; no doubt trying not to draw any attention his way. He must have managed to brace himself against the seats in front of him since he was facing forward.

"That'll be a week's detention" the bus driver growled. "Now get back to your seat, and if there's one more bit of trouble out of you, we're talking suspension!"

Kent rose to his feet and stumbled down the aisle to his seat red-faced and humiliated. He was beaten. As he sat down, James slipped in one more stab. "Pea-brain."

Kent held the seat handle until his knuckles glistened white. He could do nothing. He sat there staring straight forward trying desperately not to quiver.

James didn't disappoint at the game. His lanky six-foot-five frame was too much for the smaller Escalante team. Kent was tight lipped with his trombone, but after a while settled in and played well. It was fun, but he couldn't get James out of his mind.

When he got home, Mom and Dad were still awake discussing details of their upcoming purchase of the Tropic Cash Store.

"Mom, Dad, can I talk to you?"

Kent laid out the whole story. He didn't leave a thing out including the detention. As he finished, he shifted in his seat and waited for their response.

"Son, your mom and I know how much Betty means to you," his dad said. "We can't alter the circumstances, but Betty is a fine, sensible young lady. She won't buy into a kid like James. The next piece of advice I have for you is that time will tell all and it will heal. Kent, things may be totally different a year or two, or three from now. Be patient and keep calm."

Then Mom spoke. "This James kid seems to know how to get under your skin. Remember, the bigger man is the one who makes peace. In fact, it is your appropriate behavior that will affect him the most. In fact, I'd dare say, it'll drive him crazy."

Kent let their words sink in for a moment. "I didn't see that earlier, but I see it now. It's as if I jumped right into his trap."

"Yes, you did, son," Dad piped in. "It sounds like he's a good trap layer. You'll have to be careful. Keep a watch on him at school. You don't need any trouble. Now, let's get some sleep."

Kent went to his room, closed the door, and flopped onto his bed, his mind a battlefield of anger and frustration. "Why, God, are you letting this happen? James is no good for Betty! Maybe you think Betty can change James as she did me. Well, I'm the one who's right for her. I'm the one who loves her. I'm the one who's worked so hard. And now you've forgotten me."

With that, he turned his head around and buried his face in the blankets. He was losing hope. He was even blaming God. He was back in that desert wasteland where Betty was nowhere to be found.

He bolted upright to a sitting position. "My dream! It's coming to pass. It's for real. Maybe God gave me that dream to help me get through this, this nightmare, this desert wasteland. But what's the conclusion? I woke up before it finished! Where's Betty? What happened when everything went dark? Do I die? Does Betty? Do we never get together? Do we never kiss? What's the answer, God? I'm sorry for getting mad, but I need help. I can't do this alone. Don't leave me. Forgive me; please, please, please give me the answer to my dream."

CHAPTER 36
NO WAY OUT

*J*ames walked up the steps of Tropic High with a smug look on his face. He had created the perfect scenario. Because Kent started the fight on the bus and called him names, he'd have every right to beat his face into the ground. Everyone would understand that he was just a guy who stood up for himself.

He walked victoriously down the hall toward Kent. He maneuvered through the students, and bumped him. Kent shrugged it off. No matter. He'd get him at lunch.

Kent sat down at a table in the lunch room and began eating his sandwich, waiting for his friends to show up. But instead of welcomed friend at his side, it was a sharp push on his shoulder. He bolted around.

"So, tough guy," James said. "Want to finish what you started on the bus?"

Kent hesitated a moment then said. "No, I'm sorry for my behavior on the bus. It was uncalled for."

"Oh, trying to change your tune and become Mr. Nice Guy? I suppose you know I'd beat the stuffing out of you anyhow." There was a long pause. Kent said nothing. "Suits me," James growled. "Betty's all mine, anyhow. I help them out daily. They've all taken a real liking to me, especially Mrs. Griffin."

"That's real good. Glad you're there to help." Kent began nibbling on some cornbread. However, he did notice he struck a nerve. What a horrible thing to say about a dying woman, whose mental faculties, according to Betty's letters, were beginning to decline.

There was another pause. Kent knew his mother's counsel was working. James was probably boiling over right now.

Suddenly he felt the palm of a hand glance off his head. He instinctively jumped up, knocking his chair over, and drawing attention from others in the noisy lunch room. "Obviously you're a coward and a quitter," James scowled. "I don't believe someone should start something and not finish it." James looked around the room. He had drawn plenty of attention. "He picks a fight with me, takes a swing at me, and now isn't man enough to follow through."

"Oh, I'm man enough, all right. I just think it's a waste to throw anything at you."

James's face turned ashen white with fury.

"A waste, huh? We'll see about that. I'm going out back off the school grounds behind the trees, and you better show up." With that he walked out.

Kent looked around the room. All eyes were on him. If he followed James, he might get beat up, but at least everyone would know he wasn't a coward. Maybe he'd win and teach this jerk a lesson. If he didn't show up he'd be known as the coward from Tropic.

He put his sack lunch away, and made his way toward the trees.

CHAPTER 37
NO WINNER, JUST LOSERS

Kent knew the place well. The graders would have the snow piled up there, and a clearing would be left. It would be a perfect place for a fight.

The afternoon sun was warm, and the snow was melting. It would make the clearing a little muddy. Kent trudged through the snow on his way toward the trees, becoming madder with each step. His parents' counsel nagged at him, but this guy was an absolute degenerate. Maybe a fight was the only way to deal with him. Kent was confident he could give James a run for his money. A life time of hard work had endowed him with rippling muscles, and he was pretty thick—not heavy or fat—just right.

Kent was unaware that word of the fight had gotten out to the whole school. A large number of kids followed some distance behind, but at the moment, Kent had tunnel vision. James needed a good thrashing, and he was going to give it to him.

He walked through the trees and heard a yell. James ran at him probably hoping to catch him off guard. He cocked his right arm and let it fly. Kent ducked, but not in time. The punch glanced off his temple and sent a white-hot jolt of pain through him. But James had made a mistake. He was close now and Kent's shorter body could get inside his longer reach. Kent surged forward, driving his shoulder into James's stomach. James grunted as if he'd been hit by a bull.

Now, Kent's right arm was cocked. He sent it forward with such might, it felt like a continuation from the punch he'd thrown on the bus, fueled by the same intense emotions. Only this time it landed hard to James's ribs. He drove home three more punches before James lunged backward trying to get some distance between them. But Kent wasn't having any of that. He jumped forward, and let a last punch fly, reaching as far as he could. It was a direct blow that caught James on the left eye. He let out a cry. Blood started running down the side of his face.

They turned and faced each other. James was puffing loudly, eyes on fire, but Kent also noticed they wore a look of bewilderment. James had seriously underestimated his opponent.

James stepped in again, this time keeping his distance, taking advantage of his longer arms. Kent had no choice to go on the defensive and dodge the blows the best he could. After several swings he had to do something. Sooner or later he'd connect, and he was getting backed up into the tree line, or, oh no, it wasn't trees; it was the crowd that had gathered behind them.

Kent didn't like the thought of others watching, but there was no backing down now.

With the next swing, he ducked and charged forward. He hoped to get a good hold on his mid-section like the last time. Instead, he glanced off his side. James side stepped and swiped a fist across the side of Kent's face. Pain stabbed at him again. He backed up, but James was already lunging toward him, arms cocked and ready. Kent was near the wall of kids. He had one choice and he made it. He stepped toward him, hoping to close the gap where his fists could do their damage. He punched straight forward, hoping James' punches would go wide. Both of them now were swinging their fists with everything they had; just as fast as they could thrust every ounce of strength forward, then recoil for the next surge. By now, most of Kent's punches were blind swings, but a fair number connected. James also was connecting, but his punches were wide and didn't carry the weight Kent's did. Finally, Kent's left fist landed solidly, making a crunching sound. James lurched backward, his head in a blur holding his nose, blood trickling between his fingers.

Instead of driving forward, Kent also stopped.

"Had enough?" Kent barked.

"Never," James snarled. Kent charged him and then they were tied up in a knot, exerting all their strength to drive the other to the ground. Kent sidestepped to get behind James, and take him down. As he did so James twisted and pushed forward. Kent instinctively put his arm out to break his fall. It would have worked, but James tackled him at that moment. Their combined weight drove Kent's arm into the hard packed snow and dirt. There was a snap and a stab of pain that was indescribable. Kent lay face down, his arm curled under him.

Suddenly there was a thud on his head, and another and another. The light grew dim. He took his good arm and tried to protect himself from further blows. Then thuds began on his midsection. James was kicking him.

From a great distance Kent heard someone say, "Stop it, you imbecile! Can't you see his arm is broken?"

"What do you mean, broken?" he coughed. "I just whipped him."

"No you didn't. His arm is broken. He'd have whipped you otherwise. Now get out of here, James," the voice called out. "I'm going to let the whole county know the piece of trash you are—kicking a guy when he's down with a broken arm."

Kent raised his head and looked over at James. He looked a mess; blood was pouring from his nose, and there was blood and dirt all over his face and shirt.

James looked around at the group of students, who now numbered around thirty. A couple boys began walking toward him slapping their fists in their hands. James made a decision he'd never made before, and never thought he would ever make. He turned and ran.

Kent turned to see who had chewed James out. It was Anita. "Let's get you up and look at this arm."

Anita helped him to a sitting position. In spite of the pain coursing through him, Kent took a moment to look at her. Of all the people that attended school, he was glad it was Anita by his side. Maybe because he needed a sister figure, or more likely it was because he knew her better than anyone else. "Thank you," he said. "I'm glad you're here."

CHAPTER 38
THIS IS THE END

*I*n spite of protests from his mother and Anita, Kent insisted on attending school the next day. His arm hurt, and he was still pretty shook up. He had cuts on his face and bruises to his ribs and head, but he couldn't let Betty down. He'd still deliver her homework to her teachers, and hope for a note as well.

Mom fashioned an excellent splint, but stated he'd have to go to Panguitch for a cast when the swelling went down.

Even before he arrived at school, he was swarmed by the other students. The fight was the hot topic. It seemed that every student in the entire school, and teachers as well, had come to a conclusion about the fight. Some of the kids from the bus and the lunch room had told how James baited Kent. On top of that, everyone knew Kent. It wasn't his nature to cause trouble.

Kent was placed in instant hero status, but where was James? He never showed up for school the rest of that week. In fact, he never showed up the rest of that year because of Christmas break.

* * *

James Davis staggered aimlessly through the snow. He didn't pick a direction. All he cared about was placing distance between him and the school. He gingerly touched his nose. It moved. It was broken. He was sure one of his ribs was broken as well. He stopped and scooped up some snow and rubbed his face. It instantly reddened. He reached up and felt a good sized gash near his left eye.

He rubbed more snow and still more until the bleeding stopped and the snow remained white.

He stopped at a clearing. There was a little bench and a bridge over a gurgling stream—its sides covered with snow.

He sat down and tried to clear his head. He'd never been challenged in a fight before. It was always on his terms, him laying down the law, and now . . . he was bloodied and beaten. What was he thinking? Kent grew up here, and James was the outsider.

Okay, it was Monday. Only two more days of school until Christmas Break. He wouldn't go back—he couldn't. The whole school would run him out of town, and if they didn't they'd beat him even worse.

As for now, he'd skip his afternoon classes, and basketball practice. He'd jump on the early bus just as it was leaving.

His plan worked. He saw a vacant bench and quickly took it, keeping his head down and not speaking to anyone. No one sat next to him. Now his thoughts turned to his parents. What would he tell them? He couldn't tell the truth. He'd be grounded. They'd lecture him incessantly and express their profound disappointment in him.

No wait! Another thought entered his mind. He'd tell the truth. Word would get out anyhow. Mom and Dad would know he couldn't stand it in this ridiculous place. He'd argue his case to go live with his Aunt Millie back in Salt Lake. His parents would see it was the only choice left.

James hoped to slip straight to his room, but his mom always met him when he got home from school. She'd asked him about his day, and sometimes had a snack for him.

Mrs. Davis met her son at the front door. Instantly she put a hand over her mouth. Tears welled up in her eyes. "Oh my heavens, son. Are you all right? Oh my . . ."

"I'm okay, Mom."

"Come, let's get you cleaned up."

That evening James sat down on the living room sofa next to the fireplace. His parents came in and seated themselves in front of him. He felt somewhat better. Mom had stitched the cut near his eye, bandaged his nose, and placed a wrap around his ribs. The clean clothes felt good, and the fire was warm.

James looked at his parents. They didn't look as disgusted as they had in the past. They looked genuinely concerned. This was the start he was hoping for.

He related the whole story. He did it truthfully. "I can't stand it here another minute, Mom and Dad. I've tried for four months now. I can't do it. I'll never go back to that school. They probably wouldn't let me back, anyhow."

His parents were quiet. James wasn't used to that. Normally they'd fly off the handle and ridicule his behavior. This time was different.

They continued talking for nearly two hours. At what felt like the right moment, James mentioned living with Aunt Millie—neither parent said yea or nay.

Two days went by. James' mom nursed him as best she knew how. He hurt even worse the second and third days. He couldn't have gone to school if he'd wanted to.

The silence was probably good. For once, his parents would see it his way. He could get a car soon and visit often.

The days were strained—nothing like the joyous, peaceful Christmas season they'd hoped for. Dad looked as stressed as on his worst day of work, and Mom said little. With Millie gone, she busied herself making candy canes, cookies, apple pies, and choice dinners.

On Christmas day the gifts were given. Along with a new coat and boots, James received a fancy new camera. Mom said she purchased it so he could capture the beautiful scenery around Cannonville and Tropic.

James said thank you, but he didn't plan on ever using it. He wanted no reminders of this place after he left for Aunt Millie's.

On New Year's Eve, the Davis family gathered around the radio to listen to the New Year's celebration live from Salt Lake City. James thought of the times he'd enjoyed the fireworks and festivities in Salt Lake. In Cannonville there was nothing but his parents—not his idea of fun.

It was now or never. James was tired of waiting. He needed to know that he would soon be on his way to Salt Lake. "Mom, Dad? As you know, I can't go back to school here. I need to hear from you that I can go live with Aunt Millie."

"Son, your mother and I have given it a lot of thought. We've prayed about it, fussed about it, and even anguished about it. We want what is best for you. We want you to know we love you with all our hearts. Your mother and I have decided that there's nothing that should ever divide our family."

James couldn't believe it. It had to be a mistake! His dad was still talking, but he didn't hear a word . . .

"Son, going to Salt Lake would be detrimental for you in the long run, and your mom and I would be heartbroken. We've even thought of moving back for four years, but we don't feel that would be right, either."

James shook himself out of his trance. "Mom, Dad, you can't be serious. You know that life is over for me here."

"Son, I've already spoken to the principal of Tropic High. I've explained the situation. They know that moving is tough on anyone your age. They're willing to help you."

James stood up, and turned toward the door to his room. "This isn't happening! You don't love me. You hate me!" He stomped into his room, slamming the door.

Carl Davis jumped to his feet. Rage turned his skin a bright red. He took a step toward the door, but felt the touch of his wife's hand on his arm. "Please, Honey. He's hurting so bad."

"I'll not be spoken to like that by my son."

"Carl, please. Just imagine what it will be like for him to go back to school and face those people."

Mr. Davis paused. He knew it would be an agonizing ordeal for his boy. "Yes, but he dug this hole himself. Now he needs to dig his way out."

"That's true, and he's going to need our help."

* * *

James reached for a trophy he'd won. He sent it crashing into the wall, expecting his dad to come barging in any second. He waited. Only silence.

He paced back and forth. Now what?

174

Sleep came, but not until the wee hours of the morning. James awoke early. He had no choice. He had one more card to play. He'd run away. He'd hitchhike to Salt Lake.

He packed a knapsack full of food, put on his new boots and coat, and slipped out. Three hours later he was passing Tropic. Not a soul had driven by. "What a way to start the new year. And a warm welcome to you, 1938," he shouted.

Three hours more he topped out on the high rim by Bryce Canyon National Park. Down in Cannonville, the snow was only a couple inches deep, and it was much warmer. Up here, two feet of snow was on the ground, and the sides of the road were piled even deeper from the snow plows. This wasn't what he envisioned.

He observed a car coming. He stuck out his thumb, and the car pulled over. There was an entire family in the car. Little room for another, but it could work.

"Please, sir, I need a ride."

"Good heavens, young man. What are you doing out here in the middle of nowhere?"

"I'm going to Salt Lake, sir."

"My gosh, son," the man stated as he looked James' face over. "You've been thrashed real good. You sure everything is okay?"

"Yes, sir."

"Well, I can take you as far as Panguitch. My family and I were visiting my brother down in Tropic and are now on our way back."

"Thank you, sir." James made his way around the car only to be met by a woman who must have been the man's wife.

"I know who you are. My nephew told me about a fight between two boys. They described a tall lanky fellow." She paused. "You're running away, aren't you?"

"No, ma'am, I just have to get to Salt Lake."

"I heard about you, too," the man said. "Now listen to me. You can't run away from your problems. They'll follow you to Salt Lake. You've got a family down in this country. If you leave them it will be a mistake."

"Sir, please."

"No. I'll tell you what I'll do. Where do you live?"

"Cannonville—temporarily."

175

"I'll give you a ride home, and you can face your problems like a man. If you don't accept, I'll tell the authorities in Panguitch to watch for you. Do you understand?"

James shrugged his shoulders, turned his back to them, and continued toward Panguitch. He was cold, completely worn out, and hurt all over. He knew he'd never make it. Oh well, he decided, if I die they'll be sorry they didn't let me go.

The car pulled up next to him. One of the children was now in the front seat. There was room for him. "Get in," the woman said.

James heaved a sigh, and reluctantly got in. The man turned around, and headed toward Cannonville.

"Just let me out here," James said as they entered town.

The man stopped. "Remember my advice, James."

James shut the door, filled with hopelessness. A couple hours ago he figured he'd die on the road. Now he was back in Cannonville. He looked toward his house. The car was gone. His parents were looking for him.

A feeling of blackness—aloneness came over him and left him shaking. "What are you doing, James?" he spoke to himself. "This is real. You do this, and it will be the end. What about your parents? Aunt Millie?"

He started home. It wasn't far. But the voice inside kept taunting him. *You can't go back. You'll have to face Mom and Dad again. You can't go back to school, and you can't live another minute in this Godforsaken land. It's already over. Life for you . . . is over.*

He veered off the road. He went through some trees to a little clearing beneath the rock wall, but figured there was no good way up. He took a few more steps, and noticed a crevice in the rocks. He walked through it and gradually climbed to the top. The shaky feeling returned but it was magnified. "This is it, after all."

He made his way toward the rim, walked by a flat area that looked like sand underneath the snow, and stepped up onto the rocky plateau.

He looked over the farms, houses, and streets, all laid out in squares, and he felt isolated and alone. "There's nobody there for me, nobody, not even . . ." he looked up, "not even You. You've left me too," he whispered.

176

The feeling was dark—black. James looked over the cliff. He could picture his body lying on the ground beneath. The blackness had now enveloped him. There would be no turning back.

James.

Someone had spoken his name, so softly he thought he'd only imagined it. James looked behind him and took a step toward the flat area of snow—nothing. He turned back toward the cliff, but his boots slipped on the icy snow and he slid toward the edge. He pawed blindly with his hands. There was a crease in the rock—a hand hold. It held, but most of his weight was over the cliff, his legs dangling in the air. Now all he had to do was let go. In that moment, he realized he didn't want to die. He tried to pull himself up, but his wet gloves couldn't get enough of a grip on the icy rock and he slipped a few more inches closer to his death. A strange, sobbing laugh escaped him. What an idiot he'd been.

But, what was that? It was light—it was liberating. It was like a rustling. He heard it, no, he felt it.

I love you, my son, and I'll always be with you. I'll help and bless you. In me you'll find joy.

"I can't do it. I can't pull myself up. I'll slip!" A thought, or was it an answer, came to him. *Slip one glove off, then the other.* He shook the glove off his left hand. It slipped off the icy cliff and plummeted below. He placed his hand on the crease, and worked the snow away. It provided a much better hand hold. He did the same with the other, providing even better leverage. He pulled himself up with ease. He crawled down to the flat area.

He knelt in the snow. "Oh God, thank you for a second chance." A thought came to him of the girl next door. The one he thought was out of some nursery rhyme. Her mother, all those children—what she was doing was impossible. He couldn't do it for one day. How was it that she was always so full of gratitude? Is there something more to these people down here?

James stood up. He could still make a run for the edge and end it all. But he wouldn't. There was something more to live for.

He looked around. It was nearly dark. He set his jaw, and started walking toward the path home. He had work to do, and . . . it would be harder than anything he'd ever done in his life.

James's parents met him at the door. They'd stopped and spoken to the family from Panguitch on their way back. This New Year's Day, that had seemed the worst day of their lives, became one of the best days ever for the Davis family. It appeared that maybe, just maybe, after all those years, James had the desire to change.

CHAPTER 39
STARTING TO CHANGE

$\mathcal{T}$he lunch room was noisy. It was the first day of school in the year 1938. Kent was enjoying lunch with Joe, Anita, and a bunch of other friends. They were taking turns signing his cast. There was chatter all around the school that James was back.

Kent felt a tap on his shoulder. It wasn't a sharp tap. The entire room immediately became quiet. Kent turned and there was James. All eyes were fixed on him. James shuffled his feet. He was searching for words. "Kent, I . . . I'm real sorry about your arm. I guess I was lucky. You were working me over real good."

Kent just sat there. He wasn't buying it. James had to be bluffing.

He continued, as if speaking to the whole lunch room. "I, uh, did a lot of fighting in Salt Lake. That was how we settled things there. But, you guys are a cut above that type of . . . of stupidity. And, you're a lot tougher," he added with a chuckle. "Here is money which will cover the medical costs and then some." He set the envelope on the table and left.

The room burst into commotion, but Kent stayed silent. He'd thought a lot about this bully, and none of the thoughts included an apology. He opened the envelope and was surprised—twenty dollars.

Kent put the envelope in his pocket. He didn't know what to think.

CHAPTER 40
HAPPINESS IS THERE—
WORK AT IT

*I*t took all the courage James had to get on the bus that morning. But it was his mother's words that strengthened him. "Son, you can do this. You get on this path and you'll find more joy than you knew existed."

How did she know? Had God told her the same things He had told James up on the rock? James knew one thing. The choices he was making before would only lead to misery and sadness. Deep inside he'd known all along; he just refused to accept it.

James was surprised to find that change was so hard, even after his awakening on the cliff. The kids at school only knew the smug, unlikable facade he'd worn from the time he arrived in town. He might not ever convince them that he was changed, but he would never go back to the way he had been.

He did find a couple things that made him feel good. He liked basketball, and the coaches wanted him. Even the other players recognized his skill. And of course there was his height. He looked forward to practice and the games, and tried his best to do as the coaches advised. His ribs were healing, and the coaches fashioned him a nose guard.

His parents also made him feel good. He discovered real feelings of gratitude for them. Sure, they were a little unyielding sometimes, but now he saw the love behind their actions. In a way, it was a reminder of that overwhelming love he'd felt in his darkest moment on the cliff, and he was humbled by it.

"Stick with it," his mom would say as he left for the bus. "Happiness is around the corner." He'd lean down, and his mom would give him a peck on the cheek. They were closer than they'd been in years.

Kent had his own problems. The person who made him happiest lived nearly eight miles away. At times, the distance between them felt like a thousand miles.

But he made a decision. He would spend each day finding joy and happiness in friends, school, and family. The little things of daily life could be fulfilling and appreciated; even hard work, studying, and practicing. He attributed all this to Betty. Knowing her had changed him forever, for the better.

Kent's dad was home in the evenings now. Kent, grateful for the extra time, enjoyed his friends and school. His arm healed. He started playing the trombone and guitar again.

He wouldn't bide his time as he once did. He'd be happy with the experiences of each day, and he'd keep working at it.

CHAPTER 41
GOD HELPS US CHANGE

*I*n early March, basketball season was over, and James was home early. "Now James," his mother said. "Mr. Griffin next door has to spend more time away this time of year, which places a heavier burden on Betty. He's planning on selling some three hundred of his sheep, and he's got to get ready for the shearing in a couple months. I know it's a difficult thing to ask, but I hope you would slip over and see what you could do for Betty each night after school."

"Mom, I'm the youngest. I'm not good with kids, and I think Betty hates me for what I did to Kent."

"I thought you might say that, but I think you underestimate her, and . . . I think you may have underestimated the load she carries."

"Oh, I think I understand what she's going through. One day of her life would make me a lunatic."

"Son, you're underestimating yourself."

James paused. "You know, Mom, she's done something for me, and she doesn't even know it. That girl has grit I've never seen. How can a person give her whole life away for others and be grateful for it, and be happy about it?"

"Yes, I know. She's an incredible girl. She'd be a mighty fine wife."

"Stop it, Mom."

"Just saying."

The next day after school, James drew in a deep breath, and knocked on the Griffin's front door.

The door creaked open. Betty's little sister, Mary, peeked out at him. "What do you want?"

"Uh, hi. I was wondering if you could use some help."

"Really?"

"Yes."

"I don't know."

"Where's Betty?"

"She's out back."

"It's okay," James said. "I'll check with you another time."

"No, wait," Mary called as James turned to leave. "We could use your help very much. Someone's got to sweep all the dirt out of the house. If you could do that, we could watch Kenny and Lola, and maybe get our homework done."

"Sounds good." James busied himself with the broom and dust pan. He saw Pamela eyeing him suspiciously. "So, how's your mom, Pamela?"

"She's resting."

James swept each of the assigned areas, but all the while was growing more and more uncomfortable. He would bolt as soon as he was done.

The creaking of the back door startled him. He'd been dreading the time when he would face her.

"James?"

He turned. "Hi, Betty."

Betty looked at him, a wary look on her face. She set the armful of fruits and vegetables she'd brought from the cellar on the counter.

Neither said anything for at least a minute. James was nearly holding his breath, waiting for Betty to unload on him.

At last, he drew in a good breath, "Betty, now that basketball season is over I have some free time. I thought that maybe you could use some help."

Betty was sure his mother had put him up to this. Ever since the fight, Betty had wanted to give him a piece of her mind, but seeing James with a broom in his hand, looking awkward and embarrassed, the fight went out of her. Still, she figured he had to pay up one way or another. "Sure, in fact we do need help around here."

"Okay, what's next?"

"Our cellar needs attention. The beam in the roof is sagging. The ground is wet and heavy. I'm afraid the roof will collapse. I have a support beam to pound in place, but I can't hold it and pound it into place at the same time."

"Let's get to it."

They went to the cellar. Betty still didn't trust him a lick, but she wasn't about to turn away free help. She pointed to the beam. "If you can pick it up and wedge it right there at the crack, I'll pound it into place. Here are my gloves."

"Thanks." James grabbed the beam. It was heavy, maybe two hundred pounds. He heaved against the weight, moving it slightly. Betty slipped over next to him, and planted her shoulder against his.

"One, two, three." They lifted and pulled the beam under the sagging wood. "Ready, heave." They pushed with all their might. It was in place, but they needed to pound it straight with the sledge hammer. That would raise the roof nearly six inches.

"Do you want to hold or pound?" Betty asked.

"Maybe I'll hold," James said, grunting under the weight.

Betty grabbed the hammer and began pounding. Again and again she struck the wood. The roof raised maybe three inches, but the beam was still leaning.

"Let's swap," James suggested.

"Okay." Betty grabbed the beam.

The sound of hammer hitting wood echoed in the underground chamber. A minute, two. One inch, two . . . three. Finally, the beam was securely in place.

"All right," James breathed heavily.

The roof looked well supported to Betty. James was brushing dirt off his shirt. Maybe he was sincere.

"Here are your gloves. I'll finish the sweeping, and then I'll head on home."

"Thank you, James. I couldn't have done it without you."

"You're welcome. Betty . . . I'm really trying to make a go of it here."

Betty was silent. She was a little upset with herself. She hadn't thought of how thorny the transition from city to rural nowhere would be. James grabbed the broom.

184

Betty looked at her hands. She had a good sized splinter in her palm. "Mary, would you help me with dinner, and Pamela, would you bring me Mom's sewing needle and a match?"

"Do you have a sliver?" James called from the mud room.

"Oh, it's nothing."

The sweeping done, James came in and looked at Betty's hand. "I shouldn't have worn the gloves."

"Well, my hands are like leather. I can't believe a sliver got in there."

"My mom has tweezers, and a special needle for slivers. Hold one second, I'll be right back."

"No, I'll be fine for now," Betty said. "I've got to get everyone fed. How, about after dinner, say . . . eight o'clock."

"See you then," James called.

James showed up at eight, armed with tweezers and a fine-point needle. He thought of his feelings when he first saw her, and now he was removing a sliver from the girl in the nursery rhyme.

"Okay, let's find some good lighting." The whole bunch of them gathered around the lamp. James reached down and took Betty's hand.

Betty was still unsure about the change in James. "What is life about if it isn't change?" She asked herself. Her beloved Kent had said it not so long ago. "God sent us to earth so we could change—become better."

In just minutes, James had the sliver out. It was nearly an inch long. Her hand started bleeding, but Pamela was ready with a cloth.

"I've thanked you a lot today, James. But thanks again."

"You're welcome again."

"So, can you stay a few minutes?"

"I guess so." They sat on the sofa.

"So how is school?" Betty asked.

"It's uh, good and bad."

"What's bad?"

"It's tough, Betty. Everyone hates me."

"I don't believe that. I think the people here are quick to forgive, and prone to love and support each other."

"Not where I'm from. Well, maybe I shouldn't say that, but I wasn't a forgiving person before. If I was treated like I've been treating people, I'd never forgive them."

"That was then, this is now."

"I hope you're right, but Kent's never going to forgive me, and I don't blame him either."

"You underestimate Kent. Even he doesn't know how good a man he is. If you're trying to repent, he'll forgive you."

James was suddenly self-conscious, and quickly changed the subject.

"Wow. So do you want to hear what we learned in school today?"

"Yes, very much."

"Do you know who the first United States Postmaster General was?"

"No."

"None other than Benjamin Franklin."

"You don't say," Betty said.

"Yes. He was appointed in the year 1775 by the Second Continental Congress. Did you know that young Ben left school at age ten to work in his father's candle shop?"

"No."

"Did you know that he ran away at age seventeen?"

"Why, that's just a little older than we are. I can't imagine that."

James thought for a moment about his own experience with running away, and was glad Betty didn't know the full extent of his foolishness. He wanted her to think well of him, and found himself trying to impress her.

"Did you know that there are already planes carrying mail all over the country?"

"No."

"And, did you know that in the next few years they're going to have regular postal service here? Even post offices." James spent the next hour telling of news that he was sure Betty couldn't know. Much of the information he gleaned from the radio programs that his family listened to almost nightly. The most informative was the *National Farm and Home Hour*, as well as the *Standard School Broadcast*. If they were in a jovial mood, they'd look for episodes of *The Lone Ranger*, *Dick Tracy*, or *Amos and Andy*.

Betty forgot her animosity toward James. She was lost in a world of hope, wonder, and fascination. "You learn all this from your radio?"

"Yes, and school."

"That's amazing! I wish . . ." She cut herself off. Getting a radio for the time being wasn't possible. But she yearned for it; she envisioned it in the living room, all of them gathered around listening to the wonders of the world. She sighed. She'd put the thought out of her mind for now. But when the time was right, she'd mention it to Dad.

James left that night, amazed at what had happened. He wouldn't have dreamt in a million years that events with the Griffins would turn out as they had. Maybe God really was helping him. Maybe he'd attend church with his mom and dad again. He hadn't attended for at least two years.

He continued helping the Griffins each night after school. It was becoming easier. He'd found a third thing that made him feel good—the Griffins.

CHAPTER 42
BIRTHDAY GIFTS

*L*ife for Kent had jumped into a whole new gear. One year earlier he hoped to work many seasons for Mr. Griffin. Now, he was to become his dad's main clerk at the Tropic Cash Store. The day after school let out it would be known as the Tropic Town Store. At that time, Dad would take over. Along with the store came an old flat-bed pickup that would be used to deliver all kinds of freight to the store and to the customers. That would be one of Kent's responsibilities.

Dad had to assume a large debt, which was obviously troublesome to him, but he was determined that, in time, the store would pay it off. Even Mom and Marilyn were going to work there.

The changing family business was exciting for Kent, but it was counterbalanced by his feeling that Betty was drifting away from him. Could love really remain if they never saw each other? He determined to give her the best birthday present ever—a classy pen and pencil set he'd seen at the Panguitch Hardware Store. A dozen pens and pencils were in the set—she'd love it as she wrote in her journal. Dad said he would pick it up on his next trip.

* * *

"Dad," James asked. "Would you do me a favor on your trip to Salt Lake?"

"Yes, son."

"Could you buy a radio and a generator?"

Carl's eyes opened wide. "What on earth for, son? You know they're planning on running electricity down here next year, and besides we have all that."

"I know, Dad, but," he handed his dad a good sum of money. "Mr. Griffin would like them in his house. This money is from Mr. Griffin for the generator, and I'd like to use my allowance for the radio."

"You're going to use your allowance? Son, that's very admirable. I'm proud of you."

James had to turn away quickly to hide the prickle of tears that his father's words had stirred up. He was embarrassed, but he wouldn't have given up the warm feeling that was growing in him day by day for anything.

* * *

On Betty's fifteenth birthday, Martha Griffin made a decision. She would accept no morphine on this special day, nor the day after, which was Sunday. The pain was already excruciating from her chest to her hips. The doctor had said the cancer had started somewhere in the bowels and would likely move to the bones—it had. But she would enjoy her daughter's birthday, and would wish genuine love and thanks for her with a clear mind this . . . this one last time.

She would attend church on Sunday. She'd partake of the bread and water. This was the end. Though her frail and withered body would live a while longer, she knew her mind couldn't remain sound. She'd come home and express her love and appreciation to her family . . . and then she'd accept the morphine and slip into comfortable oblivion again.

She feebly walked to her room and looked heavenward. *Please dear God. Even now I feel the pain thrashing at my mind—threatening to make me delirious. Give me strength, this one last time.*

The party was to start at seven in the evening. Martha had sent Betty away, stating they needed to prepare for her party. Betty reluctantly left, and her mom knew exactly where she would go.

Betty walked across the little meadow under the cliff. Her heart was a lightning storm of emotion, but she'd do as her mom said. She could take the time to dig into the caverns of her heart, or she could try to relax. She chose to relax and clear her mind of the incessant concerns she carried day in and day out.

She slowly made her way to the top. She stopped at the sand she'd sunk her knees into so many times. She pictured Kent there, feeling for himself the spirit of that place.

She stepped up on the rock. She let the gentle breeze sift through her hair. Unbidden, she also found herself thinking about James. He'd said he had no friends. Well, that wasn't true. He had a friend—Betty Griffin. "None of the other kids know the real James. None except me," she said out loud.

She sat down placing her feet against a little ledge in the rock, rested her arms on her knees, and cleared her mind and relaxed. She would play a little game she once played when she had free time. She let thoughts come into her mind, then chose the one that was most appealing. Only three thoughts came. Though Kent and James were there, but the thought of her mother was the one she chose. Hers were the arms the held her close as a child. It was her patience, nurture, and love that helped her each day. It was she who listened to her woes, calmed her fears, and helped her through life's challenges. She had always been there with a kiss on the cheek, an encouraging word, and a warm smile. To think that her mother would soon be gone was almost unbearable. How would Betty face each day's struggle alone?

It was time to return to what she was sure was a surprise party. She stood up to go home. The words, when they came, penetrated her heart and mind with clarity. *You're never alone. I am always with you.* Overwhelmed by the sweet assurance, Betty dropped to her knees. "Thank you, God. I'll never forget again. I know . . . I know that you'll carry me when I think I can't go on. Thanks for sending Kent into my life. Thanks for sending James, and please help him to know that he does have friends here."

All the way down the hill, Betty continued to feel surrounded by grace. She was amazed that in spite of what was coming, she wasn't filled with sorrow or fear.

"Surprise!" Her whole family met her at the door. Martha Griffin took her daughter in her arms. "Happy birthday, my dear." Then Dad and each of the children hugged her. She entered their home. It shone brighter than noon day.

She looked at the light bulb, amazed. "What? How?" Laughter spread around the room. Pamela came out from the kitchen carrying her birthday cake with fifteen candles, and a chorus of voices sang "Happy Birthday."

"Whose present do you want to open first?" Mary asked.

"Kent's for sure."

Betty opened the package, eyes widening as she beheld its contents. She didn't know such fancy pens existed. She read the letter. "That boy loves me," she whispered softly in her heart, "and I love him."

She opened the other presents. She wasn't used to getting—she was used to giving. But she was enjoying every moment. Just seeing her mother smile was enough. There was a knock at the door. It was Carl Davis.

"Hello, everyone, and, happy birthday, Betty." He looked at Sam. "Is it the right time?"

"Perfect," Sam answered.

Carl propped the door wide. "Watch your step, son." James entered carrying something heavy, covered with a dark sheet.

"Happy birthday, Betty."

Betty couldn't answer. Tears had filled her eyes. Even covered, she knew what it was. She couldn't believe it. She'd thought about it, fantasized, even dreamt about it, and now it was hers. James set it down and pulled the sheet off. The radio was rounded on the top, about one and a half feet wide and two feet tall, with arched cutouts for the speaker.

"Are you going to thank him?" her dad asked. Betty jumped from the chair, and hugged James tightly.

Stepping back, she asked, "How? Where?"

Carl Davis said from the doorway. "Let's just say your dad, James, and I are pretty good schemers."

Sam and James found a good place for it, hooked it up, and they all listened to an episode of "Amos and Andy." Betty sat and listened for a while with eyes wide. Then her eyes gradually closed. She let her mind relish the scenes "Amos and Andy" painted. Her heart raced with understanding that a world of learning, knowledge, experience, and growth was at her fingertips.

With seemingly no room left in her heart and mind for one more thought, she yet found more space; a prayer, thanking her Heavenly Father for her family, for her life, for friends and neighbors, for her home—for every blessing she held dear, and for the young man next door—James.

Later that evening, the Davis family back home, all the little ones and Sam in bed, Martha Griffin looked into her daughter's eyes. "You're one of the finest of all God's children. What a privilege it's been to be your mother."

"Oh, Mom, it's you . . ."

Martha cut her off. "Betty, tonight I saw two young men who will love you with their whole heart and soul. How . . ."

"Mom, James is just being supportive and nice. He doesn't see me as a girlfriend or a girl he'd even like to date. He's just been . . . kind and thoughtful."

"Oh, my dear. I wish I could live to see this play out . . . you, Kent, James . . . What a story it will be."

"Mom . . ."

"Ah, ah, ah. You watch and see, my girl, you watch and see."

Sleep would not come for Martha Griffin that night. Betty had prepared her mother for bed and now sat holding her mother's hand. Betty could tell that the pain gripped her like a vise—ever tightening, ever squeezing.

Martha spoke in little more than a whisper. "I've embraced the entire realm of mortal life's experience," she said, "the good and bad, the happy and sad, the health and sickness, the pleasures and pains, the triumphs and failures. Know that I chose long ago to point my whole soul, to the God who gave me life."

She seemed more lucid than Betty could remember in several weeks. Martha panted for breath, but then she continued. "Who is God if He is not eternal? What is life if we can't discover who we really are? We are daughters of God! This life on earth is just a small step in our eternal path."

The minutes and seconds clicked by. Martha closed her eyes, and Betty thought she had gone to sleep. But then she opened her eyes and looked directly at her daughter. "I feel the most exquisite joy and peace," she whispered. "I've been looking at it all backward!

This physical suffering is but a small moment. Soon I will be in the presence of Heavenly Father. . . . 'For God so loved the world, that he gave his only begotten son, that whosoever believeth in him should not perish, but have everlasting life' . . . Remember, Betty. Remember. It is true."

Martha slipped into sleep then. Betty checked twice to make sure her mother still had breath. Then Betty gently laid her mother's hand on the coverlet and tiptoed out to let her rest.

CHAPTER 43
THE SABBATH IS MADE FOR MAN

*B*etty hadn't been able to attend church for a long while. She put on her makeup, and washed her hair until it glistened. She let it fall down over her shoulders. She wore her Sunday shoes and her prettiest dress. She didn't look fifteen. Her figure and height made her look older.

Sam helped Martha with her finest dress. It now draped over her, because she'd lost some fifty pounds. Betty came in and fixed her hair and her makeup. They were ready.

Betty and the younger children walked to church, only a block away. Sam carried his bride to their car, and they drove to the church. Sam picked Martha up and carried her in. The service was just beginning. As they entered, an immediate hush settled over the room. All eyes were upon them. He walked slowly to where his children had saved a seat, and set her down gently.

The meeting continued, the sacrament portion of the meeting began. The bread was blessed. Again all eyes were upon Martha Griffin. She lifted her hand to partake. As she did so, a teardrop was heard as it splashed upon the tray. Every soul in that congregation had the same question: "What is Martha feeling at this moment, near her last hour of life?"

As they blessed the symbols of Christ's sacrifice, Martha remembered the words, "this do in remembrance of me." Not only did Jesus give his life for her in the most excruciating way, but he took into himself the entire realm of human suffering. All her pains he'd felt, all her anguish—all her grief. But not just on that crucial night in Gethsemane. He was there! She could see his touch on the sojourn of her life. Each and every moment—assisting, blessing—comforting.

Her heart was full of gratitude. She focused on three words of the sacrament prayer. "Are willing to." She had been willing. She'd made the choice to come unto Christ.

The water was blessed. She drank of it. Again she remembered the blood her Savior spilled for her, His agonizing moments on a cold cross on Calvary, the crown of thorns, the whip. He bled from every pore in Gethsemane. How could He love so much? She now knew. With everything she had left—everything! She loved him too. But, at the same time, the decision she had made to come unto Him had blessed her, helped her grow, repent, change, find joy and hope. On and on were her blessings. That was God's loving plan for her. She kept her head bowed in gratitude.

* * *

James also had come to church. He wore a nice suit and tie, and sparkling black Sunday shoes. His family had come a little early to get a good seat.

James had been amazed with the sacrament service, and the reverence and respect given to Mrs. Griffin. Afterward, he went to the Sunday school class for his age. He sat down, saying hello to a couple of the girls who were there. They were cordial enough. It was a good start. Maybe the church thing wouldn't be so bad.

Just before the class was to start, a tall, beautiful young lady entered. Her eyes were bright, and she wore a beautiful smile with dimples and had a little curvature to her lips.

"Betty?" James said, standing up. "Betty, I . . ."

"Okay, class, let's get started," the teacher said. Everyone was already staring at James. He couldn't take his eyes off Betty.

Betty sat down and James sat next to her.

The lesson on repentance was excellent. The words, "your sins could be made white as snow," stirred his heart as he recalled his former conduct. But his mind was on the girl next to him. He'd never seen her like that. Well, maybe at that dance, but his mind must have been in another world.

After the class, they met outside on the church lawn. The afternoon was beautiful—the sky a deep blue, and there was a gentle breeze.

"Betty, I didn't think you could make it because of your mom, and she was here!"

"Wasn't it wonderful, James?"

"It was amazing!"

"What you did last night, I . . . I'll always cherish."

"The three of us had a great time planning it."

"Hey, you two." It was Sam Griffin. "We'd better get home. Your mom has something special planned."

"Okay, Dad, we'll be right along." Betty stood up.

James stood up as well. "Betty?"

"Yes."

James tried with all he had to get out the words he really felt. He was good with words. "Betty, when I first came from the city I was a different person. When I first saw you, I figured you for a character in one of those nursery rhymes, but Betty . . . I think I see things more clearly now."

Betty stayed focused on him. What was he trying to say? Could mother have been right?

James had to say what he felt. He'd never felt like this before. All he knew was that Betty had to hear it. "Betty, you're beautiful. You're beautiful both inside and out."

CHAPTER 44
HER LAST WORDS

The Griffin family gathered in the living room. Lola struggled to get onto her mother's lap, but Martha was too weak to hold her. Betty positioned a chair so that Lola could sit as close to her mother as possible. Even the little ones seemed to sense that something holy was happening. The room filled with a spirit of reverence, of love, of gratitude, and of God as Martha Griffin began to speak.

Her words were soft, but they were precise, and her eyes were aglow. "My precious family, this will be the last time I'll be able to talk to you with a clear mind. I want you to know that my family is the most precious thing on earth. You are my dreams, my every thought, my joy, and my fulfillment. Anything I've accomplished in this life pales when compared to you.

"I wish . . . I wish I could stay with you, and watch you grow, watch you learn the meaning of being true children of God—honest, hard-working, loving, forgiving, courageous, and yes . . . repenting. I wish I could watch you relish in the most precious gifts of life— falling in love, marrying, and bringing more of Father's spirit children here that you may teach them the principles of happiness that your dad and I have taught you. For as you do, you will become as your Heavenly Father intended you to be.

"Soon I will return to my Father in Heaven who gave me life." May each of you know that I know that God lives, that Jesus is the Christ—our Savior and Redeemer, and that the Holy Ghost will always lead you right. Learn to feel Him. Learn to recognize Him, and follow His promptings, and you will do and be what God wants. You will know Him, and you will be happy, and when your day comes, as it will soon come for me, you will be comfortable back with Him—home again. Please know, that as the weeks or months pass, and I'm not the same as I am now, that I'm at peace. I love you with everything that I am. I love you . . . I lo- . . ."

She dropped her head, and clutched her side. She was exhausted and began shaking. Dad picked her up and carried her to bed. Betty got the morphine. The medicine quickly circulated to her brain. Her arms relaxed, her quivering stopped. Martha Griffin slipped into peaceful oblivion.

CHAPTER 45
I LOVE YOU

*K*ent started work at the store the day school let out. Some days, he worked fourteen or fifteen hours with barely time to eat. He became good friends with just about everyone in town. Dad paid him well and promised that the money would improve.

Kent grew closer to his dad. He quickly became his right-hand man in helping to meet the obligations of managing the store, and also their home, garden, livestock, orchard, and the rest of the farm.

The summer months evaporated quickly. Kent still didn't have that balance he hoped for, but it wasn't as painful now. He was making good money, and learning to be a businessman. He handled all the transactions exactly as his dad told him. Some of the farmers were upset when they couldn't intimidate him with business matters such as asking for more credit, but in the end they respected him. The only real respite he had was on Sundays. The Wilson and Johnson families still got together for barbecues, gatherings around the radio, or a game of cards, so Anita was pretty much the only friend Kent saw. They were back to the brother/sister relationship, except now Anita was dating a lot. Kent didn't like it, and he let her know it. It was because she was fifteen. He was no one to talk, but he felt it had been different between him and Betty.

James had a different row to hoe. Gaining confidence and trust in small towns was a slow process, but he felt that some were warming up to him.

Now that school was out, he had more free time. Mom and Dad would probably let him spend some of the summer with Aunt Millie, or he could get a job. His dad was getting his hand in some of the local businesses. But it didn't feel right. There was a young, beautiful girl next door that needed him, and this time of year would be very tough on her since it was the busiest time of year for her dad.

James continued helping the Griffins week after week. Something was happening inside of him. He'd never been in love before. It was ... exhilarating. Betty inspired him. He wanted what she had. His heart was softening. It was becoming easier for him to give compliments, and even express love and gratitude to his parents. He was finding the happiness his mother talked about.

"Betty," James called from the front door.

"She's out back," Pamela said, peeking out from her mother's room. "But tell her mom's getting restless, and Kenny's hungry."

"All right." He walked to the back. "Betty!"

"Down here," came a muffled cry from the cellar.

James descended the steep, wooden ladder. "What are you doing down here?"

"Hi, James. A rabbit got in here, and I'm trying to get it out, but I can't catch it."

"Do you have another pair of gloves?"

"Over there on the bucket."

"So, what's our strategy?" James asked as he slid the gloves on.

"Hum, if we can herd it into that corner, we could pin it down and grab it by the ears. Be prepared for him to squeal and kick."

"Okay."

The rabbit was crafty. James and Betty lunged and darted all around the musty cellar knocking over shovels and chairs, and kicking aside buckets and baskets.

"He's in that bin," Betty shouted. They ran to the bin and prepared to reach in and pin it down. Suddenly it hopped out right between them—they lunged. They didn't come up with the rabbit, but they found themselves hugging each other.

"That rabbit brought us together," James laughed.

Betty giggled as she slowly removed her arms from him.

"Smart rabbit," James whispered.

Fifteen minutes later they had the wily bunny cornered. "Now what?" James asked.

"You hold it, and I'll grab its ears."

"Okay, but maybe I'll let it go, I'm enjoying this."

Betty grinned. "You better not."

Betty ascended the ladder holding the kicking and squealing rabbit. With about three rungs left, she lifted the rabbit out, and set it on the ground. "Well, go on then."

James worked his way up around Betty for a look. The rabbit just sat there.

"What's the matter with it?" James asked.

"Maybe it's in shock."

Betty gave it a little tap. It made a couple hops then stopped. It finally hopped away slowly.

They entered Betty's home. James began playing with Kenny. They'd developed little rituals. If Kenny made a noise or a peep, James answered with a yip of his own. It seemed to never get old—they'd go on and on. Sometimes, James would pin Kenny's hand to the floor. Kenny would wriggle it out, but he'd put his hand back on the floor so James could pin it again.

Betty grinned and entered her mother's room. She looked upon her, her jovial mood fleeing as if it was evilly rooted from her soul. She felt catapulted back to real life. But, she was strong, and she had developed means to keep her heart from breaking as she watched her mother deteriorate. She would relive her mother's last testimony, her birthday, the radio, and . . . what? Her mother's last coherent words. "I wish I could live to see this play out, you, Kent, and James."

What was happening to her? Her love and devotion was eight miles up the road. But, James was so frequently with her. Always kind, always generous, always supportive. She knew he was falling in love with her. Was she starting to have feelings for him too?

It was late August. School was starting in a few days. Betty rested her head on the wall and sighed. Everyone was in bed. It was her favorite time—her time to reflect. She wasn't ready for school. Homework would be an added burden and . . . James wouldn't be spending as much time with her. How long did Mom have? Her tall frame was a shell now—maybe eighty pounds. She couldn't speak. She could only make gurgling noises like Kenny. Her behavior was hard to read. Mom went through the motions of eating, trying to move or stand, but it was neutral. She showed no emotion or feeling. Betty wondered if her spirit was still there, trapped, or if she was allowed to visit her Father in Heaven. They'd given up walking. She'd sit the chair in her room for meals, and that's all. She had become incontinent, and Betty struggled to keep the house smelling nice.

Betty also had lost weight. She hopped up, remembering a basket of peaches she'd left on the back porch. She reached in the dark to gather a couple and savor their sweet taste, as she reflected on her life a few moments longer. Quickly she retracted her arm. She'd felt a sharp twinge. "No," she gasped. She ran to the living room. The red mark on her arm was growing bigger. It was surely a black widow. "Not now," she moaned.

She sank back in the rocker, wondering what the effects might be. She couldn't afford to be sick or injured, not when so many people depended on her. She'd just rest here a bit, and then go doctor up her arm. At least that was the plan.

Betty awoke. She was still in the living room. There was a haze—a blur. She tried to stand, then sat back. She was dizzy. She leaned to the side, and threw up. There wasn't much in her stomach but green bile, but she heaved and heaved again. It wouldn't stop. Her stomach ached.

Mom was awake and moaning. Dad was already gone, but he'd said he'd back in the early afternoon.

Betty made her way to Mom's room. It smelled, and mom was delirious. "Pam, get a cool cloth."

They worked with her, cleaned her, and this time Pamela gave the morphine. Martha calmed down. Betty began dry heaving again and again. The baby awoke and started crying. Betty made her way toward his room. She was dizzy. She fell, slamming her head against the corner of the wall. She couldn't feel the blood trickling down her face. All she knew is that she had to keep going—caring for her family. Tears sprang from her eyes. What if she couldn't do it?

She crawled on her hands and knees, leaving a trail of blood as she went. She found little Ken. She didn't dare lift him. The crying increased. "Pamela, where are you?" She felt strong arms lifting her—holding her.

"There, there, everything will be all right." Somewhere she heard a deep voice. But it seemed distant—foggy. "Mom, I can care for her. Pamela says her arm is red and puffy."

Another voice—a woman's, came next. ". . . a spider. I have antibiotic and antihistamine in the cabinet. I'll be right back."

Betty's eyes were blurry. She continued to struggle. "It's okay, it's okay, I've got you, and we'll take care of Kenny and your mother."

Betty stopped and tried to focus.

"Mary," James said. "Please grab two cool wash cloths for your sister." James nestled her head against his chest and held her—speaking softly. He cleaned her bloody head and face, and held the dry cloth over the wound.

"James." Tears began leaking again.

"I'm here. Let's sit you up. Mom has medicine for you."

The day slipped by. James sat with Betty, her head nestled against him. Betty was in and out of consciousness. She was aware of people in her home—Carla Davis, people from church and from around the neighborhood, and Dad—but then she'd doze off again.

It was night. James and Carla Davis stayed with them. The house was clean, Martha was comfortable, and Betty relaxed and slept.

The sun brightly beamed over the eastern mountains. Betty awoke, mind clear, and aware of what had transpired. She felt her forehead. There was a bandage—the fall in the hallway. She looked at her arm—the black widow. She made her way into the living room. James was playing with Kenny, the others were gone, probably at the park. She glanced in the back room. Dad was sitting on Mom's bed.

Noticing Betty, James smiled and stood up. "Good morning. How are you feeling?"

Betty stopped. She was barefoot, hair a mess, a bandage to her head, eyes surely bloodshot. She cupped her hands over her eyes and turned to scoot away. She felt James's arms around her.

"Good morning to you too, and, just in case you're wondering," he turned her toward him and moved her hands from her eyes, "you look as beautiful as the day we sat together in front of the church."

"You're blind."

"Ah, but you forget. You're the most beautiful young lady I've ever known . . . both inside and out."

Betty let out a cry. She wrapped her arms around him and hugged him with all her might. Her back shuddered, tears landed on the hardwood floor. It was a good while before she let him go. James took her hand. It was the first time he'd held her strong, sturdy hand. They went to the sofa.

"James?"

"Yes."

"Thank you . . . thank you for . . . for being you."

"Thank you, Betty. Thanks for being you. Did you know that of all the people that showed up yesterday, every one of them mentioned special things you had done for them over the years? I think everyone that knows you is grateful for you."

"You're sweet to say that, but our neighbors are good people."

"Are you ready for something to eat? Mom has a nice breakfast for you, and Ken's at our place."

"Yeah, I'm famished. Thank you."

"Betty?"

"Yes."

He still held her hand tightly in his. He took the other one, turning to better face her, knowing that the moment was perfect. He knew in his heart he was sincere. He'd worked on this new path for eight months now. He had no desire to return to his old ways. He truly, deeply, had love in his heart. He was in love with Betty Griffin.

"Betty, would you do me a favor?"

"Sure, anything."

"Would you picture us out in front of the church?"

"What? . . . Okay."

"You're in a beautiful dress. You have on your fancy black shoes. You have your make-up on with bright red lipstick."

"Okay James, whatever you say."

"Good, now close your eyes and capture the scene real good."

"Okay."

"Now open them."

She did, hesitantly.

"Betty, I, I want you to know. I want you to know that I'm in love with you. I love you with everything I am."

Betty's eyes opened wide. She stared deeply into James. His countenance was soft—his eyes deep. His mom had told her he was a most kind and loving child. He was sincere, he had changed, but, but Kent. A deluge of the experiences and depth of love she felt for Kent nearly overwhelmed her. The final coherent thoughts of her mother resounded in her ears.

She was in love with James, too. He was there for her. She would let him know . . . but not right now. She'd know when the time was right.

"Betty? Do you think, maybe, you could say something . . . something about me?"

She smiled. She reached a hand over and nestled it against his face. "I will, but I need a couple of days, and . . . it will come with a letter."

CHAPTER 46
A CHOICE

*B*etty penned the letter several times. She used an elegant pen—the one Kent gave her. She still loved him. She knew that he still loved her and that he wasn't seeing anyone else. But she was in love with the young man next door.

There were no witnessing angels, no voices from heaven telling her whom to choose, only the feeling in her heart. She would devote her heart to James.

Tomorrow would be the first day of school. She'd gotten the idea from Kindra. Betty met James out near the Davis' front porch. She was dressed in casual nice clothes like the ones she'd wear to school if she could go. Her hair was down, and she had makeup on. She'd removed the bandage, hoping the scar wouldn't be too noticeable.

"I made something for you. Try these out."

"Cookies," James exclaimed. "I'm not having a bad day, and . . . and you're so beautiful!"

Betty giggled, knowing he was thinking of Kindra, but her heart softened even more. James was good with words, and he knew when to say them.

"Oh, just try one . . . here."

He bit into it. It was sweet and . . . but it was hard, no leathery, no . . . it was a piece of paper.

"Oh, how neat. A message in a cookie."

"Would you just read it?"

James read, "James Martin Davis, in case you're wondering. I love you with all my heart, but I need you to make me a promise..."

James stopped and took her hands in his. "I promise I will always love you ... with all my heart."

"Thank you, however, you have shown me your love every day for months, and ... I don't think there's anything in the world I'd appreciate more, but..."

But what? James thought. What more can there be? He gripped her hands even tighter. He wanted to kiss her. He'd dreamed of it, pondered it, and hoped for it ... it had to be the perfect time. He started to pull her closer.

"Read," she said again.

"Oh, yeah." He read, but he did so silently. "Promise not to kiss me until my sixteenth birthday." James stared at the words in disbelief. Betty hadn't laughed or grinned—she must be serious. He knew his mom would approve as well, but ... his heart was sinking—that was nearly eight months away!

"And," he read out loud, "promise me you'll make me laugh every day."

"That's not what it says."

"Well, that's what it looks like. I chewed it up pretty bad."

"Oh, give it to me."

James dodged her hand, and brought her close. Hugging her would be fine for now. Fine because she was hugging him back. "Okay Betty. You're right. That's what my mom would say, and I'm sure yours would too if she could."

"Thank you, and ... one more thing." She reached down and pulled out a letter from under the plate of cookies.

"Wow, a letter, too?" He looked at it, and then the recognition hit him hard. He stepped back. The envelope read: Kent J. Wilson.

CHAPTER 47
THE LETTER

*K*ent was waiting in the parking lot when the bus arrived. He felt restless. Betty's letters had contained fewer expressions of love and were simply informative. He hoped to rekindle the spark somehow. It would be easier now with Kindra to deliver daily notes. Surely Kindra would have a note for him today.

James hopped out first, then Kindra. "Good to see you, Kent," James said. He put a hand on Kent's shoulder. Their eyes met. But James was hard to read. He seemed friendly enough, but seemed worried. "Perhaps we should talk later," James said.

Kindra walked up. She had a rather disconcerting look on her face. She did have a letter, but as she handed it to Kent she said, "I'll be here with a plate of cookies tomorrow."

Kent stood there frozen—unwilling to move. The realization of what was happening began smothering him. He turned and walked. He wanted to be alone. He arrived at a wooded area, the place where he and James once fought. He sat down on a fallen tree and read.

My Dearest Kent,

Please understand what I'm about to write. This is the hardest thing I've ever done, for I know for sure that what we have is sent from God. I shared with you the deepest dreams of my heart in the most sacred places to me in the world—our nearly first kiss, the angels that surrounded us, saving each other in the wash, and every moment we shared together. I'll cherish these thoughts forever.

And you, you're so noble and kind; so hard working and fun loving—so dedicated to goodness. I'm a better person because of you, and I'm always proud to be seen with you.

As for me, I'm worn out. I often wonder if I can keep going. I don't sleep. I don't eat much. I'm edgy. I get upset and yell at the kids. There have been times when I've wondered if God abandoned me. But even as I write these words I know it's just selfishness. I know deep down that God hears and answers my prayers. He would never give me more than I could handle.

He did answer my prayers and sent me strength. He sent the Davis family to live next door to us. They have literally saved my family. Six months ago, James started coming over to our home to help. He has never let up, and he's literally carried me through the toughest times.

Kent, he comforts me, he loves me. He's changed.

Kent, no one can replace what you've given me. I'll cherish what we have forever. But I've given my heart to James.

With deepest affection,
Betty

Kent held the letter in his hands. He wanted to go down there, and tell her that she was wrong. She and James could never have what they had. Surely she knew that. She saved my life in the wash. This can't be happening. Why did her mom have to get sick? Why did James have to move next to her?

He looked heavenward. "Oh God, how could you let this happen? I thought that what Betty and I had would last forever and ever. I don't understand." He buried his face in his hands. He sat there numb; his mind a blur, his heart broken.

The lunch bell snapped him out of his trance. Kent stood up and made his way toward the schoolhouse. Students were pouring out the front door. They seemed so energetic—so happy. Didn't they know what just happened? The world had just come to an end.

CHAPTER 48
APPROVED BY GOD

*K*ent had no choice but to continue on with life. It was harvest time. He was busy at home harvesting their fruits and vegetables, and busy at the store because almost everyone else was harvesting as well.

At school he was asked to be the junior editor for the school paper, and he made first-chair trombone and assistant director of the band. Not bad for a sophomore.

But he was back in that same rut again. Try as he would, he couldn't find enjoyment in family, school, or work. He was going through the motions, but without feeling. He was numb.

James was now good friends with several kids from Cannonville. Since he was liked by them, the rest of the students started to soften toward him. He continued to practice basketball, even if it was off season. Basketball would be his in, his gateway to being respected and liked, and hopefully his full-ride scholarship to the University of Utah some day. He enjoyed school and learning, and continued to help his sweetheart Betty every night after school and on weekends.

Anita was blossoming in school. She was the only sophomore to make the varsity cheerleading team, was excelling in her classes, and was considered the prettiest girl in the school. She was the life of any game, activity, dance, or gathering, and was very popular. She was dating a senior, Derek Sutherland, the star guard on the basketball team. This brought her respect from her tenth-grade classmates, because normally seniors would only date other seniors, or at least juniors.

Life was good, at least until that day during the first week of October when James announced in school that Betty's mom had taken a real turn for the worse.

The news caught Kent off guard. He retired to his bedroom early that night, his mind bombarded by questions. What would he do when Betty returned to school? Could he keep his feelings for her suppressed? How would he feel when he saw her with James? The questions haunted him.

Martha Jane Griffin held on valiantly for one more week, then passed away on October 12th, 1938. The funeral was set for Saturday. Kent was asked to be a pall bearer, which surprised him, but he was grateful to be invited to take part.

Saturday was cool, overcast, and raining. Kent and his parents arrived at the Cannonville church with a little time to spare.

He made his way to the front of the chapel, which was packed with people, to sit with the rest of the pall bearers. Betty would surely be there. It had been nearly a year since he'd seen her. He was eager, but also troubled—James would likely be with her.

He saw Betty in front of the casket with James next to her, and the rest of her family on the other side. He walked up to offer his condolences. She turned, and their eyes held.

Hers were bloodshot and her countenance strained. She quickly stood up, stepped toward him, and hugged him tightly. Could she know that he'd have been there for her every moment if it was he who lived next door? Would he ever be able to show her? He melted into her embrace.

He felt more arms around him—what? He was surrounded by all of Betty's little sisters; right down to little Lola who had wrapped her arms around his leg. They remembered him! He hugged them and kissed their foreheads.

The minister cleared his throat and looked at Kent. He sat down. Betty and the older girls resumed their seats, and James gathered up Lola and Judy and sat them on his lap.

He couldn't concentrate on the talks, the songs, or anything. In just one year all the promises, hopes, and dreams he shared with Betty were no more, and worse yet, his former arch-enemy now held her heart. He couldn't help but feel it was unfair.

At the conclusion, everyone stood up. Kent joined the other pall-bearers as they reverently carried the casket out of the chapel. They placed the casket on a flatbed truck.

The rain had slowed to a slight drizzle. When everyone had arrived, and the casket was placed at the grave site, Mr. Griffin stepped forward.

"On my daughter Betty's birthday, Martha's eyes radiated focus and clarity. I'll never forget her words. She said, 'What is God if he's not eternal? And why, of all the titles he could carry, does he prefer to be called Father? Are not we, his children, eternal as well? This is not the end. We will be back together someday.' I believe her. I felt the witness of the Spirit when she spoke. Martha's greatest joy and fulfillment was her family. She often said that every experience of life paled when compared to the family. I don't remember my mother. She died when I was two. But in Martha, I know what motherhood is. There is nothing," he said, struggling to keep his composure, "there is nothing in this world that compares to motherhood. There is no greater influence, no sweeter spirit, no greater love and concern that can be conveyed in any fashion, than that of a mother. May I express my love and gratitude for my children? Betty has not attended school for more than a year to help me with Martha and the little ones. She doesn't know this, but one night I heard her crying. I was afraid she was buckling under the weight of caring for her mom and siblings. I watched in . . ." Again he choked up. "I watched in . . . amazement as she thanked God for the privilege of helping her dying mother. Betty is a gift from God, I have no doubt. She demonstrates to me a favorite scripture in the Bible: 'There is no greater love, than to give one's life for another.' Betty has done that. All of my children have helped where they could. I believe, as did your mother, that you also will join us in the realms of eternity.

"I'd like to thank the Davis family, all the church members, and our neighbors for helping us through this trying time—you too, are gifts sent to us from heaven.

"Martha Griffin, in her short thirty-eight years of life, has showed us why we came to earth. Her qualities were that of love, of nurturing, of caring, giving, and teaching. She worked, she studied, she served . . . she prayed. She never tired of doing good for somebody—anybody.

"I believe all of us here are Christians so we'll understand what motivated Martha to be the great person she was. She had faith in Jesus Christ. She made his investment in her effective. I know when she slipped up she repented. I want all of you to know, that I know that Martha Jane Griffin's life on earth is approved of God, and that she's happy and comfortable, back home with Him again.

"I believe now that her eternal soul is free from her mortal diseased body, that she is going about doing as she's always done—loving, serving, and giving. And what a better day to go home to our Father in Heaven, because today, as some of you know . . . is her birthday."

There wasn't a dry eye of anyone that heard Mr. Griffin speak. Everyone felt it. It was the Spirit of God.

CHAPTER 49
THERE IS ALWAYS MORE

A drop of water hit the pale yellow paper. Charlene Harris wiped her eyes. She felt warm inside. She felt intelligence and knowledge. She knew it was the Spirit of God witnessing to her the truthfulness of Sam Griffin's words.

"Sam and Martha were incredible folks." Dad's words jolted her from her thoughts.

"Richard and I will be together, Dad. I feel it in my heart."

"Yes, that's the Holy Ghost witnessing to you that you will. He'll always communicate to your heart and mind."

"Dad, thank you."

"Oh, my dear, you're welcome, but you're just getting your feet wet."

"What?"

"Char, my girl. With God, there is more—there is always more."

Char thought of her mother. She thumbed through the rest of the yellowed pages then noticed additional papers at the end.

"Your mom did write her deepest thoughts—her book, and I wrote some more of mine. That's part of your treat. I pray you'll be understanding and accepting of the events that will transpire in the next couple days. Please know that I will be happy—happier than I've been for a long time."

"What are you saying, Dad?"

"Just trust me, my dear—trust me."

CHAPTER 50
THE BODY IS A TEMPLE

*K*ent's worst fears came to fruition. Each time he saw James and Betty together, he felt betrayed. He hoped that they never kissed. She'd surely have James wait until they were sixteen, but they did hold hands and that irked him something fierce. Although he still loved her with all his heart, or perhaps because of that, he often found himself angry with her. She should have kept her promises. She had promised that her love would never dim.

The scriptures say "after the trials come the blessings." They must be wrong because after his trials came heartache and despair. Somewhere deep inside he knew God was there, but he couldn't get out from under his depression. It only deepened.

He felt distant from his friends. Joe, Sam, and Bob were dating. Anita was dating Derek so he didn't see her very often. His one source of comfort was his family. The words Sam Griffin had spoken about Martha were right.

Christmas Eve rolled around. Each year Dad would round their family up, and would read the Christmas story from the second chapter of Luke. Some years, especially when Mom was expecting or if they had a little baby, they would re-enact the birth of the Savior. This year there was no re-enactment, but Kent found his heart softening and his faith in God returning.

They had a closing prayer, and were preparing for bed. A knock came at the door. Kent opened it, along with David and Jillian. "Hi, Anita. Is everything okay over to your place?"

"Yes, we're fine. We just finished reading the second chapter of Luke, as I'm sure you did. I'm surprised we didn't do it together this year." She shifted then looked away.

"Anita?"

She looked restless. She folded her arms. "Kent, can we talk?"

He looked at his little brother and sister. "Shall we go over to your place?"

"That would be good."

"Mom, Dad, I'm going over to Anita's for a few minutes."

"Very well, son," he heard from the back bedroom.

Neither of them spoke as they crossed the road to the Johnson home.

"I know it's late, but I have to get this out, but I don't know where to start." She paced back and forth, and kept twisting her hands. "You know I've been seeing Derek and we've been getting pretty close."

"I know. I do live next to you, and I see his car here a lot."

Anita's eyes filled with tears.

"Anita, what happened?"

"It was after the Christmas play last night. Derek and I watched it together. It was so beautiful. I felt so good. I felt so close to Derek." She paused, and drew a deep breath. "He touched me!" She began sobbing. She turned away. "We were kissing; we sat on my bed, next thing I knew I was lying on my back on the bed. His hands were on me. He bent over and kissed me."

Kent didn't dare speak.

"I didn't know what to do. When I tried to move away, he pinned me. He kept touching me. He kept saying this was our moment. I was ready to scream, and he . . . he put his hand over my mouth. 'Be reasonable,' he said. He finally took his hand off my mouth and threw his hands in the air. I ran out. He was mad, but finally he left."

Kent was furious. "What were you thinking with that guy?"

"Kent I, I . . ."

"How could you not see this coming?"

"Kent you're not helping." Her sobbing increased. "Maybe you should go."

Kent stood there a moment, watching Anita sobbing pitifully, her face against the wall by her bed. He looked away. He couldn't stand looking at her in such anguish. "I'm so sorry. Please forgive me."

He waited as she continued to sob. "I can't bear it to see you this way," he said. "I can see how hurt you are." He thought of putting his arm around her, but that didn't feel right. "Are you through with him?"

"Of course. I've had a whole day to relive this. I don't want to ever see him again."

"Good. How can I help?"

"You can be my friend. You can still think of me as a good person."

"You're one of the finest girls I've ever known. You're true and honest, kind and loving. You're beautiful, inside and out."

Her sobbing returned, but Kent knew they were different tears now. He waited. "Anita, you're a good person. You're still pure and clean. I know you are."

She looked up, making unsuccessful attempts at drying her eyes. "I'm not, Kent. I'll never forgive myself."

"Of course you will, Anita. Just looking at you, and your suffering, I think God is forgiving you right now."

"Do you think so?"

"I do."

She smiled. "Kent, I know deep down I'm a good person, but do you remember what we learned in Sunday school?"

"We learned that you're a daughter of God, and you should be treated as such."

"Oh, Kent." Her tears returned again. "We also learned that our bodies are temples."

"Yes."

"A temple is holy and clean. A person needs to be worthy to enter, and we need to wait until we're married to do such things, and I failed."

"You didn't fail. You stopped him. He was wrong to do that."

"I'll bet you never did anything like that to Betty."

"No, I wouldn't, I couldn't. I was tempted, but I couldn't hurt her. I love her."

"I'll bet you miss her warmth, and love . . . and her kisses."

"We never kissed."

"You're kidding."

"I'm not kidding. We were going to, but I didn't feel it was right. We were going to wait until April 23rd next year."

"What does April 23rd have to do with anything?"

"It's her sixteenth birthday."

"Oh." She looked pensive for several moments. "I wish I would have waited until I was sixteen for my first kiss." She looked into Kent's eyes. "Thank you for being here."

"I love you like my own sister you know." Kent moved toward the door.

"Kent, one more thing." She stood up, walked over to her lifelong friend, and hugged him.

He knew she loved and appreciated him for who he was—a lifelong, understanding friend. And as for him? Well sure, of course he loved her, but as a sister.

CHAPTER 51
NO MORE DEPRESSION

*1*939! It was as if a light bulb had turned on. Dad's business was prospering. He was completely pleased with himself. He'd paid off a good portion of the loan, and was thinking about replacing the family car. Kent was only too quick to offer to buy the old one.

Electricity arrived to the little towns. No more generators! There was even talk of a switchboard in Tropic and one up to Bryce Lodge for phone service. Even indoor plumbing was on the table.

The upgrades in the standard of living were thrilling to Kent. His dismal poor-me attitude was beginning to fade. But was it the electricity and the prospect of a nice car that lifted his spirits, or was it the pretty young lady next door?

Since the night he and Anita had talked about Derek, he began to look at her differently. He found feelings for her that he hadn't known he had. When she was near, his pulse rate went up a bit. He walked her to school every day, feeling a jump in his step.

Anita worked through her pain. She had dumped Derek, and word quickly spread through the school that she was once again available. Again, upperclassmen had their eyes on her.

James was outstanding on the basketball team, and he was only a sophomore. The boy once rejected was becoming popular and respected.

Truly it was a time of new hope and possibility for the people under the painted cliffs. The depression was ending.

CHAPTER 52
IN LOVE AGAIN

Kent felt an exhilarating new spark growing inside of him. Once, he had thought he had nothing in common with Anita. That didn't matter now.

Anita wondered if Kent would fit her plans and goals. Things change as you grow older. They were no longer two six-year-olds kissing in the bushes. She would be sixteen in a few weeks. A relationship now could mean marriage. Could she could find true love with her oldest friend?

A knock came the door. "Who is it?"

"A salesman, I want to sell you some shoes."

"Very funny." Anita stepped out, her long golden hair waving to the small of her back. She had lipstick and makeup on.

"Annie . . . you're . . ." He tried to think of something she didn't hear all the time.

"I'm lost, fallen . . . what?"

"No, no, silly, you're . . . oh never mind."

"You're smooth, Kent Wilson. Do you want to come inside?"

"How about if we just sit on your porch swing?"

"Okay."

"Great." He tugged her toward the swing.

"You're sure jovial tonight."

"I am, huh? Well, I've been forming a plan."

"Does it include me?"

"You know, as a matter of fact it does."

"Does it include holding my hand?"

"Oh my gosh!" He let go of her hand. "I'm sorry. I forgot I had it in my hand."

"Are you funning with me?"

"No. Well, maybe. But brothers and sisters don't hold hands."

"You're right. They probably don't sit next to each other on a swing either."

Kent didn't move. "You know, Annie; that brother-sister thing I used to feel with you?"

"Yes."

"I'm not sure how to say this . . . but I lost it. I don't know where it went."

She was silent.

He hesitated, "I was hoping you'd go on a date with me. I mean a real date. I was thinking May 13th. I know it's your birthday, so I won't keep you all day."

"Really, I suppose a walk to the park would be all right."

"I was thinking . . ." He'd been thinking about it for a good while, "fine dining and a ride to Panguitch."

Anita's eyes grew wide. "Really? That's fantastic!" She placed her hands to her face.

"You'd really go with me?" He grabbed her hands in his.

"I would." She gave his hands a squeeze. But then a look of worry flooded her. "But Kent, you don't really like fine dining, do you?"

"Believe me, Annie, I do."

"What about the store . . . and how will we get there?"

"Well, let's see. Dad and I are going to Salt Lake this weekend to buy his new car, and . . . I am buying his old one. And, I've already asked for the day off."

"You've thought all this through?"

"Uh, yes."

"Kent." She searched for words. "I can't believe it. Is this for real?" She squeezed his hands even tighter, then let go of one of them, and gently rested her head on his shoulder. She was in love. She had always loved Kent.

Kent looked deep inside himself and knew he loved her, too.

CHAPTER 53
SHALL I KISS YOU?

*T*he next morning, Kent was waiting for Anita when she came out for school. He grabbed her hand, and slipped his fingers through hers.

"Kent, you're holding my hand."

"I know."

"Everyone will see."

"I'm planning on it."

"Aren't you moving fast?" Anita teased.

"Annie, it doesn't feel fast to me. I mean . . . I feel like I started loving you about fourteen years ago when you fell into the ditch."

"I don't remember that. Well, I started loving you when we danced in your living room."

"I don't remember that."

"Your parents invited our family to dinner. After dinner your dad played music on the phonograph. We danced. Everyone cheered."

"My gosh, I remember. I think we were three."

"Yep, something like that."

"Annie, at the risk of moving too fast, I was thinking of something that happened when we were in first grade."

She stopped. She turned and faced him. They were near the school. "Well, you can't. I'm not sixteen yet, and my temple doors don't open for a kiss until then."

"I've been thinking. No, actually I've been dreaming of kissing you. But it has to be in a very special place—at Mossy Cave on our way back from our date in Panguitch."

Anita was silent.

"It will be beautiful this time of year. The green trees will con-trast beautifully with the red rock. It will be nice and cool in there, we'll be able to hear the water in the creek bouncing over the rocks, and no one should be around."

"You've really thought this out, haven't you?"

"Yes."

"How about if I kiss you right now? Just kidding. The temple doors will open in the early afternoon, on May 13th at Mossy Cave."

CHAPTER 54
MAKE YOUR GIRL HAPPY

"*A*re you awake, stranger?"

"Nope, still asleep," came a muffled response.

Kent waited a moment longer wondering where her parents and brother might be.

"Oh, that's right," came another muffled tone. "Something about a date?" The front door opened. "Stranger?" she announced, placing her hands on her hips. She wore an exquisite dress reaching just past her knees, a dainty blouse just covering her shoulders, and a necklace.

Doing everything he could to recoup, he said, "Uh, yeah, I haven't seen you since, uh, yesterday."

"That sure is a long time. Maybe we should get reacquainted. Hi, I'm Anita Johnson." She stuck her hand out cordially.

"Hi, I'm . . . spellbound, and you're . . . who did you say? Breathtaking?"

"I could have sworn my name was Anita, and by the way, your name is Kent Wilson."

Kent couldn't help it. He pulled her close, hugged her, and swung her around. Then, setting her down gently, grabbed her hand and ran to the passenger side of his car.

"That was quite the introduction," she grinned, snuggling back against the seat.

"Yeah, you make quite an entrance, breathtaking." He paused, putting the car into gear. "I was afraid you slept in, or forgot."

"Not hardly," she grinned.

They drove along talking freely, both thrilled with the new adventure. They drove by Mossy Cave.

"So we're going for a walk up there on the way back?" she asked.

"I sure hope so. I've been there a time or two."

"I've never been there, but I'm always hearing about it."

"It's the most beautiful walk ever up there. I have it all pictured."

"Oh, what's the picture?"

"Well, I see us walking up there hand in hand," he said softly, taking one hand off the wheel and slipping his fingers between hers.

"Kent, where did you get so smooth? Oh, go on—then what?"

"Lots of oak trees hide the cave. It's like a secret hide-out." His mind was in such a whirlwind that one wheel left the road. Joggling over the brush, he let go of her hand, grabbed the wheel and swerved back on.

"Be careful," she said, "We don't want . . . to miss our first kiss." She smiled and brushed her fingers under his chin.

Kent's heart beat even faster. "Annie . . . I've never kissed a girl before. I'm probably a very bad kisser."

She was quiet for some time.

Finally she breathed. "Well, I know two things. I'm positive you're a great kisser, and I can't wait to find out."

They began descending into another beautiful area called Red Canyon. It also had spectacular rock formations like Bryce Canyon, but right in the middle were two tunnels. They were small, looking more like arches.

"Anita, I want to start a new tradition."

"Oh,"

"Yeah, I feel like shouting to the whole world, this is Anita Johnson—my girlfriend. But since the whole world can't hear us, I just feel like honking the horn. But . . ."

"Let's just honk the horn, then. Let's honk it under both tunnels."

"Ready, here they come!" *Hooonk, Hoooooonk.*

They laughed and laughed.

"From now on, it's a tradition," Kent announced. "Every time."

"That's a terrific tradition," Anita chuckled.

Arriving at Panguitch, Kent parked on the main street, ran around to Anita's door, cordially opened it, and stuck his hand out.

She took it daintily. "Thank you, Mr. Chauffeur."

They darted from store to store on either side of the street. Kent liked the photography shop most, with the pictures of Bryce Canyon, Zion, and the other canyons. Next, he enjoyed the outdoor shop with all of its fishing tackle and camping gear.

Every store caught Anita's eye. Appliances, furniture, fabric, it didn't matter. She spent a while marveling at the fine dinnerware and interior décor, and she was fascinated with the jewelry store.

Stopping a gentleman, Kent asked, "Where's the finest restaurant in town for a beautiful lady?"

He looked over at Anita, and broke into a broad smile. "Oh, that'd be the Canyon Country Inn, just across from the hospital."

"Thank you."

They were greeted warmly by the hostess and were shown to their seats. Anita couldn't help but stare as she took it all in. "Look at all the décor, the shutters, drapes, and fixtures," she whispered.

"Yeah, sure is beautiful."

"Don't you just love the architecture?"

"It's okay, but what I really love is the . . . ambiance."

"Sorry, but I don't know what that means, Mr. School Editor."

"It means, this is a lovely setting for the two of us, but you could throw all this out, and I'd just be thrilled being with you."

Smiling warmly, she reached her hands across the table and took his.

"Here are your menus," the waitress said, setting glasses of water in front of them.

Anita picked up the menu and scanned its contents. "What's the price range?" she asked.

"The range is whatever is on the menu. By the way, happy birthday!"

"Thank you." She disappeared behind the menu then popped her head up again. "You're sweet, Kent Wilson."

CHAPTER 55
A TRUE KISS

*T*hey started back in the early afternoon. Hardly a cloud was in the sky, and it was warm for the middle of May.

"Kent, thank you so much. I've had such a wonderful time."

"Thank *you* so much. You make every moment . . . out of this world. But, our date isn't over yet, right?"

"Oh, I thought you were taking me home."

"Well, I was thinking that we might stop first."

"This has been the most thrilling date of my life. I can't imagine how it could get any better."

"You haven't forgotten about . . . uh . . . Mossy Cave have you?"

"Oh, that's right," she said, laughing.

"You really had me there. You know you really could be the finest actress in the world."

She smiled, but then sobered. "I just know that I'm happiest when I'm with you. And I can't wait for Mossy Cave. Step on it!"

They parked at the turnout, jumped out, clasped hands, and started up the trail. The scene was nearly unbelievable. Canyon walls of red rock rose on either side. They counted six, no, seven arches. They could look through and see the clear blue sky on the other side. All around them were the majestic spires and pinnacles of Bryce Canyon. They could hear the gurgle of the brook tumbling over the rocks nearby. Oak and juniper trees lined the trail, their deep green color contrasting pleasingly with the orange landscape.

As they neared the cave, the trail got steep. The air was still quite warm and Kent could feel the sweat trickling down the small of his back.

Abruptly, they were there. The entrance was nearly hidden by trees and shrubbery. They entered, and were met with a refreshing burst of cool air.

They stopped, each taking in the new world they'd entered. It was more of a half dome than a cave. Boulders were scattered across much of its base. In most of the area, a grown person couldn't even stand erect, but near the middle it was a good ten feet high. They could hear the drip, drip of water that seeped from the roof in at least a dozen places. The water trickled toward the center of the cave, forming a little stream.

They made their way to the middle; it was the perfect sanctuary.

"Welcome to Mars," Kent said, putting his arm around her. "Starting to get cold?"

"Not with your arm around me."

He noticed his heart was pounding. "Annie, I'm not cold at all. I think my heart is on fire."

She turned and planted soft loving eyes up to Kent's. Placing her arms around his neck she whispered, "Mine is on fire too."

He placed his hands under her chin. "Annie, I . . . I love you."

"And I love you."

He melted. He pressed into her lips with passion that he had no idea he had, wrapping his arms around her. She felt so incredible! So smooth and soft, but it wasn't just her lips. It was this timeless soul. This beautiful person was loving him back, was putting everything in her life on the line. For him! How could he deserve such devotion?

Anita let a lifetime of dreams, of worries, and of thoughts about the young man that held her in his arms float gently away with the trickling of the water. She was his. She could feel his love. At last she was at peace.

They finally parted and looked at each other.

"Annie, I, I can't believe what I'm feeling. I know now."

"Know what?"

"I know what it's like to kiss a daughter of God."

"And I know what it's like to kiss a son of God," she paused, "and a man who tries to do God's will."

They made their way back out of the cave. The air was warm. They descended the hill, and made their way toward home.

"Annie."

"Yes."

"I'll cherish my first kiss forever." She was silent. "I know that wasn't your first kiss, but . . ."

"Kent," she placed a couple fingers on his lips. "It's true I've been kissed before. But, if I was asked if I'd ever been kissed before I'd say yes and no. Yes because of the other times, and no because I never knew what truly being kissed meant until today."

CHAPTER 56
THE FANTASTIC FOURSOME

After that date, Kent and Anita saw each other nearly every day. Word was all over school. Everyone seemed to expect them to get married. Even James and Betty did.

Kent had become one of the more popular boys in the area, much of it because of his business dealings at the store, and Anita was the most popular girl. Charlie hired Anita to handle the cash register at the store for the summer. Kent and Anita spent the little free time they had that summer talking on the porch swing, going for walks or drives, and listening to the radio.

James now was admired and well-liked. Besides his popularity from basketball, he had his own car. His dad had begun several business ventures in Cannonville and Henrieville. Some of them involved Charlie Wilson and his store. James was his clerk, salesman, apprentice accountant, and even assistant manager. He and Kent found themselves interacting in business. Carl Davis had worked a deal with the Tropic Town Store to purchase goods at a wholesale price through them. It saved him the expense of transporting goods. They became good friends and workmates—unlikely because of their first interactions.

Betty was popular in her own way. Part of it was the choir. People were thrilled when she was given a solo part, and at each basketball game, everyone hoped she would be the one to sing the national anthem. She still kept her extracurricular activities to a minimum because of her responsibility at home without a mother. But everyone in school admired her, and she was with James.

On April 23, Betty and James shared their first kiss on Heaven's Rock. During their free time, they enjoyed drives. James, almost every time, found an opportunity to take pictures of his girlfriend. They enjoyed walks, listening to radio programs, and a swing in the park.

The school year of 1939/1940 began with an unusual twist. Only ten seniors were graduating that year, and few wanted to accept school leadership positions. Kent became the chief newspaper editor and senior band leader. Betty accepted the role of assistant senior editor, with responsibilities of all news from Cannonville and Henrieville, and senior vocalist in the school choir. Anita became the student body activities chairman, which included being chairman of the yearbook committee—a role that had always been occupied by a senior. She accepted graciously, although she was concerned about the work load. She was also head cheerleader.

There was an enthusiasm that hadn't been felt in years. The Tropic High basketball team made it to the state tournament for the first time in its history. James carried the team. Anita and her cheerleading team added heart and soul to the players, providing new cheers and added talent.

Kent and Betty added a flair to the paper—more drama, more detail, and wider coverage. The circulation doubled.

The band, with Kent's assistance, became recognized in the whole area, as did the choir, under Betty's help and talent. The band and choir held more concerts and were asked to play for various programs and events.

Through all these activities and events, the foursome worked together. Bus rides, planning committees, rehearsals, noteworthy news—they each contributed. They became ever closer. A saying became popular throughout the school—the fantastic foursome.

It was the final day of school, the spring of 1940. They were now considered seniors—the "big wigs" of Tropic High. After they were done signing yearbooks, the four of them stood up. They kind of naturally placed their arms around each other as if in a huddle. "Hey look, a four-way hug," James exclaimed. "This could be the symbol of the fantastic foursome."

"Suits me," Anita said.

"Me too," Betty and Kent said in unison.

"And ... how about if we put our hands together and shout, 'let's do it,' " Anita added.

They all agreed.

They parted, James and Betty striding over to his car, and Anita and Kent heading for their homes. It was now crunch time. One year left. All their decisions had increased meaning and importance. They were the expected leaders of Tropic High, and they would return in three months as the fantastic foursome.

CHAPTER 57
TAKE HER ON DATES

"So Kent, Kent . . . come back to earth . . . Kent."

"I'm here," he said, chuckling.

"I have a need, and I want you to help fill it."

"Oh, what might that be?"

"A date . . . one like the one when we went to Panguitch."

"Wow, that's a hard date to copy."

"Oh, knowing you, you'll probably top it."

"Sounds great, Annie. I'd like a date, too. Does it come with an experience like in Mossy Cave?"

"Probably not. That was once in a lifetime." She laughed and tugged on his arm. "Kent, sure it does. But for the past year we've been too busy for time alone. You know, just you and me."

"I'm sorry. I don't need to work so much any more. We have plenty of money, and Mar and David are old enough to help out more. Annie, I'm running too fast. I . . ."

"Kent, why don't you quit running and just enjoy me?"

"You paint a beautiful picture. I'd love to dive right into that scene, but I can't for a few weeks."

"Yeah, I know what that is. Its seed time, spring cleaning, plowing, and whatever-else time. You're building your new family room, and the store is busier now than any other season."

"That's right, Annie, but I promise to come see you each night after work. And I promise to take you on a date that will knock your socks off."

They reached their homes.

"Deal," she said. And they kissed on it.

CHAPTER 58
HELP FROM ABOVE

*I*n mid-July, Kent and his dad finally began catching up with home and store. Kent's promise of a special date with Anita was prominent on his mind. It was way past due. But, as providence often shines, his date quandary was answered in a way that he'd never dreamed.

"Thank you," Kent said as Mrs. Sorenson left with her purchases. He heard the shuffle of another customer to his other side. He turned.

"Hi," the fellow beamed, sticking out his hand.

"Jeepers, James. Good to see you. How are you?"

"Things couldn't be better down Cannonville way. Betty and her family are fine too. Sam raked in a huge profit this year."

"Wonderful news."

"Say, I want to surprise Betty with a special date, but my mom says it's not a good idea for just the two of us to go so far."

"What are you talking about?"

"Have you heard of *Gone with the Wind*?"

"Sure. It's the most expensive movie ever produced, it lasts about four hours, and it's sweeping the country."

"Well, it's going to arrive in Cedar City, July 26th."

"James, that's fantastic! Anita and I would love it. I can't wait to tell her. We've been planning a special date that will knock her socks off. This one will do it."

"I'll get word to you. It's a three-and-a-half hour trip one way, and the matinee starts at one thirty. We should leave around nine to be safe. We won't be getting home until ten at night. Mom and

Dad said we can take their car. Betty and I will probably drive up to let you know a day or two before."

"That sounds great. I'll make all the plans on this end. See you then."

CHAPTER 59
SURPASS HER EXPECTATIONS

"nnie?"

"Yes."

"How long does it take to close the cash register?"

"What's the hurry?"

"I have a surprise for you."

"All right, in that case, I'm done."

"Come on, hurry."

"I thought our families were getting together to listen to a preview of *Gone with the Wind* on the radio?"

"We are."

"So what are you so excited about?"

"Can't say."

Anita, her parents, and the whole Wilson family gathered in the living room around the radio. "Tonight's program," the announcer said in his deep sonorous voice, while Charlie worked with the radio knobs to get the best sound possible, "is about a movie that is sweeping the country. Its total cost of production has surpassed seven million dollars. The main characters are played by Clark Gable as Rhett Butler and Vivien Lee as Scarlett O'Hara."

"Talk about a story of civil war, political unrest, marriage, a child, a miscarriage, infidelity, miscommunication, this movie has it all. The crux of the story is whether Rhett and Scarlett will ever truly understand each other. Will Scarlett ever squelch her desire for Ashley, and truly love Rhett? Will Rhett ever put off his pride and truly communicate his love for Scarlett? Would Scarlett accept that love if he gave it?"

"The movie keeps you guessing, hoping, longing, and it keeps you downright bewildered at how such a movie could be put together."

They listened to the narration for another fifteen minutes. Then Charlie turned the radio off and stood up. "Okay, everyone, we need a master of ceremonies to field our thoughts about this movie. We need the person who is most familiar with the movie. I think Kent would be best. Would you come up here?"

Kent looked startled. He just sat there, but quickly all the kids started chanting, "Kent, Kent, Kent." Even the adults joined in, and Anita started pushing him.

Kent rose, and hesitantly walked to the front, but inwardly he was smiling, and he felt warm all over. He looked out over his audience.

"*Gone with the Wind*," he began, "is sweeping the country, and why?"

Mrs. Johnson raised her hand. "Because it's laced with problems. Look what happens if you marry for the wrong reason or if you don't communicate in that marriage."

Dad raised his hand. "War is awful. I hope we're not going to war. It would affect us all."

Kent was searching for words to continue, but Mom's hand went up. "It's heartbreaking to see the needless pain and anguish a couple goes through when they won't commit, when they won't love. I believe God gave each of us the gifts to love, to nurture, and to commit to someone or something. If we're committed to good things, like our marriages and our families, we'll avoid all of these problems that *Gone with the Wind* depicts."

"Wow, those are impressive thoughts. I think I was the wrong one to do this, but I do have one thing to say. This movie is sweeping the country for a reason—it's captivating. I think each man who takes his wife or each young man who takes his girlfriend would have the time of their lives."

He glanced again at Anita. Her mouth was open. "Of course the ride over to the theater in Cedar City would be suspenseful. You know, with the anticipation of the movie, it would be completely enjoyable to talk to your sweetheart and to the others that would be present." Anita was standing up. She looked like she wanted to speak but was unable. "Namely James and Betty, next Friday, July 26th. What do you think, Annie?"

She had to jump over a couple of the little ones, but no matter. She wrapped her arms around Kent. They hugged and even shared a brief kiss. Everyone clapped their hands and cheered.

"Excellent job, son," Charlie boomed.

Anita looked around the room. "Who all knew about this?"

One by one hands went up.

She couldn't contain her smile. Now she knew why Kent was so anxious to get home. Just thinking of the adventure less than a week away thrilled her from her head to her toes, but her deepest feelings were for the young man sitting on the radio. She was truly in love.

CHAPTER 60
GONE WITH THE WIND

*A*nita and Kent were on her porch swing twenty minutes before James and Betty were to arrive. Their fingers were intertwined, but every minute or so Anita would jump up. "I still can't believe it."

"Can't believe what? That you're the most beautiful girl in the country?"

"Oh, for crying out loud—that James has turned out to be such a nice guy. Do you remember the first words I ever spoke to him?"

"No, I remember him kicking me, though."

"Yeah, well, I remember that too. I called him an imbecile, and a piece of trash, but now he's nice to everyone at school, he's popular, well liked, and very generous."

"You're right. A girl like Betty wouldn't have fallen for the old James. He's turned his life around, all right. I'll bet God helped him like He did me."

"Now look at us. We're the fantastic foursome."

They paused. Tires crunching on gravel could be heard from the road.

James and Betty pulled up. Anita pulled on Kent's hand and they scrambled into the back seat. They all quickly burst into chatter about the movie, the car, and Cedar City.

Then James began telling about the operas, plays, movie theaters, ski clubs, and universities in Salt Lake City. Anita drilled him with question after question, and added the experiences she'd had during the summer she spent there.

"So have you heard about the plays on Broadway?" Anita asked.

"You bet," James eagerly answered. "Plays like *Hamlet* and *Romeo and Juliet.*"

"On Broadway? Those would be delightful," Anita stated—a hint of longing in her voice.

"My mom and dad took me to *Romeo and Juliet* in Salt Lake. It's very sad."

"No kidding, I saw it too," Anita said eagerly. "Maybe we were there together and didn't know it."

They chatted back and forth about their experiences nearly the rest of the way to Cedar City.

They pulled onto the main street. It was lined with stores, restaurants, motels, gas stations, and repair shops. There was no problem finding the theater. There was already a line of people gathered outside, and a huge painted billboard with the words, *Gone with the Wind*.

"Okay," Kent said. "Since James drove us here, when we get inside, I'll buy popcorn for all of us, and you can save the seats."

"Fair enough," James said.

The lights dimmed. The audience clapped their approval. The film began. The story unfolded. Kent glanced at Anita. Her eyes were straight ahead, her hand dipping back and forth in the popcorn. This was the date of her dreams. A smile spread across his face. He'd outdone himself—thanks to James.

The movie was heartbreaking, mind boggling, upsetting, and frustrating. It affected all of them in different ways.

When it ended, again there were claps of approval. *Gone with the Wind* did not disappoint.

Afterward, James purchased fuel for his car, and they ate at one of the restaurants. They spoke of the movie the entire time.

"I think Rhett should have been more sensitive to Scarlett's needs," Anita said.

"I think Scarlett should have been more committed to Rhett," Betty said. "A marriage needs to be completely committed, with no second thoughts. Rhett would have noticed, and would have loved her like inwardly if he had wanted to."

"Well, seems to me that a couple needs to communicate," James said. "They both figured the worst in each other. If they'd shared their true feelings, that wouldn't have had such problems."

"I'm just glad we got to see it," Kent said. "Thank you, James." Each of them expressed their gratitude to him as they got back in the car, Kent in the back seat behind James, and Anita behind Betty. The sun was at their backs, shining on the majestic cliffs of Cedar Breaks. Mountains covered in lush green forest were on every side, and an occasional deer pranced across the lonesome one-lane dirt road—the scene was one of pure beauty.

James said. "My parents told me that moving to Cannonville would be a tremendous blessing in my life. I thought they were crazy. Now, three years later, I can see they were right. I should be thanking you."

"So you think we backwoods people are okay?" Anita jabbed James in the shoulder.

"More than okay, I'm more impressed every time I turn around."

Anita began talking about the movie again. Then they spoke of anything that had to do with big cities, fame, and fortune.

Suddenly James cried out, "Oh, no!" A deer froze on the road, perhaps blinded by the headlights. James swerved sharply toward the middle of the road, barely missing the deer. Something crunched on the back window, and glass shattered. They skidded to a stop. James jumped out thinking he'd hit the deer. He could see nothing in the darkness.

"James," Kent called out. "It's Annie! Turn the dome light on, quick! Annie, are you okay?"

"Yes, I think so," she said removing her hand from the back of her head.

James turned the light on. Anita's palm was streaked with blood. "Let me have a look," Kent said. Her hair was full of glass fragments. Spreading her hair apart, he found a piece wedged in her scalp. He removed it, and blood oozed. He covered it with a finger.

"It's a small cut," Kent said. "Well, Annie, looks like I get to hold your beautiful head the rest of... Annie! What's happening?" Anita's eyes rolled up. She fell limp toward Kent.

"She's fainted," cried Betty. "Give her air." Anita's legs twitched convulsively.

"She's turning blue," James screamed.

"She's dying," Kent sobbed.

"No," Betty said. "She'll make it! She'll be okay. She's got to be okay."

Agonizing seconds passed. "Betty," James pleaded. "You have more faith than anyone in the world. Please pray for her."

"Oh God, our Father, Anita has hit her head and is unconscious. Please . . . please bless her that she'll be okay. Help us to know what to do to help her. In the name of Jesus Christ, Amen."

"Her skin is turning pink again."

"She's breathing," Kent said.

James let out a gasp. "I'm so sorry. I should have just hit the deer."

"James, it's okay," Kent said. "Anyone would have done the same."

"We've got to take her to the hospital," James said. "We're still too far out from Panguitch. She needs medicine. She needs an x-ray. We should go back to Cedar City."

"James, let's give her a little longer. She's going to be okay," Betty said.

"Well, we've got to do something," James said. He walked into the darkness. Dropping to his knees, he begged. "Oh God, I've hurt Anita. Please bless her. I can't live with the guilt—please . . ." Several moments passed. His pleading continued. At last, he made his way to the car.

"Look," Kent said. "Her eyelashes are moving! She's opening her eyes!"

"What's going on?" Anita whispered faintly.

"Anita! You're okay!"

"What's all the fuss about?"

Kent said. "There was a deer in the road. Your head hit the window."

"Did you hit the deer?" She asked, looking up at James.

"I should have," James said. "I'm so sorry, Anita—so, so sorry."

"Sorry for what?"

"For swerving."

"What's the matter with swerving?"

"Anita, I can't forgive myself, I've hurt you."

She struggled to sit up. Kent let her rest against his shoulder. "Surely, you don't think it's your fault."

"Well, I was driving."

"Oh hush."

They got back in the car and headed east. Anita had no recollection of the accident. Her last memory was sitting in the car talking. But she said that she felt a fogginess that made everything dim. By the time they arrived at the turnoff to Panguitch, Anita said she didn't need a doctor. "I'm fine, I promise. I feel much better. Our families will be worried sick. Let's just go home."

James reluctantly turned toward Tropic. It was nearly midnight. The lights were still on in the Johnson and Wilson homes. James and Kent helped her out of the car.

Anita was regaining strength but still was a little dizzy. The Johnson and Wilson families appeared on the porch. They'd seen the headlights.

"I'm fine," Anita stated. Kent quickly outlined the story of the accident as Anita rested on the sofa.

"God smiled upon you today," Mr. Johnson said.

As Kent spoke, James had a different view of the story. He thought of the horror he'd felt watching Anita pass out. "I'm so sorry, Mr. and Mrs. Johnson, and Anita. I pray you can forgive me." He shifted back and forth nervously. His voice was hoarse.

Anita, sensing she'd better speak up, lifted herself off the sofa. "I'm sorry, too." James braced himself for what she would say. "I'm sorry I broke your window."

James eyes widened. She wasn't mad at him! Betty slipped her arm around him. Kent went over as well. Even Anita went to him. All of them placed a hand of reassurance on him. "Thanks for taking us, James," Anita said. "I can honestly say that I'm never going to forget this day."

CHAPTER 61
OH, SHE SHINES

*O*n the first day of school, Kent and Anita walked hand in hand. She had recovered fully from her accident and was back to normal. But today was different. Normally, they talked and joked with each other the whole way, but today Kent's mind was exploding with a thousand different emotions.

Sleep hadn't come easy for him since Annie's accident. He relived it frequently, each time recognizing how fragile life was. He understood how life could change from one second to the next. It took effort to take charge, and tell himself to do his best and God would do the rest.

His love for Anita had deepened. But his love for Betty had deepened as well. He felt grateful at how Betty's faith had helped during Anita's accident. Kent was shocked at how James had reacted to Anita's plight. He was a mess. Was he in love with her as almost every other boy was? Did he have feelings for her that even he didn't know about? There's no masking one's true self in such a panicked situation. And the conversation during the long ride had been mostly between James and Anita. They each loved the city and everything it had to offer. Kent and Betty had just listened.

Now, his first day of school, what a contrast! Three years ago he and Betty agonized when they learned they would not be together while she cared for her mom. Two years ago he tumbled into despair when he learned Betty had fallen in love with James. One year ago he was thrilled to be with Annie. And now they were the fantastic foursome.

Betty and James hopped out of the bus, and hand in hand ran toward Kent and Anita. They all made their way to the gym for the opening assembly. Anita and Kent sat hand in hand, next to Betty and James.

Anita's hand began to perspire.

"First day jitters?" Kent teased.

"Very funny."

Anita was student body vice president, activities chairperson, head cheerleader, director of assemblies, head of the yearbook committee, and head of just about everything else. She got ready to take her place on the stand.

The school principal and the rest of the teachers and staff gathered near the podium. Anita jumped to her feet.

"Knock them dead," Kent yelled, as she daintily jogged up to the stand.

Everyone took their seats, and a gentle hush settled over the gym.

"Welcome Tropic High," she shouted, throwing her arms in the air. The whole gym erupted with cheers and stomping of feet.

"Welcome class of 1941."

All eighteen seniors threw their arms in the air and cheered.

"Class of 42," Anita yelled. Again there was cheering from the juniors.

"Class of 43, 44."

"This is going to be the best year Tropic High has ever seen." The whole assembly cheered again. She continued dazzling her audience, and Kent found himself just sitting there admiring her. All the other fellows were probably eating their hearts out. What a catch! And she was his!

She was beautiful and talented. She'd told him, though reluctantly, that she'd stay in this area, as long as she could travel some. Travel was easy now. No problem to go as far away as Cedar City and back in one day.

Maybe he should change his plans. Perhaps there was more out there. It would be nerve-wracking and awkward. He'd miss his homeland beneath the painted cliffs, but Anita had so much talent. She could play Vivian Lee's part in *Gone with the Wind*, or Dorothy's in *The Wizard of Oz*. She could act on Broadway. He didn't want to stifle her dreams, ambition, and goals.

"I'll tell her," he decided. "I just need a little time."

CHAPTER 62
THERE ARE TWO THAT POINT TO HEAVEN

The mid-October afternoon was perfect, not a cloud in the sky. Anita wanted some photos for the yearbook, and was dragging the foursome along. Their first stop was the sliding hill overlooking Tropic. Each couple ascended the hill hand in hand.

Kent reflected on the times he'd climbed to that very spot to work through his problems. He chuckled as he thought of the time, blood trickling from his face, when he heard his parents talking of laying the whole farm on his shoulders. He looked at Betty, her arm around James as they looked out over the patchwork quilt. How times change.

When the pictures had been taken, the foursome went down the hill and drove to Henrieville. Their last stop would be Cannonville, where they would drop James and Betty off.

They drove to a spot near the cottonwoods and started toward Heaven's Rock. They crossed the clearing and entered the crevice. Anita and James entered as if they had done so many times.

This can't be happening, Kent thought. *I wonder what Betty is thinking?*

This can't be happening, Betty thought. *The two men I love more than any other in the world are going to Heaven's Rock. And Anita . . . she's the only other one in the world that knows some of my secrets.*

They reached the top. Anita let go of Kent's hand and ran to the sandy patch. "I can't believe it," she yelled. "It's been years since I've been here." She ran over to the slit in the rock. "I found this hole in the rock, and Betty started putting her writings in here."

"So, Betty," Anita questioned. "You now call our cliff Heaven's Rock?"

"Yes."

"How come?"

"It's because I feel closer to God up here."

"Yeah, there is a special spirit up here," Anita answered. "Didn't I hear you say you point to heaven, too?"

Betty finally answered. "Yes, I stand right here and point to heaven."

"What a great idea," Anita responded.

Kent thought that both Anita and James were oblivious to what had transpired between him and Betty. Anita pointed upward. "What do you point at, Betty?"

"I point to heaven to thank our Heavenly Father for the gifts he's given me."

"I know what I'm going to point to heaven for," Anita announced, pointing her arm even straighter. Then she turned her head and gave Kent a wink.

Kent was inundated by memories.

He looked over his shoulder. In a few minutes it would be time for their shadows to jump off the cliff. Had Betty shared that treasured secret with James?

"We'd better be getting back," Betty stated. "I need to check on the little ones."

They made their way back. Betty's mind was in a frenzy. She hadn't shared her shadow with James. Why? She didn't know. But she could not allow her devotion to him falter—she would not. But the memories she had with Kent were there, and they could not, should not be erased.

On the way back to Tropic, Anita and Kent were alone. "Annie, what were you thinking of when you pointed to heaven?"

"Can't tell you. It just wouldn't be right."

"Oh come on." He slipped his hand in hers. "It's not like a wish or something."

"Yeah, I know. I was pointing to heaven to thank God for the gift he'd sent me." She reached her free hand up to his shoulder then rested her head there as well. "I was thanking him for sending me you."

Kent withdrew his hand from Anita's and placed it on the steering wheel where they both became frozen in place. Again he couldn't believe it. There would be better odds of getting struck by lightning than having the two loves of his life pointing to heaven on Heaven's Rock, thanking God for him.

"Kent. What's the matter?"

He placed his hand back in hers. "Annie, it's you that is the gift sent from heaven, not me."

"Oh shush. Just accept that it's you, and keep driving."

CHAPTER 63
ONE TORN, ONE NOT

*T*he afternoon the foursome spent taking pictures sent Kent into a tailspin. He had everything worked out, so he thought. Everything that he felt for Betty he'd tucked away deep inside, and he'd devoted his whole heart to Anita. And now . . . he felt torn. A flood of promises he and Betty had made to each other had suddenly come from nowhere. The sacred moments they had spent together burst before him as if on a movie screen.

They both wanted the same things, right down to staying in the land beneath the painted cliffs, raising children, having a farm, and on and on. *Stop it*, he scolded himself. *We were so young. Mom always taught me that love is a verb. Choose your love and love your choice. I've done that.*

He forced his mind to Anita: her beauty, her outgoing loving personality, her love and devotion to him, her many fine qualities. But somewhere from the back burner, a plethora of concerns scooted his peaceful thoughts offstage.

She would prefer to leave Tropic. She wanted a career in dance and theater, along with the fine dining, and social events. She didn't have the desire to work a farm, or raise children on that farm. Sure she'd do it. She would give it all up—all her talent, aspirations, and dreams.

He couldn't do that to her. He would compromise. That's what marriage is all about. Maybe they'd figure out a way to do both. He'd have to get hold of himself, but, for now, he was torn.

Betty Griffin contemplated the evening with their foursome. She questioned herself. Why hadn't she shared her shadow with James? Was it subconscious? Was it something she would treasure for her and Kent alone? The memories of her and Kent flooded her heart—the expressions of love, the angels, and the promises.

Stop it, Betty, she scolded herself. *I will not fight an inner war over Kent and James.* She looked up. *Mother, if you're listening, I'm putting an end to this right now.* She gritted her teeth. *James is my decision—I will stay true.*

CHAPTER 64
A HAPPY BIRTHDAY

*A*nita was keenly aware of all seventy-eight students in the school, and made sure every one of them was involved in some activity or event. She welcomed everyone over the intercom every morning, and with Betty's help would come up with a saying for the day.

Kent was just getting comfortable at his desk in first period class when Anita's voice came over the intercom. "November 15th," she announced. "This is a very special day for Tropic High. No, not that it's Friday. It's something else."

Kent began grinning. He knew what was coming.

"Today Kent Wilson turns eighteen."

The students in his class began shouting "Happy birthday," and shouts and the stomping of feet could be heard from other rooms. Not thinking, he jumped up and ran toward the front office where the microphone was. Anita saw him enter the room as she was telling everyone to wish him a happy birthday.

"Oops, here comes Kent now. Have a dandy day, everyone." She handed the microphone to the secretary. Kent didn't dare to try to take it from her.

"You are such a tease," he blurted. He tried to glare at her, but there was no holding back. They both burst into laughter. He took her hands, pulled her close, and hugged her warmly. "But you're the cutest tease ever."

He smiled at the secretary and went back to class. Before he got there he heard over the intercom.

"Please pardon the interruption, but Mr. Wilson just came in and gave me a hug. Change of plans. Everyone who sees Kent today, give him a great big birthday hug."

He couldn't even get into his classroom. He received a hug from every student in the room and the teacher as well. A chant came from other classrooms, "Kent and Annie, Kent and Annie, Kent and Annie," along with stomping of feet.

When class ended, he gathered his books and out to the hall, only to be greeted by Betty. She hugged him tightly. He let his books fall, and wrapped his arms around her. It was a good while before they parted.

"Happy birthday," she exclaimed. "Can you believe it? Eighteen! Talk about getting old. You're old enough to . . . to do whatever you want."

He felt a tap on his shoulder, and James also gave him a big hug. Kent got birthday hugs all day long. It was a day to remember.

That night Kent went to bed exhausted, thinking of Annie. It seemed like the whole school had picked up on the nickname he'd given her. She'd made his birthday . . . exceptional. His feeling of being torn was over. What a lady!

CHAPTER 65
MORE TO THE CHRISTMAS STORY

The Christmas plays put on by the Tropic schools were, without question, the biggest inside events of the year. Anita had given much of the responsibility of directing the high school play, and she had gone all out to make it extra special. She went to the grade school and invited them to take parts in the high school play. They were only too eager to be involved with the big high schoolers.

Anita was finishing the final dress rehearsal just an hour before people would start arriving at the high school gymnasium.

"Anita?"

"Oh, hi, James."

"I have a favor to ask. My role in the play is real small, and I'm fine with that, but, I feel impressed to add a little something. What do you think?"

"James, it's too soon before the play. We don't have time to rehearse it."

"Annie, I promise it will fit."

"I'm sure you would do a terrific job, James, but I don't feel we should try it. I'm sorry."

James left reluctantly.

Soon the gymnasium was filled to overflowing. The play began. Joseph and Mary, who was riding on a real donkey, traveled to Bethlehem to be taxed.

They arrived at the inn. James answered the door. "Can't you see the sign—NO ROOM."

"Yes, sir, but my wife—the baby."

The tall innkeeper looked at them a moment, then glanced at the crowded stage. "There's no room," he repeated. He started to shut the door.

"Please, sir," Joseph said again.

"Listen," James said, irritation in his voice. "There's no room in the inn. You can stay at the end of the road. There's a stable there and straw and a manger." With that, he shut the door.

Mary and Joseph turned, heads down, and continued to the end of the road, and took shelter in the stable. The next scene showed the shepherds keeping watch over their sheep. Suddenly, a light shined brightly upon them, and the voice of an angel was heard from above declaring good tidings of great joy—a Savior for ALL people!

Dressed in white, the school choir sang "Away in a Manger." A bright light was turned on, and a star appeared high above the stage. The audience began singing "Silent Night," its sacred lyrics casting peace into the heart of everyone present.

The curtains opened. The shepherds, who were supposed to be walking toward the manger, were not there. Instead, a tall man appeared. It was the innkeeper!

Anita and the other directors looked on in disbelief. What was James doing?

He walked across the stage, head down, holding the piece of wood from the inn that said, NO ROOM. "I can't sleep. What have I done? What's that?" He looked up. "A star?" He traced the beam to the stable. "What do I hear?" The baby was crying. "A baby? It's true; it's really true. The new king is born!"

He dropped the sign, and placed his face in his hands. "But now I can't face him. I sent him away." He turned, and began to walk away.

A voice pierced the silent auditorium. In a beautiful, deep voice, Andrew, the head of the men's choir, sang "O Little Town of Bethlehem." James stopped. As the hymn finished, he turned and exclaimed, "Where meek souls will receive Him still / the dear Christ enters in."

He bent down and picked up the piece of wood, and wrote upon it, and then walked to the front of the stage.

"I shall throw away my sign of 'no room.' It will have place in my heart no more. Instead, I will receive him!" He lifted the sign high so all could see. LET CHRIST IN! "I shall . . ." James bowed his head bursting into tears—his sobbing audible to everyone present. His shoulders heaving. He brought the sign down, holding it close to his heart. He took several deep breaths. Then he thrust the sign high again. "I shall let Christ in. I will let Him in."

James walked off stage and the shepherds entered. From the back of the stage, the choir sang "While Shepherds Watched Their Flock by Night." Not a sound could be heard in the audience.

Anita and the rest of the cast could only stare at James as he left the stage. Was this the bully, the tormentor of just a few years ago? He'd lived the part of the innkeeper. The dear Christ had entered his heart.

As the play ended, the younger children from the elementary school sang "Hark the Herald Angels Sing." Their little voices, even though off key, pierced the room with innocence and pure love. They then sang "Oh, Come all Ye Faithful."

At the close of the first verse, a change occurred. The voice that sang the second verse was powerful, resounding, and beautiful. Betty Griffin stood on the stage, the spotlight upon her. The dramatic change from the voices of the little, off-key children to Betty's voice brought an "ooh" from the audience as she sang, "Sing, choirs of angels."

As she closed, the crowd seemed to bask in the spirit of Christ their King. Betty nodded her head. The music began for "I Heard the Bells on Christmas Day," and she started singing. A new dimension of spiritual high filled the room. She became stronger with each verse, but then . . . she made the kind of mistake that singers can make if they allow emotion to fill their heart as they sing.

She hadn't prepared for this. "And in despair I bowed my head. There is no peace on earth . . ." She thought of James and Kent. War was on her mind, looming overseas, threatening each day to pull the United States, and all their loved ones into it. Her voice cracked. She couldn't sing. Her sobbing could be heard on the microphone—her shoulders trembled. The audience too began pleading for her with their eyes.

Betty looked up. She'd made a mistake. She would not let it beat her. She wouldn't care that she didn't verbalize the words, "for hate is strong and mocks the song."

Then it happened. The music changed to one key higher. Betty nailed the notes of the fourth verse with power and conviction. "Then pealed the bells more loud and deep / God is not dead nor doth He sleep." Mouths dropped open at her recovery.

When she reached the fifth verse, "A chant sublime, of peace on earth, good will toward men," the spotlight dimmed and the play was over.

Betty was swarmed by hundreds of people, including James. Almost everyone said a similar line. "I had no idea of the treat I was in for when I came tonight. Thank you, thank you."

At just the perfect moment, just a few seconds between the accolades being presented, James leaned over. "Betty, I'm so in love with you."

She leaned back and said, "I'm so in love with you." The two of them had not realized the spirit they would bring to the play.

When most of the crowd had dispersed, Anita caught James in the dimly lit area back stage. "James, what you did, I . . . I can't believe it. I . . ."

"Annie, I'm sorry. As I thought of my part over the last few weeks, it just came to me. I hope I didn't ruin the play for you."

"Ruin it? Your rewrite and Betty's singing are all everyone is talking about. The innkeeper is you, but really . . . the innkeeper is all of us. James, you've truly become . . . a wonderful man."

"Oh, Annie, I have you and Betty, Kent, my parents, and . . . my Savior to thank for helping me turn my life around."

Anita stood there looking at the person whom she once had called an imbecile and piece of trash. Without thinking, she pulled his head down by the neck and kissed him on the cheek. "James, I lo- . . . I'll see you at school Monday morning."

When the last of the spectators and cast prepared to leave, Kent was on the back steps, alone in the dark, weeping. As Betty sang, he tingled from his head to his toes. She was a daughter of Almighty God. He loved her. He loved and treasured everything about her. He could see himself playing the guitar as she sang to their children. He pictured her in this beloved land, raising a family in righteousness, truth, and nobility.

He . . . what was he thinking? He was in love with Anita. But there was a difference with Betty. There was transcendence of time. He profoundly loved every trait, every desire . . . everything about her. He was mesmerized by who she was. What was happening to his heart?

CHAPTER 66
THE BIG GAME

$\mathcal{B}$asketball season started. Tropic High went undefeated through February. There was talk that this year they could be state champions, if they could get past the squad from Panguitch. One of the Panguitch boys had grown five inches last year, and was pushing six feet five inches like James. It was expected to be a real duel.

The Panguitch team arrived ready to play two games. The first was the junior varsity game, and then the varsity would be the finale.

Panguitch thrashed the younger team by twenty-two points. It was sad to see the bigger school work the little one over, but the real show was yet to come. A record crowd, many of them from Panguitch, showed up for the varsity game. There was standing room only. When Tropic High took the floor, the building exploded with cheers. James took his turn first with the lay up drill, and slammed the ball through the hoop. The crowd roared.

And then, a hush settled over the room. Betty Griffin stood at the microphone. The sacred lyrics of the national anthem begun. Betty's voice permeated the stillness. Mouths dropped open as she solidly hit the high notes of "and the rockets' red glare." The mood was set. The game began.

The first half ended deadlocked at 30 to 30. Panguitch pulled ahead by five points by the end of the third quarter. In the fourth quarter, the Tropic coach had one strategy. Get the ball to James before a shot is taken. If James was double- or triple-teamed, he could find the open man. It was working. The cheers and screams from the crowd were deafening in the little gym. Anita and the cheerleaders cheered their hearts out. In the band, Kent played his trombone like there was no tomorrow.

With fifteen seconds left, Tropic was down by one point. The ball was worked to James, who was playing high post on the left. He wasn't double teamed. This play had worked three times before; when two men collapsed on James, he'd kick the ball out to Sam.

Now it was big man against big man. One bounce, now eight feet from the rim, James leaped high. His defender jumped high as well to block his shot. With two seconds on the clock, James palmed the ball with his right hand only, and used the new "hook shot" he had read about to swing the ball over the outstretched arms of his opponent. As time ran out, the building hushed; only the swish of the ball through the net could be heard.

Students, fans, cheerleaders, band players, all stormed the court. Everyone was trying to get to James. The final score was 60 to 59. Tropic High would be going to state.

It was minutes before Kent was able to work his way through for a turn to congratulate the star player. He finally reached James and was shocked at what he saw. James and Anita had arms wrapped around each other. It wasn't just a hug, it was as tight as an embrace can get.

Finally they relaxed their grip, but as they parted they peered into each other's eyes. James spotted Kent and came over and gave him a huge hug—sweaty and all. Betty made it through the crowd jumped into James's arms as Annie came to Kent's. Was it all innocent enough? There was no question James had taken his play to a new level when Anita cheered him on, but was there something more there?

Later, Kent parked his car in front of his home, and slipped around to give Annie a hand.

"You don't need to walk me to my door tonight," Annie said.

"What? Of course I do."

She leaned over and gave him a tender kiss on the lips. "Not tonight. I'll see you in the morning."

She turned and walked away. Kent stood watching her. Then it hit him. He turned toward his home. Their porch light was on. He walked up to the door. He didn't know how he knew, but he knew. It was because of what he'd seen earlier. If he turned to look for Anita, it would signal his continued love and devotion to her. If she was looking back at him from her porch, it would signal the same.

He stood there frozen. They'd need to talk and soon. Was it time to let her know of his concerns? Maybe she just needs reassurance? Or . . . could it be true? Maybe she wants to signal she's falling for James? But he loved her. He couldn't handle the thought tonight. He turned.

Anita was at her door, her back was to him. Was she telling him? Would she step inside and not look back?

That thought pressed heavily on Kent's heart. But she turned. Kent threw his arm high and waved. Annie blew him a kiss. He caught it, rubbing his face. A last wave, and they entered their homes.

CHAPTER 67
MARRIAGE PROPOSAL?

The remaining three months began to evaporate quickly. The fantastic foursome was obliged to immerse themselves in the state basketball playoffs. James took Tropic High to the state championship game. They came up short to a whale of a team from Salina.

Several scouts were at the state tournament. James had requests from nearly every school in Utah, Nevada, and Colorado. He would accept the offer from the University of Utah.

Anita too, had several offers for scholarships, including one from the University of Utah. Kent and Betty didn't receive as many offers. Each of them contemplated what to do, much of the decision resting on their sweethearts.

Spring brought added work to Kent and James, as business nearly tripled very quickly. The last Saturday of March they began making deliveries again. Kent's first delivery was to Mr. Stevenson.

"So, Kent," Mr. Stevenson asked as he was unloading several sacks of oat seed. "Are we going to be hearing wedding bells soon?"

Mr. Drake had the same question, as well as Mr. Richards, who had sold Kent his first car. As he drove to the different stops, his worries became even more disquieting. Maybe it was already too late? James was probably receiving the same questions. Maybe James was in the same quandary as Kent was. He'd talk to him first.

Both James and Kent stayed late after school to work on their senior projects. Betty and Anita had both gone home. The timing was perfect.

"James?" Kent asked, glancing around the room. They were the only two left. He finished pasting the last word strip describing the do's and don'ts of entrepreneurship on his wallboard and turned to face him. "James, for some time I've wanted to talk to you. It's . . ."

"Yeah, me too."

"Really?"

"You bet. We've got quite the foursome going on, huh?"

"You can say that again. I've never heard or seen anything like it."

James took on a somber look. "Betty Griffin has changed my whole life around. When I arrived to this area, I had no clue about life—real life. When I saw Betty struggle, pray, cry, and toil with her family, I grew up. I learned."

"The Servant and the Princess," Kent said under his breath.

"I dove in and helped her. It was so hard, but I started looking forward to it. I began loving and giving for the right reasons. I fell in love with her—true love." He paused a moment, remembering.

"And as for you and Anita, why, you're the luckiest man in the world. She's beautiful, talented, cheerful, . . . everything! Her manners, her professionalism, her dress, her personality . . ."

Kent interrupted. "That's what I want to talk to you about," Kent said. "I think the four of us love each other for sure. Are we all aware of what's happening? Just look at you. Your hopes, dreams—ambitions . . . they're all perfectly in line with Anita's. And it's the same with Betty and me."

"Kent, you can't be serious. You're not planning on making a play for my girl?" James's tone was laced with concern . . . and maybe a little anger.

"James, I just want you to think about it. Have you thought about Anita? Can't you see that I would squelch her talent and her goals if we did what I want? I want to stay here. She wants to spread her wings and fly away."

James was silent, but Kent could tell his mind was racing. At last James threw his arms in the air. "Kent, I'm not having this conversation. I'd never make a play for your girl and . . . and I was just going to tell you. I'm planning on proposing to Betty the day after school gets out. I've thought about it, dreamt about it, visualized it . . ."

They were both silent for a good while. "Thank you James. Thanks for sharing your feelings with me. I hope I didn't offend you. I was trying to think of all four of us."

"Kent, you're reading too much into this. I can compromise with Betty. Sure I'd rather get out and conquer the world. I could manage a big business and get in the spotlight. But I've accepted that won't be my life. I'll stay here, build a hotel, a campground, build cabins and run the store. Everything will be fine, because I'll have the most beautiful, amazing woman at my side."

Kent went home that night in a bigger quandary than he was before. He'd heard the phrase since he was a boy: "follow your heart, and it will lead you right." But he couldn't follow his heart. Circumstances and the others of the fantastic four wouldn't allow it. Now what?

CHAPTER 68
WHAT DO YOU REALLY WANT?

As weeks went by, Anita began to feel restless and impatient. She also was getting a lot of inquiries about marrying the man next door. He wasn't making any moves or giving her any clues. What was going on?

Aside from school, her dream was to fly away with Kent. But she didn't even know if he'd go to the university with her. Why did he always avoid planning for the future? They'd go and get their education, but then they'd come back. She'd do anything for Kent. She would compromise. He was worth it.

But scholarship deadlines were coming. They needed to plan. She had a lot on the table. Her whole high school career rested on the coming weeks. It would be the thrill of her whole life if a marriage proposal came with her jubilant school finale.

Kent tried with all his heart, but he couldn't relax. He knew he was hurting Anita. It hurt him to the core. He knew of her wishes and dreams. A proposal of marriage and his acceptance of a scholarship to the University of Utah would send fill her with joy. But would it completely? Was she still thinking of James?

Kent learned that James and his family were going to Salt Lake City. This was his chance. Since the Davis' family was away, he arranged to deliver a shipment of goods to ranchers and farmers in Cannonville and Henrieville.

He finished the last load of goods at four in the afternoon, just in time for a surprise visit to Betty.

Taking in a deep breath, he knocked on the door. Pamela answered the door. Kent could hardly believe she was already sixteen. The door to the back of the house slammed. "Who's here?" came a questioning voice.

"It's a surprise," Pamela yelled. "Come and see."

In a moment, Betty entered the kitchen from the opposite side of the room. When she saw Kent, she dropped several apples on the floor. "Kent, how wonderful to see you."

She quickly placed the food on the counter, brushed her hair back with her hands, and took a few swats at the dust on her dress. Her dress was worn; she wore no makeup, and had the look of "toiling in the dirt" on her. She looked opposite from Anita, but it was a look Kent knew in his heart he preferred.

Kent picked up the dropped apples and placed them on the counter. Betty asked, "What brings you to Cannonville?"

"I was hoping we could talk."

A quizzical looked flashed across Betty's face, but she said, "Sure." Turning to her sister, she asked, "Pamela, would you get dinner started, so Kent and I can go for a walk?"

"No problem."

They slipped out the front door.

"Let's go to Heaven's Rock," Betty said. "I don't get up there much anymore. So how is Anita?"

Kent paused. It was a little quick to start, but he had to find out Betty's true feelings. They were entering the crevice where he'd first held her hand. "Betty, that's why I came down to see you. It was clear back when we returned from *Gone with the Wind*, that questions started to churn in my heart."

"Kent, I know where you're going with this. You should stop."

"Betty, I can't. Please, please let me speak my mind."

She could see how important this was to Kent. She'd already worked through it. She had it all resolved. Well, everything but the shadow. "Okay, Kent."

They topped out on the rocks, and made their way to what was once their piece of heaven on earth: the place where their first kiss was to be.

"Betty, since *Gone with the Wind*, since we came up here to take pictures, since the fantastic foursome became so close, I've watched us. We all love each other."

"Yes, we do. It's amazing."

"When we went to the movie, Anita and James talked the whole time. They hugged at the game. Then there's you and James. You want different things. Anita and I want different things. She and James have full scholarships to the university."

"Kent, hold it right there. Surely you're not suggesting James and Anita get together?"

"Betty, can you imagine what they would do? They'd go to New York. They'd travel the country."

"Kent, there's more to life than fitting lifestyles together."

"I know, Betty, and that's why I wanted to tell you once again . . ." Betty knew what was coming. "Yes, I love Anita. She's beautiful, a thrill to be with. Sure, we could compromise. I'd accept a partial scholarship to the U of U. I'd tour the country, I'd manage her plays and support her career. I'd adjust to the city. Or, I'd squelch her dreams and keep her here. She could teach at the high school and start her own dance studio, but neither of us would truly be happy with that."

"Kent, you're reading too much into this."

"You're right. I'll throw all that out. The real reason is you." They stepped onto the soft sand. His voice started to shake. "You." He worked his shoes into the sand. "I love everything about you. There is not one thing in your entire being that I'm not completely, madly, profoundly in love with. I love your family. I love Heaven's Rock. I love this whole area. I love you. You're the most courageous, giving, caring, thoughtful, wonderful person on this earth. You make everyone around you better. You're committed to everything good and everlasting. Your faith in Heavenly Father and Jesus Christ is mighty. And . . . and the little things, they touch you to your very core. These things about you I adore and admire."

She stayed silent, but he'd stirred something in her.

"I know we were young. It would seem to any adult that it wasn't real, like puppy love; but it was real! Every moment, every horseback ride, walk, talk, competition, activity, every moment with the angels, everything we did together was real—was forever."

"Betty, I would have been there every moment for you while you cared for your mom if I could have. You have to know that."

They held their eyes for a good while. Had he said his piece? He felt himself becoming desperate. "Betty . . . what do you really want for *you*?" Tears were nearing the surface. "You probably know, but I want you to hear. I have great faith in God. I know we are His children. When the whole farm was placed on my back, He carried me. I know He did. Instead of running from my responsibilities as I once did, I shouldered them, and I know it's because God sent angels to strengthen me as He did for His Son in Gethsemane. I've felt His love so many times throughout my life. So much so that sometimes I feel I'm on fire from within. I love Him."

"I know why He sent me here; to have faith in Him, to try to do as He would do, to earn my bread by the sweat of my brow. I will work my hardest all the days of my life. I hope to give and to serve and to love as you do, for I know those qualities will bring fulfillment and happiness."

"Kent," she whispered. "I . . . I . . ." She began fighting tears, her body began to shudder. She began sobbing. She turned and walked up to Heaven's Rock.

He ached for her as he watched. He didn't want this to happen.

It was several moments before she spoke. "Kent, I love James. He's going to propose to me after school gets out. And you're going to hurt Anita. She's already starting to worry. Surely you see that? She's put her whole life on the line for you. I can't . . ."

"Betty, Anita and I will be all right. I feel it in my heart. We've known each other since, well, since we were born, you know." But even as Kent mouthed the words, his heart became heavy. He was hurting her. It pained him to the core. Was there no easy way out of this?

"Kent, are you ready?"

"Ready for what?"

"Our shadows."

Their shadows jumped off the rock and slowly moved across the meadow. They climbed the trees and then vanished into soft dimness.

"Let's go home," Betty said. They started back.

"Betty?"

"Yes."

"I can't stand not knowing. I need to hear something from you. Surely I deserve it."

Betty thought about Kent's petition for a while. It felt like being dishonest to James. But at the same time, she was hurting Kent, and that was painful to her. Not just painful. She recognized again how she loved and adored the man next to her. He was everything she could hope for.

"Kent...we were so young. Please understand, everything I did with you, every feeling I had for you, every time I felt the angels with you, was more real than anything else in my life. Yes, I love you. You're one of the finest men I've ever known. But James was there during the darkest time of my life, and he is also a good man."

"Kent, things don't always pan out like we figure. I'm going to marry James. I'm going to the U of U with him. Sure we'll have to compromise, but we're each willing to do it. Yes, he was raised in the city, but it will all work out. He, like you, is one of the finest men I have ever met."

"Thank you, Betty. I'm sure I knew all that you just said, but I had to hear it from you." They walked in silence until they emerged on the meadow below. "Betty, I'm still haunted by something—my dream. I never got to see the ending. Is what we've experienced these last few years with our relationship the windswept wasteland I saw?"

"Perhaps."

"Does the darkness mean the end of us, and we go our separate ways?"

She was silent.

Kent stopped at the cottonwoods. He faced her. "Betty, please pray to Heavenly Father—what do *you* really want? I think you're thinking of everyone but you."

"Kent, please don't ask me that. James and I have our plans, and you and Anita have yours."

"Well, I think time will tell."

Again she was silent. But at last, maybe it was just a flicker, but the corners of her lips curled. "Yes, it will. My mom used to say that."

"Yeah, my mom says it too."

CHAPTER 69
NO PEACEFUL WAY OUT

*E*xcitement mounted as they neared the end of school. They were ready to make their marks in the world. Well, the other seventeen graduating seniors were. Kent put on a good face, but inside he was a mess.

Kent began doing a better job of communicating warmth and love to Anita. But despite his efforts, he noticed sadness in her face. She was the last one of the foursome to whom he hadn't yet spoken his mind. He needed more than just a few minutes in passing at school or on the porch at night. A drive after church on Sunday fit the bill. And Kent knew just where to take her.

At the morning service, he found his moment. It was a favorite occasion for each of them because they could rub shoulders, hold hands, whisper sweet thoughts, and of course learn from the speakers.

"Annie."

"Yes," she answered, bending her head toward him.

"I have something special planned for us after the meeting."

"Sorry, I spend Sunday afternoons with my family."

"I know, but I thought you might make an exception this time."

"Sorry, no exceptions."

He could see she was a little ruffled. It was the most thrilling time of her life, and her boyfriend was out to pasture.

"Annie, your parents said it would be just fine."

"You asked my parents?" her head bobbing up. "What about your parents?"

"They're fine."

She turned sideways. "You're serious aren't you?"

"Yep. So after church, please hurry and change clothes. I have everything ready."

"Okay, Mr. Preparedness. So that's why you drove to church on such a beautiful day."

"Shhhh, the speaker."

"Don't shhhh me."

"Just be ready."

"Okay."

They were on their way shortly after the meeting. The day was ideal—warm and not a cloud in the sky.

"So where are we going, Mr. Secretive?"

"Oh, now I'm secretive. Well, we're going up on the rim."

"Bryce Canyon Rim?"

"We sure are."

"Kent that's wonderful! We can sit on the log chairs, and look out over the hills, canyons, and valleys?"

"Yes, I figure with the trees, orange cliffs and spires, and the lodge behind us, it's the most romantic setting this side of the Mississippi."

"What's on the other side of the Mississippi? I want to go there."

"You're such a tease. Actually, it's the company that I'm most thrilled about."

She softened with that. Her breathing a little heavier, she spoke softly. "Where has this loving and affectionate man been these past several weeks?" They were passing the Mossy Cave turn out. "He's reliving a dazzling memory that took place right up there."

Up on the rim, the snow had recently melted and was replaced with green shoots of grass and shrubbery. The smell of pine was abundant and there was a cool gentle breeze. Just a few people were at the lodge, but in a week or so it would be bustling with tourists from all over the country.

They walked hand in hand to Sunrise Point. He needed to tell this beautiful soul that he loved her, but he also had to let her know of the battle launched within him.

They looked out over the rim at the splendor of God's creations. They walked over to the log bench with its back against the trees.

Annie started talking before they sat down. "Kent, I've wanted to have a heart-to-heart talk with you for a while now."

Kent was startled but waited patiently. "Kent, don't you think after all these years that I know you better than about anyone? Probably as well as your own parents."

"Sure, Annie. Too bad you know all my faults and failings."

"Oh, stop it." She slapped his leg with her free hand. Then she turned, looking at him squarely. "I'm madly in love with the most genuine, honest, sincere, loving, generous, kind man I've ever known." She paused. "Who happens to struggle every moment of every day with his feelings for two women. Oh yeah, I can tell. I think you started thinking about her clear back when we took pictures at Heaven's Rock."

Kent jumped to his feet and looked out over the horizon blindly, his mind scrambled like eggs in a frying pan.

"Kent," Annie's voice was calm. "The four of us are together almost every day—the fantastic foursome. Do you think James and I don't see how you and Betty look at each other?"

"Do you think Betty and I don't see how you look at James, and he looks at you?"

"What? You're not serious? Why would you think that?"

Kent faced her. He had to know how she felt about James. "James is smart, talented, has a full scholarship to the U of U. He will be very successful. He's from the city. He wants to return there. He loves the city and all it represents . . . as you do."

"My gosh, Kent. Why do you read so much into this? He and Betty are getting married; you and I . . . love each other—end of story."

Kent bit his lip. Why did everyone keep saying that?

"Kent, I know you love me. I feel your warmth and tenderness. Sometimes I feel you're ready to commit your whole heart and soul to me, but then you falter and turn away. It's hard for me. This is the most thrilling time of my life. I'm ready to spread my wings and fly out into the world. People keep asking me of my plans. They ask me when you and I are going to tie the knot. And I would love . . ." she stood up this time. She was quiet for a good while. "And I would love to lay out a picture of a romantic wedding and our plans for the future."

272

Kent sat at the edge of the bench, yearning to jump up and proclaim an exquisite scene for each of her dreams, but he couldn't. He sat there . . . wanting, but waiting.

Anita was keenly aware of the empty hole in her heart that needed to be filled. A void that she felt had every right to be filled.

"Kent, maybe there are a few things I don't understand." Her voice now echoed frustration, her eyes narrow. "You and Betty were young. You were just kids! We are adults. What is it about you two that could be so enduring?"

Kent jumped up, and stepped toward her. She took a step back. "Annie, I've tried and tried to erase this, this mayhem within me. I want to love you and only you. I want to somehow, someway feel at peace with myself. Instead, this battle rages on until I feel guilty, traitorous, and foolish."

She didn't move. She just stared at him. Finally, she turned, arms folded, and began walking along the rim.

"Annie," Kent said walking up beside her. "I know I'm shattering your dreams. It's killing me."

She abruptly stopped and faced him. "Then stop it." Her voice was sharp. "For your sake and my sake, stop it. You've got to know I'd fulfill every one of your dreams and more."

Kent remained silent, wanting to speak but not finding words. Anita turned and walked on. He caught up. They walked in silence.

Kent felt the ice getting very thin, but he'd ask anyway. He had to. "Annie, are the decisions of our fantastic foursome all up to me?"

"What are you saying?"

"Do you know James's heart for sure? Do you know Betty's?"

"What? Yes, if you must know. I've talked to them both at length."

"I have too. You've all told me the same thing."

"So you don't believe all three of us?"

"I, I . . ."

"You know what, Kent. Let's go home." She turned, walking quickly.

The ride home was long and tense. They drove in silence. Kent felt he'd dug a hole so deep he couldn't dig his way out.

"Stop here," Annie suddenly said. It was the Mossy Cave turn out. He pulled in. "What do you feel when you think about this spot?"

"I relive what I figure to be the most beautiful moment of my life."

"Let's just say that Betty turns James down and marries you. Then what? Are you going to think of me and torment yourself and her as well?"

Kent stared at the steering wheel, speechless.

"That's what I thought."

"Annie." He was a little irritated now. "There's more to me than that."

"Prove it."

"I will, Annie, I will."

CHAPTER 70
GOD WILL ANSWER

*T*he next two and a half weeks proved impossible to prove anything. Each of the fantastic foursome was swamped. Kent's work was at its busiest point of the year. He also had to study and take finals, make graduation preparations, practice a final piece for the band, and somehow write columns in the school paper.

Anita was every bit as busy, preparing for the graduation ceremony and all her final tests. James and Betty didn't have a spare second to call their own, either.

The foursome was often together. James and Betty could see Kent and Anita were withdrawn, but said nothing. Kent and Anita didn't hold hands or share kisses here and there as they always did before. They muddled through the remainder of school, with finals, newspaper columns, yearbooks, goodbyes, and thank yous.

Kent felt exasperated and angry with himself. It could have been delightful for him and Annie. They could have created life-long memories, but now it was over, and he couldn't change it.

He hurt for Annie. He hurt because of what he had taken from her. She had every right to be upset. But still, he was determined to "prove it," as Anita had challenged him. It was the hardest thing he'd ever done in his life. He was zero for three. The other three felt he was reading too much into it. Maybe he was, but he had to be certain of what he should do.

If he chose Anita, surely, hopefully she'd forgive him. They would realize all their dreams since childhood, and he'd never look back.

If he chose Betty, it would be the biggest news in the territory—that was, if she chose him as well. If Betty didn't accept, and he hurt Anita, he'd probably get run out of town on a rail.

There was no school for seniors on Friday the 23rd, the day of graduation. Dad had already given him the day off. The whole morning and into the early afternoon he'd be free.

He began the drive just as the sun was rising. He'd studied every aspect of his decision in his mind. It was now time to take his dilemma to the Lord in prayer. He was going to prove it, just as he'd told Anita. He would return home with devotion and commitment to one of these women only, and he'd never look back.

He arrived at the headwaters of Kanab Creek. His dad had taken him fishing and hunting there. He was pleased with the setting he'd chosen. Aspen and pine trees were scattered across the foothills. Orange mountains rose at his back, and a pristine meadow stretched for about a half mile to the front. Kanab Creek with the high run-off wound through the middle. Majestic mountains rose steeply on the far side of the meadow. Several deer grazed at its base. This was the perfect setting. Surely God would answer his prayer.

At the head of the meadow, in a little clearing beneath the pine trees, he knelt. It was a long prayer. Longer than he'd ever prayed—maybe nearly an hour. Finally he stood up. He felt good, but that wasn't an answer. He wasn't expecting thunder and lightning, but he'd felt the warmth in his soul before. He'd listened to that still, small voice before. It was undeniable, but right now, he wasn't feeling it.

He walked, pondering, for a good distance down the road. A heavenly setting of aspen trees spread before him. This was the place. He knelt again. This time he prayed only about Betty for a long while. He waited, searching his heart and soul. Sure, he felt warmth and good feelings about her. He pictured a home, love, and children with her. But there was no still, small voice, no burning inside.

"Please, God. I can't do this anymore." Kent spoke as if his Heavenly Father was walking with him. "I need to make a decision and stick to it, and never look back. My mom and dad have taught me that your spirit can touch us and teach us. Yes, I fell in love with two women, but the circumstances, well . . . you know everything that happened."

A tear trickled down his cheek. "Father, I need to know what to do. Mom and Dad say it's the most important decision I'll make in my life." A thought came to mind. *Maybe I'm not in tune with the spirit? Maybe it's there, but I'm not feeling it?*

Kent felt the glow of the sun and a gentle breeze on his face, and . . . he listened. A lark was singing. A squirrel was scurrying up a nearby tree. The wind purred gently through the trees, and then . . . Kent had the sudden assurance that the Lord had heard his prayer.

A blast of warmth filled his heart and mind with burning. He burst into tears and dropped to his knees. His shoulders heaved. Though he was praying about Annie, he could picture the angels on the rock where he . . . and Betty once blended their souls, sounding trumps of love, oneness, and eternity. He could see more. He could see as if he was looking down from the sky—Betty, children, a home, and their own land. He knelt again, this time pouring his heart out in gratitude.

The feeling began to dissipate. He jumped up. *Please don't leave me, Lord.* The feeling was fading, but the burning in his soul was unforgettable. He could never forget what he'd just experienced.

He knelt again, this time thanking God for his family, for Betty, and for James and Anita.

At long last he stood up; he felt like singing and jumping. He had the memory and he had felt the Spirit of the Lord.

"He did it!" he yelled. "God answered my prayer! I know what to do! I'm free!"

He broke into a run. He would embrace this new life. He'd made his decision.

CHAPTER 71
NOT A NORMAL GRADUATION

*I*t was a pleasant, warm spring evening. The good weather meant the ceremony would be held in the park instead of the gym.

Kent drove his car about thirty yards to pick up Anita. She came out in her cap and gown. He smiled, hoping to disguise his anxiety.

He opened the car door for her, and hurried to his seat. He'd been desperately rehearsing speeches in his mind, but so far—nothing. He slipped into his seat and stammered, "You look lovely tonight."

"Thank you."

"Anita, I have no doubt that because of you, the program will be splendid."

"I hope so, but it was a team effort."

"So what's this new announcement that's going to be made?"

"You'll just have to wait and see."

"You mean you can't tell me?"

"Oh, I could, but you haven't told me either."

"What was that?" he questioned as he pulled to a stop in front of the city park.

"Well, actually, I guess you have. You've proved it, and for that I thank you."

A rush of their friends showed up, laughing and talking. He knew what Anita was saying, but he could only say hi to his friends, and join in their animation. For now, he would enjoy the evening, but the gravity of his decision and answer to his prayer were setting in. It wouldn't be easy.

Near the entrance to the park, James and Betty joined them. "Hey," James called. "All seniors come join our foursome. Let's have an eighteen-some hug." They wrapped their arms around each other, leaned over, and shouted, "We did it! Way to go, seniors!"

Joe and his girlfriend, Sara, were next to Kent. Joe whispered to Kent. "Man, have I got some news for you."

"What is it?"

But even as he questioned, he could hear the school principal saying to the town folk who had arrived, "Go ahead and form a line so you can greet them all." They did so, and they began filing through.

Anita came and took her place next to Kent. Eight of the seniors had paired up and entered the line together. James and Betty were in front. There were congratulatory remarks such as, "you two are going to have a bright future together," or, "we're expecting to hear great things out of the pair of you."

When Anita and Kent went through, similar statements were made. Kent's determination faltered.

He slipped a glance at her. She was smiling, waving, and shaking hands warmly.

They took their places. Eight of them sat on the row of chairs, and six took their places in the band. Anita, and Lance, the senior class president, and two others took their places on the stand with the faculty and district superintendent.

The three hundred seats were filling fast. It would be the biggest turnout in Tropic High history.

Kent took the moment to take a deep breath and ponder what his decision would demand. He knew he had received an unmistakable answer, but how it would all play out was a mystery. He knew James and his family were driving to Cedar City tomorrow, and James would buy the ring. He'd mentioned that there had been no opportunity to get it until now.

Somehow Kent would have to find Betty and talk to her alone. There would be a lot of rushing around, noise, and confusion after the benediction. That would be his moment. He hoped that if he could get Betty to think about it and pray about it, the Lord would bless her as He had blessed him.

Annie's voice jolted him from his trance. She welcomed every-body, and announced the person giving the invocation.

After the prayer, the band played a medley of songs Kent had put together including the theme songs to *Gone with the Wind* and *Wizard of Oz*. The cheers afterward could be heard in Cannonville.

Next, Lance spoke a little about the seniors, giving a warm tribute to each of them.

Now it was Anita's turn. She delighted the crowd by highlighting each activity and event of the year. She made special mention of the state basketball championship and their all-star, James.

The school principal recommended the graduates, and was fol-lowed by the district superintendent. Then it was time for the seniors to receive their diplomas. One by one, they were summoned to the stage. Betty's name was called, two more names, then Anita's. Loud yells and applause erupted from the crowd. She accepted her diploma, smiling and waving. When Kent's turn came there was more applause.

He accepted his diploma with bitter-sweetness in his mouth. Sweet, due to the feeling of tremendous accomplishment; the pic-ture of him contemplating dropping out of school so his family could keep the farm burst into his mind. Bitter, because of the hurt he would shortly cause Anita.

Anita and Lance began their closing remarks. Grabbing the micro-phone, Anita announced, "We're going to make a slight change in the program. We'd like to have the benediction now. And then we have some exciting news to share with you."

After the benediction, Lance yelled, "Is anyone ready for some big news? News of some big changes for our little towns beneath the painted cliffs?"

There were cheers and chants from everyone.

"Okay," he paused, "the date is not set, due to circumstances here and perhaps throughout the world, but the plans are all made up for . . . a new school right here in Tropic. It will be much more modern that our little Tropic High and it will serve from kindergarten all the way to twelfth grade. How about them apples?"

Cheers erupted.

Then Anita joined in. "That's not all, there will be no more Tropic High! Instead we'll go by a new name: Bryce Valley High, and our mascot will be . . . the Mustangs!"

Again, cheers burst through the dark night air.

"These little towns are known for growing spectacular weeds," Lance continued, "but they are also known to produce some of the finest young people anywhere. The tradition will go on!"

"And now," Anita's voice resounded. "And now to declare our class slogan for Tropic High, class of 1941. 'We're ready to spread our wings and fly! Class of 41, Let's fly!' "

She removed her cap and let it fly, as they all did. The entire scene boiled to life with people running everywhere, shouting, laughing, hugging, and kissing.

Kent knew this was his chance. Instead of finding his parents for congratulations and hugs, he headed toward the area where he'd seen Mr. Griffin. Sure enough Betty was there, being embraced by her dad. "Hi, everyone," he shouted above the noise. He grabbed Betty's hands and began to pull her close for a hug, but then without really knowing what he was going to say or do he stepped back, and tugged Betty toward him.

"Betty, I need to talk to you." She followed but was hesitant. When they were some distance away, where he figured James wouldn't find them too easily, he turned, letting go of her hand.

"Betty," trembling evident in his voice, "please hear me out before you respond. Please. Betty, I love you more than life itself. I can't live another minute until I tell you this. I'm breaking up with Anita. Betty, you're the love of my life."

Betty stood there speechless, uneasiness in her eyes, her face hesitant. "Betty, I want to spend eternity with you, only you. I know things happened in our lives, but they were not meant to drive us apart. They were meant to make us strong—bring us together."

He paused a moment, tears began trickling down his face.

"Kent, I love you more than life itself, but I'm marrying James."

"Betty, please! I know this is happening so fast. James will be gone to Cedar City tomorrow. Just take the day to ponder, and pray on Heaven's Rock. God will answer you. I will come and see you tomorrow after I get off work at six o'clock. Just be on Heaven's Rock, and point to heaven so I will know you want me forever and ever just as I want you."

Just then, Joe and Sara burst through the crowd.

"There you are," Joe shouted. "We've been looking all over for you, and so is your family." He tugged on his arm. Kent looked back at Betty in a panic. "Six o'clock tomorrow," he yelled.

Joe reached down and grabbed Sara's arm. "Guess what transpired today," he announced, grinning from ear to ear. Sara was sporting a shiny engagement ring.

Kent was stunned. Never did he think Joe would get engaged before he did. For a moment his tension subsided, and he relished Joe and Sara's exuberance.

"I can't believe it, Joe. Congrats, you two."

"I can't wait to tell everyone that this fine lady is mine," Joe announced giving Sara a kiss on the lips. "Hey," he began tugging on Kent's arm, "let's go tell your mom and dad, and I believe I saw your future mother-in-law talking to them. We can tell her too."

"Stop, Joe, stop," Kent yelled. "My future mother-in-law is dead."

Joe's eyes widened and then widened some more. "What in the world are you talking about?"

"Please Joe, Sara. Don't say anything. I don't know what will happen tomorrow."

Joe placed a hand on his forehead. "Good golly," he stammered. "We won't say a word." He grabbed Sara's hand, shook his head, and ran into the main gathering of people.

Kent stood there in the dark by himself. He'd done it. It was now up to Betty.

He found his family and Anita's too, visiting together.

"Kent," his mom said. "Where have you been? It's kind of customary to hug your family when you graduate from high school. We'd like to congratulate you, you know."

He hugged his mother, then Dad, all his family, and the Johnsons. "Anita, that was the most beautiful ceremony I've ever attended. What a terrific job you did."

"Thanks."

They talked for a while longer, then, noticing that the evening was drawing to a close, began making their way to their cars.

"Anita?"

"Yes."

"I don't feel like driving."

"Sounds great," she said, turning. "I don't either."

They began walking back across the field toward their homes, both of them still wearing their gowns. Kent swallowed hard, and braced himself. He pictured years ago when he'd hurt Anita as they walked that same path by saying the wrong words. There were no right words again, and he knew what Anita had to say wouldn't be pretty.

He was surprised at his thoughts. They weren't a jumble. They were astonishingly clear. The problem was his heart. It was broken. When he made his decision on the mountain, he didn't see all that it entailed. He had no idea of the pain.

He found himself wanting to grab her hands, apologize, express his forever love and make everything right. But he squelched the thoughts quickly. He could not resume that inner battle ever again.

"Anita, I think you've left a mark on Tropic High that will shine bright through the years. All of us were touched by your enthusiasm, your spirit, and your courage."

"Ah, Kent. You haven't lost your smooth touch. But thank you. I hope that some people benefited from the activities and events. But, let's talk about why we're here, walking home, not holding hands, you calling me Anita, the night of graduation."

"Yeah, I . . ."

She interrupted. "And by the way, since I went first last time, I think it's only fitting that I go first again."

"Oh, please, I've got to go first."

She stopped, and placed a hand over his mouth. "Kent, do you think I can't see how much you hurt? Do I not know you? I'll help you, because I love you."

Kent came to a stop. What an incredible woman.

"Kent, sure I was mad after our talk on the rim. I felt cheated out of the best time of my life. I felt I'd put my whole heart and soul on the line for you, and you just trampled it. But, as busy as I was the past few weeks, I had time to ponder. Come on, let's keep walking."

He stayed with her this time.

"Do you remember how the Sunday school teacher taught us that as soon as we think we're humbling ourselves, if we look closer we'll see how prideful we still are?"

"I remind myself of that every day."

"Kent, after that first week I began seeing how prideful I was. I started seeing beyond myself. I began feeling your heart. I felt your love and affection for me. I know you're sincere, genuine, honest, and true. You would never ever wish to hurt me. I began thinking of words you'd said. I thought of all your efforts to make decisions for the four of us. I had never done that. I knelt down and prayed. I've prayed every night for an answer. You've prayed about the four of us for a long time, haven't you?"

"Annie, I've prayed every morning and every night since . . . since our trip to *Gone with the Wind*."

"That's what I thought. And I want you to know, I'll always point to heaven thanking God for the gift he sent me your friendship. Kent, if anyone is worthy of answers from God, it's you. And just so you know, now that I've prayed I believe you're right. As hard as it was for me because of all the love I feel for you, I feel in my heart that you're right."

Kent hugged Anita, filled with emotion. He did love her, as a friend, as a child of God, as an amazing woman he had been privileged to share part of his mortal journey with.

Several moments later, each of them made their way to their doorsteps, dying to turn and look back.

Kent ascended his steps. He would always cherish their friendship, but it was time for their paths to part. Heavenly Father had different plans for them, and Kent trusted God that those plans would work out for the greatest possible happiness for all of them. He entered the door . . . and didn't look back.

Anita ascended her steps, as thoughts of dancing with Kent when they were three, and memories of every other event she held dear coursed through her heart. He had been the love of her life. But like Kent, she had faith that God was directing her life, and she would wait to see what glorious things He had in store for her. Still, that didn't mean that her heart didn't break. But there was sweetness and peace there as well. She placed her hand on the knob, and wondered briefly if Kent had turned. She fought back tears; she drew in a deep breath . . . and walked forward into her new life.

CHAPTER 72
HEAVEN'S ROCK

*K*ent had a terrible time keeping up with all the business of a Saturday. Several times, his dad had to reorient him to what he was doing.

At last, the customers started thinning. Around five thirty, he received permission to leave and go to Cannonville. The last words he remembered his father saying were, "Son, I'm proud of you. You've shown such courage of what you feel to be best. May the Lord bless you, son."

The drive to Cannonville seemed interminable. Kent began trembling as he neared the corner where he'd be able to see her. This time, his whole world would be shattered if she wasn't there.

He arrived at the corner. He began rounding the corner. Straining his neck he began peering into the sun to see Betty. Stopping at the side of the road, he stared in disbelief. She wasn't there.

His mind raced. "Now what?" He pulled out onto the road, and continued toward Cannonville, stopping at the stand of cotton-woods that sheltered the clearing underneath Heaven's Rock. He sat there, each moment becoming more frantic as he internalized the consequences of his decision.

With that, the tears flowed. Here he was, a grown man now, crying like a baby. Of course Betty couldn't come back. She'd made her choice. By tomorrow, she'd be engaged to James. The wedding was probably already planned.

He sat there for some time, then stepped out of his car. He made his way through the cottonwoods to the meadow. So he didn't get an answer to his prayer. What's the answer then? "Father," he yelled out loud. "I don't understand. So what were all those miraculous times Betty and I shared? We complement each other more than any two people in the world. We could have done wonderful things you know. We'd have been the best parents ever. We'd have stuck to any challenge. We'd have been great!"

He hung his head in despair, and dropped to his knees. To add to the gloom, darkness suddenly gathered around him. "So that's the end of my dream. At first the whole world is bright and rosy with Betty at my side, and then I go through awful trials, and now the end, dark and alone."

"Oh, God, I trusted you, I trusted you! Couldn't you just cast this shadow away and . . . and . . . shadow . . . shadow?" Taking in a huge breath, he questioned, "The darkness in my dream? It didn't end in darkness. That shadow was . . . Oh please God, please." He whipped his head up, and there stood Betty, tall and straight on Heaven's Rock, arm pointing to heaven just as the last ray of sun melted into the horizon.

He jumped to his feet. "Betty!" He felt as if he was caught in a whirlwind—his feet not touching the ground.

"Well, are you going to come up here or not? I think we have some unfinished business."

"Oh my gosh," he gasped, the realization hitting him. Slapping himself on the forehead to assure himself that this wasn't a dream; or better yet, this was his dream! "Give me ten seconds." He broke into a run. He ran all the way to their piece of heaven on earth where Betty was waiting, arms outstretched.

He swept her into his arms and spun her around until she was laughing breathlessly.

"Kent, I promised you at the flood that my love for you would never dim—never, never, never, and it never has."

He stepped back to look into her eyes. He could read in them the depth of her love, her devotion, the timeless beauty of her soul. A panorama of pictures of every moment they'd ever enjoyed flashed into his mind: the angels attending them on the rocky ledge, their near first kiss there on Heaven's Rock, the picnics, the walks, the horse rides, the numerous days and nights he'd spent dreaming of her—the oneness.

At long last, the tears stopped, they loosened their hold on each other, and looked into each other's eyes.

His heart began to pound, his whole being aflame as it once was long ago. It had been a long journey over six emotional years, but the moment he would cherish forever was finally here. He stepped back, brought his hands over her shoulders, up her neck, and rested them on her cheeks. He drew closer ever so slowly. "I'm so in love with you," he whispered. Closer, she closed her eyes. He waited just a moment, and beheld his future bride. He closed his eyes.

Their lips met. They pressed into each other with passion, warmth, feeling, caring, love . . . he didn't feel they were just another son and daughter of God on this huge earth. He felt the whole earth revolving around them. This was true love. This was endless love. He felt her press upon him with fervor and devotion. Again, the innumerable angels were present.

Tears mingled with their kiss, but they only added to the sweetness of the moment. He was awed that this incredible daughter of God had agreed to join her life with his for the rest of eternity.

At long last their lips parted, and they dropped to their knees in the soft sand. Kent bowed his head. "Oh God, I thank you! I will never, never let her go again!"

After a moment, Betty embraced him a little tighter. "Well, Kent, you won't ever have to."

Darkness began to spread over the valley. They sat down, placing their feet against the little rock ledge, and watched a full moon rise over the mountains. Betty looked heavenward. What was she doing? "Okay, Mom. You were right. You were so right!"

"What was that all about?"

"My mother, shortly before she could no longer speak, told me she wished she could live to see the love story play out between you, James, and me."

"She knew all along?"

"Yes."

"So, Betty, what happened today?"

"Well, I came early this morning. I prayed a while on my patch of sand, then decided to walk up to Heaven's Rock and ponder as I looked over the valley. No sooner did I get there, that I knew my shadow was meant for only you. I always knew it was meant for just you—the fulfillment of your dream."

"You knew?"

"I did. And the angels. They were only with you and me."

"You should have come to Tropic and told me. I was in sheer agony all day!" Betty laughed. "And you still let me bumble down there until your shadow was cast." He gave her a rap on the arm. "I didn't figure it out until the last second."

"Well, the dream had to be fulfilled, don't you think?"

"I suppose, but . . ."

"So how is Anita?"

"She's good, Betty. You've probably noticed we've been working on it the last few weeks. She's an incredible woman. So, how about James?"

"I'll have to let him know tomorrow. I don't think it will be too big of a surprise. Things have been a little pensive the past couple weeks with us, too. I just need to find the right words so that he won't be too hurt. Did you talk to him?"

"Maybe a little. Who knows? Anita might stop him before he proposes, or maybe he'll talk to her."

Betty smiled. "You're so sly. Kent . . . I must tell you. I'll always love James. I'll always be grateful for . . ."

Kent interrupted, "It was James's arms that held you close while your mother lay dying. It was his love that lifted you and sustained you during your darkest hour. I, too, shall love and respect him always."

Betty broke into a beautiful smile. "Kent, you were my first love. I named this place Heaven's Rock because of you. It's always been heavenly because of you. Whenever I was lonely I would come up here and I'd be with you. I can relive those feelings, desires, and dreams each and every day forever. Can you believe that we were just kids? We were thirteen and fourteen, and yet we formed a bond, a love that wouldn't recede no matter what the obstacle."

"We sure had to grow up fast, but as I look back, I wouldn't change a moment of it," Kent acknowledged.

"I feel the same way, Kent. Everything that's happened, no matter how horrible, unfair, and difficult to bear, made us stronger."

"Yeah, you're not going to believe this, but . . . I want to write it. Our own book."

Betty pulled him close. "I have a feeling our story is yours to write . . . for certain, Mr. School Editor."

Kent looked into her eyes. It was time. The moment he formed the thoughts in his mind warmth and confirmation flooded him. Again the earth began revolving around them. The angels were present. He dropped to one knee, and took her hand. "Betty Griffin, would you . . . marry me?"

"Yes, yes, yes, yes!" she shouted, smiling ear to ear. "But does it come with something round and shiny indicating eternity?"

"Oh my," Kent answered, chuckling. "Can you give me a week?"

"One week. That's it."

He jumped to his feet and they kissed again, warmly and tenderly. At long last, they took a final look at the moon and the valley below, and with arms still lovingly placed around each other, began their new walk home.

CHAPTER 73
MY BOOK TO YOU

October 11, 2009

 $\mathscr{I}$ t was nearly midnight when I retired to bed. My precious companion of sixty-nine years had succumbed to a deep slumber a couple hours earlier. I sat looking at her in the dim light. She looked tired and frail. Her fingers, tucked up under her chin, were twisted with arthritis. Her spinal column had a marked curvature, dropping her height nearly five inches. Her expression bore a weight of pain that plagued her constantly. And yet, she still maintained that little curvature of her lips indicating the makings of a smile, or simple contentment. She never expected to come to a world that wasn't full of challenges, as painful as they may be.

I reached for my pillow to ease up next to her. My hand hit something knocking it back between the bed board and the wall. I gingerly bent my aging frame to my knees and fumbled my fingers on the floor looking for the . . . there it was. It was an envelope. It was pretty thick.

There would be no sleeping for a while now. I made my way to the living room, and turned on the light. Although I greatly anticipated the words my treasure had to say to me, I also noticed my heart growing heavy. It was sinking. I knew what this meant. I knew my sweetheart plenty well after being side by side for so long.

I slipped the cover of the envelope off and read.

My beloved Kent,

You deserve a book of your own. One that typifies the wonderful man you are—the loving companion, the gentle provider, the fun-loving father, my one and only.

It's been seventy-four years since the day we first met. I consider myself blessed among women to have been at your side whether we were an ocean apart or snuggled tightly in each other's embrace. I knew the caliber of man you were the first time you rough-housed with my little siblings, and from there, you only reinforced your goodness with each event of life.

As with any marriage, we had our differences. Though our long-term desires were the same, we each had our own opinions, quirks, and points of view, some of which caused us each to walk a difficult road of compromise, struggling to understand and accept. But our foundation was solid—rock solid. We began laying it at the tender age of thirteen, based on pure love, devotion, and commitment, and always rooted with the approval of Almighty God and his angels.

I've been writing your book in my heart for the past sixty-nine years. Although short, it's from the deepest corners of my heart, complete with some of the poetry that I love.

My Book to You

It seemed that from the moment we were married, the plans we had for life weren't in line with the plans Heavenly Father had for us.

You were always so full of hope and dream.
Such zeal for life I'd never seen.

291

But, almost without fail, each dream was not to be.
It was altered or changed with whole new scenery.

So, through it all you remained steadfast,
And made the very best of life's contrast.

Your faith undaunted, your will to remain,

You worked God's plan for its every gain.

Even if we didn't get to live our dream from the start, it didn't slow us down, and it certainly didn't dampen our love for each other. Our marriage is the foundation of every good thing. Especially when we learned that little Char was on the way. I cherish the oneness that it brings.

During those special moments when we are one,
I want you to know that it's totally fun.

But way beyond that, are the feelings I treasure,
My heart, my soul, my everything, is yours beyond measure.

My will, my devotion, my love will forever endure,
Because this gift is just you and me—clean and pure.

And now my heart soars, my thrill just begun,
For we'll soon be blessed with a daughter or a son.

We had it pretty good there for a while. Both of us studying and broadening our horizons. Anticipating the day our little boy or girl would be born. But life throws us curve balls when we least expect it. I'll never forget the day the draft notice came.

The call to war was an awful thing
I thought my heart would burst.

What changes now would come to pass?
Would you be leaving first?

Confused and with child soon to be
I will remain faithful and true,
For it is to my eternal love,
That I'll stick to forever, like glue.

You embraced the call to duty
Your life you would lay down
Holding true our countries flag
While lying on the ground.

For more than self, your country loved,
Your devotion and commitment pure
Your love for God and fellow man,
Would each and every day endure?

So as the months and years go by,
And oceans separate us apart
Don't worry, I love you, I'm with you
Every single moment, deep within your heart.

And I will look for that shining day
When you'll return home to me
The hopes and dreams will then be ours
We'll love and cherish each other for eternity.

I was terrified at the thought of losing you. What a horrible and gruesome war, and you being half a world away somewhere in the Pacific. I would shudder when the news came in. For four and a half long years there was no comfort. Just stress, frustration, and a relentless tormenting strain on my heart and soul.

But, in saying that, there were times of relief—precious moments when a letter would arrive or when I'd feel a still, small voice whisper comfort to my soul.

I'll always cherish the day you met our little Char for the first time. Well most of it. For me it was wonderfully gratifying and terrifying at the same time. I know I've told you the story, but I wrote it for you.

Whole at Last

"Mommy, is Daddy tall?"

"He's just like me."

"Where is he, I want to see him now."

"Yeah, where is he? After four and a half years, one more minute will be too long."

It was San Antonio's Missouri/Pacific Station where we waited. We got there an hour early, and I was beginning to feel that that was a mistake. However, there would be no missing a first glimpse of my forever love, and little Char's daddy that she'd never known.

A train whistle was heard in the distance. That would be the Iron Eagle. Char began to jump and pull on my arm.

Kneeling down and pulling her close, I whispered. "Do you remember what your father looks like?"

"Yeah, he's, he's . . . well, I remember his picture."

"He's handsome, and he has soft, loving eyes. He'll be dressed in his army uniform."

The whistle blew again, and a crowd began to gather. "Here it comes!" Char cried.

The train came to a stop. People began spilling from the doors. Many of those returning from war were dressed in their uniforms. The gates opened. Char shook loose of my grasp and ran though the gate right into the flood of exiting passengers. Crying her name, I ran after her, dodging and colliding with the people. It took only seconds, but the wall of people thwarted all my efforts to catch her. She disappeared from my view.

Pressing forward, panic stricken, I worked my way through the crowd. The rush of people was relentless. Running headlong into a tall bearded man, I stepped back, fixing terror filled eyes upon him. Shockingly he smiled at me.

"I'll bet I know who you're after," he bellowed. With his vantage point above the crowd he raised his hands high and yelled. "Where's the little girl? Here's her mother." Others of the crowd responded by backing up and creating a space as if they'd seen her. As the space began to grow, at the far end was little Char . . . in the arms of her loving father, Sergeant Kent Wilson.

I learned to cry double tears that day. Many tears were for your safe return, and the rest for finding Char safe in your arms. Kent, I literally melted into your embrace that day. I remember hugging and kissing and even smashing little Char between us, but she didn't care because she was busy kissing you on your head.

The crowd witnessed an incredible reunion that day. They clapped and cheered for us. The Wilson family was once again whole and complete.

Our Little Sammy

Three years after your return from the war, we lost our little boy. I didn't know I could hurt so much. I must admit I buckled. I blamed you, I blamed the doctor. I even blamed God.

I became keenly aware of the words *agonize, torture,* and *suffering.* But when my selfishness began to dissipate, I noticed your agony and suffering as well.

To this day I chasten myself for throwing away our book—adding to your torture. But somehow, some way, I have this feeling *that our book will endure.* To this day, I wish I could remove the blame I placed on you, God, and anyone else involved. But I did do it. But, as you know, I've repented as best I can. I must leave the rest to God.

I've prayed and pondered now for nearly fifty-four years in behalf of our little Sammy, and I know you have as well. I've come to know or come to feel the Spirit of God. Deep in my heart I know, I have no doubt that he's still ours, and that he'll always be ours as long as we're worthy of him. Some glorious day, we will know the joy of raising him. How could a just and merciful Father in Heaven not have it so? We're his work and his glory—we're his kids! So rest at ease, my love. Just as we became whole upon your return from the war, so it will be again when we reunite with Sammy.

The Park Service

You used your excellent skill with numbers to handle the money for different national parks, starting with Bryce Canyon. Bouncing around from park to park wasn't in line with my plans for us. I know it wasn't for you as well. We would never feel at home until we were nestled under the orange-painted cliffs of Bryce Canyon.

However, much good came from the parks. We raised four wonderful children, and saw them grow, fall in love, and start families of their own. What could be more beautiful? You made it happen, you know. You were such a good provider. You never complained. Thank you, thank you, thank you.

Back Home

It took twenty-eight years, but we did it. What joy we felt as we purchased our land and built our home beneath the towering orange spires! It became a veritable sanctuary for the kids. Countless visits rejuvenated their weary souls, and bolstered them up to return to their busy schedules. But more than that, we had thirty-five years of just you and me. I didn't think it was possible to grow more in love with you, but I did. Very much so, I did. I began to appreciate your goodness even more. I keenly felt your efforts to build and bless others. I witnessed your struggles, rejoiced in your triumphs, and honored your undying commitment as husband and father. I enjoyed our travel together. The new experiences and new people only augmented our union with greater depth and knowledge.

And then to relive my first love here in the land of our dreams—home again, and whole. I often picture us, full of energy, full of life, and full of love for each other; running upon the rocks, jumping on the wool sacks, knocking each other in the dirt, riding the horses, having picnics, and falling deeper and deeper in love. And we were again close to Heaven's Rock. Whenever I was lonely or sad I could go up and be with you and remember our young love.

My Fall

A broken neck, compounded with osteoarthritis! I found I couldn't care for myself on my own. I knew I would need nursing care, but never in my wildest dreams did I think it would be you. You volunteered, or perhaps better said, told them that you'd be the one caring for me. Oh, how I appreciate your continued support and care day in and day out.

It felt horrible to receive care. I felt like I was my mother, and it shook me to the core. My whole being cried out, "This cannot be!" I remember how exhausted, how dreadfully depleted I became, and I could not stand that for you. I've watched you and worried for you. I prayed continually for you.

But you carry on, undaunted and unwavering. I want you to know that your thoughtful, kind, loving manner of meeting my needs has, over these past five years, gradually softened my heart. You've given everything to me—your whole life. You gave to me what you would have given to my mother, but couldn't.

So, as for you, I love you with everything that I am. You're my favorite person on this earth. I'm forever grateful for you, and as I told you so many years ago, you're my gift sent from heaven. I'll point to heaven, and there, I'll find you.

My Conclusion

My dearest Kent,

The day I give you this letter, or "your book from me" as I call it, you may know that I will pass on soon. But I want you to know what I know to be true. And what I say is backed by the Spirit of Almighty God. For His Spirit has witnessed to my soul countless times that there is more; much more for you and me, and our family.

I know that the love we've shared for the past sixty-nine years, the challenges and trials that have bound us together, and the experiences that are ours alone, amount to more than this life—much, much more. There is no way that a divorce decree could be written between the two of us as in death do we part. God is eternal. Truth is reason, truth is eternal, tells me that our foundation and our love spans the eternities. WE WILL BE TOGETHER FOREVER, for we have a Savior, even Jesus Christ, who realized the resurrection that we also may be resurrected with bodies full of life and youth again, fully capable of enjoying each other and rejoicing in our posterity—forever!

I make you a promise. I will be waiting for you. I hope you won't be too long. I'll try very hard to get permission to come get you on Heaven's Rock just as I did so many years ago. You'll again know that you have my whole heart, because I'LL POINT TO HEAVEN, there on Heaven's Rock. That day you'll come home to me, and we'll be one—forever.

I will love you forever,

Your fondest admirer, your forever love, your devoted companion, and truest friend,

Betty

CHAPTER 74
HER LAST MOMENTS

I checked my watch. It was three thirty in the morning. I had spent hours reading and pondering the words of my forever love. I sat there on the couch, my mind a blur. I drifted in and out of sleep, my heart trying to push away the events that would soon occur.

"The book, the book," I heard Betty's voice from the bedroom. "The book, the book!" I scooted into the bedroom as fast as I could.

"The bo-..."

"Betty dear, wake up—it's okay. You're just having a bad dream."

"Wha-... What?"

"Just a bad dream, my love," I reassured her tenderly, stroking her forehead.

Rubbing the sleep from her eyes, she looked up at me. "Was it about the book again?"

"Well," I said, opening the blinds so she could look out at Escalante Mountain. "I suppose, but..."

"Kent, I'm so, so sorry. I was just crazy in my mind with grief over Sammy."

"Oh, my love. We've put that behind us a thousand times. But, my miracle, you know that we'll be able to raise him in the hereafter— right?"

"That's right."

"And just think, this time he won't get sick—he'll just be ours to love and teach and adore."

We sat silently for a few moments. I was troubled as I observed anguish spreading across Betty's face. "Oh, just look at me; all bent over with arthritis, my neck broken, and I can hardly move—I'm no miracle anymore."

"You're just as much a miracle today as the day I saw you jumping on the wool sacks, my love."

"Oh shush, too bad you're blind."

"Blind, huh? Let me see. Ah yes. I see a daughter of God, who captured my heart from the first time I saw her. The love of my life, who brought five children into this world. The only person who ever held me spell bound, and caused me to dream of her each and every moment of every day for the past sixty-nine years. The one lady who kept me in awe, as I watched her love, build, comfort, reassure, and bless anyone she was around. The one woman who caused me to look heavenward and ask God, 'Is she for real?' Is it possible for someone to be so genuine, so full of integrity, so . . . heavenly?"

There was no answer, just complete silence. I looked down and noticed the tears filling the space around her eyes.

"Kent, are you still looking in the mirror? You are the miracle—for certain. You were the one who was in tune with God with our fantastic foursome. You made all the right things happen then, and every day since. Who are you but a son of God, forever following His paths, and blessing everyone in your wake? You're the miracle. You have my whole heart. Always and forever."

I remained silent, the world spinning around Betty and me. No heart could contain the love and admiration I had for this woman.

"Kent, I, I feel it's time."

"Time for what?" I mumbled, but deep down I knew. I remembered what she'd written in the letter.

"My chest is tight, my breathing is hard. I think I'll be going home," drawing in a breath, "to Heavenly Father today. I'll start . . . my new journey. I know . . . I'm selfish, but . . . I hope . . . you join me soon."

I sat there motionless. I felt it too. She'd struggled so valiantly since her fall.

"Kent?"

"Yes."

"How I wish, wish you could tell . . . our story to the kids. Char was so little when we read it to her."

"I'll do it, Betty. Don't worry, I'll do it."

"Tell them of the wool sacks, and . . . Heaven's Rock, and our . . . first kiss. Tell them to tap their fingers, tell them of the flood, and your proposal . . . without the ring."

"I will, my love."

The morning drew on and brightened into a beautiful Indian summer afternoon under the painted cliffs. I held my precious companion's hand in mine. By now she was too weak to talk. I read her stories and poems that she'd written over the years. Every now and then she would squeeze my hand perhaps to express her gratitude for reading to her.

"Betty, my love, of all the things I've done in this life, the best decision I ever made was having the courage to put everything on the line and go after you." I felt a squeeze on my hand. Drawing in a deep breath and fighting back tears, I continued. "Every accomplishment I've achieved pales in comparison to my relationship with you." Another squeeze of my hand. I began stroking her forehead. Just as the valley wisped into gentle dimness proclaiming that the sun had settled behind the cliffs, Betty opened her eyes, even if it was just to a slit, and held up her hand; "Mother, Sa . . ." she whispered. Her hand settled again back into mine, and she lay still.

I sat there pondering, as darkness settled over the valley, our hands still clasped. Holding her hand represented the same unity, love, and feeling it did the first time I took her hands in the crevice. I reflected on all the ups and downs of our lives. Very little of it was the script that we had written. It was a completely different script—the script of God. Knowing I had to call, I gently laid her hand down for the last time and dialed 911. I then called Char, asked her to inform her sister and brothers, and then placed my head in my hands and wept.

After a few minutes, I could hear the ambulance nearing my home. I lifted my head, dried my eyes, and tried to clear my head. The front door opened. I quickly jerked my head back for a last look at my forever miracle. The corners of her lips were raised just as they always did when she was pleased. "Betty, I'll do as I promised—our story!"

CHAPTER 75
SHE CAME?

April 22, 2015

I slowly closed the cover to Dad's sacred book, tilted my head back in my seat, and closed my eyes. The words of my mother were firm and undeniable. The uncertainty that once filled my soul was no more. I literally had no further questions or concerns. I would be with my Richard again! I would again enjoy my brother! And oh, what a love story! I could now bask in their youthful exuberance to the unfathomable devotion of Mom's last day any time I desired.

I was surprised to see Dad just sitting there smiling, looking up at Heaven's Rock. I reached over and placed my arm around him, and pulled him close. My whole being was on the brink of bursting with joy and gratitude because of him. "You were right, Dad, I have no more questions." I placed my head on his shoulder and wept.

After some time I looked up. Dad still wore that gentle smile, and was still peering up at Heaven's Rock. I looked up as well, squinting into the sun, now low in the sky.

"Dad, there could not be a more beautiful love story. Thank you, thank you. And thank you for answering all of my questions in such a lovely manner."

He closed his eyes and whispered, "You're welcome, my dear." Then he opened them again. "Did I answer all of your questions?"

"Oh, yes, Dad. I . . ."

"Are you sure?"

"Well, I think so."

"Any thoughts of Anita and James?"

"Oh my goodness, yes! What became of them?"

"Well, James never proposed to Betty. He pondered and prayed the whole way to Cedar City. He bought the ring, but he swung by Anita's home first to ask her if she had any reservations about him marrying Betty. She did! Come to find out, he was having an inner battle of his own with Betty and Anita. And Anita confessed. She started falling for James sometime around the big basketball game. Can you believe it? They were engaged three weeks after we were. Neighbors and townsfolk would walk by and just shake their heads. Others would comment, 'What on earth happened? What did we miss? We had no idea about the four of you,' and so on."

"Anita and James spent several years in New York City, where Anita dazzled many an audience on Broadway. They realized all their dreams of the city, raising three fantastic children, then settled down and lived the remainder of their lives in Salt Lake. They were as happy a couple as I'd ever seen. The four of us stayed in touch and visited when we could. We would relive the fantastic foursome, and the three of them would thank me for having the courage to set the four of us straight. And yes, we'd talk about the two loves of my life pointing to heaven for the gift God had sent them—me."

I looked over at this amazing man that I felt I was just beginning to know. This marvelous husband and father, so dedicated, so deep, so faithful, and so loving. He was sitting with his head down and eyes closed. He looked so old, tired, and frail. I'd better get him back to the care center. Hopefully they'll save him his dinner. I pulled onto the highway and began the trip to Panguitch.

"I wonder if this is the place where Dad would wave to Mom," I muttered to myself, casting a glance over to Heaven's Rock. The sun was just heaving its last glow of warmth and light for the day. I hit the brakes and skidded. It couldn't be. It . . . it couldn't. I ran off the road, and my SUV bounced over clumps of grass and sage-brush. I whipped the wheel sharply and came to a stop partially back on the road. I looked toward Heaven's Rock, but the sun's last ray was gone. But surely as I sat there alongside my dad, a figure was standing straight and tall on the rocky ledge. I looked back at Dad who was now awake.

"Dad, I . . ." Again I looked at the rocky ledge, now deserted and lonely. He smiled and bowed his head again, closing his eyes. He was exhausted. "Dad? Oh, what am I thinking? I've been living in a different world these past four days." I hesitated a moment longer, then, pulled back onto the highway. "Okay, Dad, let's go home."

CHAPTER 76
UNTIL WE REUNITE AS ONE

*I*t was well after dark when I pulled into the nursing home. I was helping Dad from his seat when several care center employees showed up.

"Mrs. Harris, Mrs. Harris, have you heard the news?"

"Oh my gosh, no!" I answered, stepping back.

"You left your phone on the sofa this morning."

"So, is it good news?" I asked while they put Dad in a wheelchair. He was too tired to make his way in with his walker.

"Oh yes, yes!" came their reply. "You are now a brand new great-grandmother!" Then Annabelle knelt down, putting an arm around Dad.

"Kent, you're a new great-great-grandfather." He smiled from ear to ear.

I waited a few moments while the nurse's aide sat Dad down for a late supper. I then excused myself, returned to my hotel, and immersed myself into a reunion over the phone with my children and grandchildren. Well after midnight I finished the last call. "How marvelous, how beautiful, how powerful, how wondrous is the family," I proclaimed to myself. I've enjoyed five generations of family today.

I lay back on my pillow, hoping for some good rest for a beautiful drive through Zion Canyon later that day. It seemed I'd barely drifted off to sleep when I awoke abruptly to the sound of the alarm on my cell. Through the cobwebs I determined that I must have forgotten to dismiss the alarm I'd set for my drives with Dad. With hazy eyes I grappled for the blinking blur on the bed stand. I noticed that it was a call rather than the alarm. I answered groggily as best I could. "Wait . . . wait a minute, now who is this?" Finally, the voice registered to my mind. It was the care center. "Hi, this is Samantha. I'm the LPN in charge of the night shift. Is this Charlene Harris?"

"Yes, it is. Is something wrong? Is Dad okay?"

"Mrs. Harris, we have some bad news. Your father passed away in his bed early this morning."

I lay there, stunned. Yesterday was the most fantastic day of my life, and now . . . "Mrs. Harris, we're so very sorry. Is there any way you could make the trip over today?"

"Oh, well, yes, in fact I'm right here in Panguitch. I'll be right there."

When I arrived, there was a faint hint of light on the horizon. The mortician's van was just leaving. I'd made prior arrangements in case of his passing. I walked in and was met by Sandra, a nurse's aide who had cared for Dad since he entered the care center. She gave me a hug, and offered her condolences. The LPN also came over. "Hi, Mrs. Harris, I'm Samantha. Your dad passed this morning between four thirty and five. Best we can tell he passed in his sleep—no pain or suffering. There were no changes in his routine."

"Thank you all so much for the wonderful care you've always given Dad." I remained silent for a moment, wondering what to do next.

"Oh, by the way," Sandra said. "I'm not sure how it got there, but there's a note on your father's bedside stand with your name on it. It wasn't there when I put him to bed last night."

For a very brief moment, I stood perplexed. "Please excuse me." I ran toward Dad's room. Could it be? I entered the room and turned on the light, and there it was, on top of his beloved book. I gingerly picked up the envelope. It was addressed to "Char, my girl." Sliding the letter out, I read.

My dear Char,

How wonderful it was to be with you the last four days, and share the sacred story of your mom and me. That decision I made, that courage, that

307

determination, led to a life of hard work, of children, of family, of . . . the greatest success story on this earth, and as you now know, in the world to come.

Today, I will reunite with my Betty again. She came for me just as she'd promised, standing tall on Heaven's Rock, arm held high pointing to Heaven, letting all the holy angels know that her whole heart was still given to me. She always told me she named her rock Heaven's Rock because I made it heavenly. Whenever she was lonely, she would go there, and I would be with her. I know she has been alone long enough and so I will go to be with her. Never to be alone again.

With my last few minutes I'll spend in this life, I wish to add my witness to what your mother and grandparents testified. GOD IS OUR ETERNAL FATHER. WE ARE HIS CHILDREN—HIS WORK AND HIS GLORY. HE HAS A WONDROUS PLAN FOR US. AN ETERNAL PLAN. WE WILL BE TOGETHER AS FAMILIES FOREVER!

I love you with all my heart. Give your mom's love and my love to all our family. Until we all reunite again as one.

Dad

CHAPTER 77
THE BEGINNING

I could not stop the tears. I sat on the bed, placed my head in my hands, and cried. It was not a sorrowful cry. Rather, it was one of gratitude. Gratitude for the miracles I had witnessed. I had received new knowledge and enlightenment. This new understanding brought peace and comfort to my soul, casting out all doubts and all fears.

I raised my head, and looked up through tear-filled eyes as once my dad did so many years ago. I placed my hands together, and pointed them to heaven. "Thank you, God, for answering my prayers as once you did for my father many years ago—thank you."

I pictured the reunion that was taking place with Mom, Dad, and Sammy. The words from his letter took on a deeper significance. He was with her. He really was with her! And Mom, at the moment she passed on, had been met by her mother and my brother. That's what she had been saying.

Drying my eyes the best I could, I picked up *The Book*, found the last page of Dad's addition, and began to pen my own addition.

Charlene Harris, eldest daughter of Kent and Betty Wilson.

April 23, Mom's Birthday, 2015

My loving father passed away this morning at the Panguitch Care Center, in his own room and in his own bed. His precious book that he and Mom wrote lay on the bed stand.

For all who are blessed to read this book: this is the end . . .

I crossed out "the end" for emphasis and changed it to say:

This is the BEGINNING of the life and courtship of Kent and Betty Wilson.

ABOUT THE AUTHOR

*R*hett G. Wintch grew up in the National Parks of the Northwestern United States primarily in Yellowstone. He graduated with an associate's degree in Psychology from Ricks College, a Bachelor's degree in business administration from The University of Phoenix, and a registered nurse from The New York Regency. He's made his career as an emergency room nurse, although his passion is writing. He's filled fourteen journals, and enjoys writing poetry, romance, spiritual, medical, and nature books. He's the youngest of five children. He currently lives in Idaho Falls, Idaho, is married to his wife Lisa, and has four children and nine grandchildren. You can contact him on his facebook page, "Rhett Wintch-Author," as well as on his website writtenbyrhett.com.

CPSIA information can be obtained
at www.ICGtesting.com
Printed in the USA
FSOW02n1316180816
23928FS